Heaven on Earth

Heaven on Earth

God's Call to Community in the Book of Revelation

Michael Battle

WESTMINSTER
JOHN KNOX PRESS
LOUISVILLE · KENTUCKY

First edition
Published by Westminster John Knox Press
Louisville, Kentucky

17 18 19 20 21 22 23 24 25 26—10 9 8 7 6 5 4 3 2 1

Book design by Drew Stevens
Cover design by Allison Taylor
Cover art: Vesica Pisces #3 *by Eric Cross*

Library of Congress Cataloging-in-Publication Data

Names: Battle, Michael, 1963– author.
Title: Heaven on earth : God's call to community in the Book of Revelation / Michael Battle.
Description: First edition. | Louisville, KY : Westminster John Knox Press, 2017. | Includes bibliographical references.
Identifiers: LCCN 2016032995 (print) | LCCN 2016048201 (ebook) | ISBN 9780664262549 (pbk. : alk. paper) | ISBN 9781611647945 (ebook)
Subjects: LCSH: Bible. Revelation—Criticism, interpretation, etc. | Ubuntu (Philosophy) | Communities—Biblical teaching.
Classification: LCC BS2825.52 .B375 2017 (print) | LCC BS2825.52 (ebook) | DDC 228/.06—dc23
LC record available at https://lccn.loc.gov/2016032995

For my sister, Dr. Constance Battle, OBGYN
Who valiantly practices God's will on earth as it is in heaven.
She brings life into the world as she battles cancer.

Contents

Foreword

The Revelation of John is one of those biblical books that are very readily consigned to the Too Difficult box. We know that even in the early church it caused problems: intelligent readers recognized that it didn't sound very much like the St. John who wrote the Gospel; anxious bishops worried about the way it seemed to make the world to come rather too much of an intensified version of the present universe. And throughout Christian history it has generated a wild profusion of fantasies about the details of the world's last days and a useful repertoire of scenarios and characters to be used in theological and ecclesiastical polemics—whores, dragons, and apocalyptic horsemen.

It is prophecy, poetry, and politics all at once; a heady mixture. It is a testament to almost superhuman heroism under persecution, the voice of communities that are facing a completely ruthless and murderous state. It is a gift to the volatile and unsettled and disturbed, offering consoling pictures of divine vindication and the torment and death of enemies. It reveals not simply the purposes of God but also the complex mechanics of how communities and individuals manage impossible stress and suffering in their imaginative lives. And just because of all this, it is not a book to ignore, however tempting it is to do so. It tells us essential truths about how God weaves the divine life into the experience of the dispossessed and threatened. It creates extraordinary and endlessly fertile metaphors for conflict and homecoming. It also creates a world in which we can get badly lost, a world where shock, fear, and resentment can breed nightmares.

To read the book sanely and Christianly but still to keep our ears and eyes open to the depth of its imaginative challenges, we need a sane Christian expositor who also understands what matters about poetry and politics, and who knows what prophecy is and isn't. Michael Battle is wonderfully well equipped as a guide to such a reading, and his reflections are going to be a really valuable framework for many people willing prayerfully to "sit under" the holy text but wary of the seductions of theological fancy and self-justifying mythologies. It is an unusual and creative book which will be a welcome addition to the resources of critical and obedient biblical discipleship.

Rowan Williams
Cambridge, summer 2016

Acknowledgments

As always, I thank my wife, Raquel Battle, for providing the time and space to do this peculiar and emotional thing of writing—especially to write about the end of the world. This appreciation is also for our children, Sage, Bliss, and Zion, who weathered the storm of my being away to write this book at the Episcopal Divinity School in Cambridge, Massachusetts. The Louisville Institute provided support and an inquisitive community to delve into the controversies of Revelation. I am also indebted to the Episcopal Seminary of the Southwest in Austin, Texas, for letting me first try out all of this in their Blandy Lectures. Also, thank you, Calvary Episcopal Church in Memphis, Tennessee, for inviting me to provide content from this book for their phenomenal Lenten Series. General Theological Seminary provided the vital experience for putting the finishing touches on this book through the Paddock Lectures in which my colleague Prof. Todd Brewer and I discussed the goodness of upheaval. I am grateful also to Kurt Dunkle and the faculty at General for trying out the later stages of this book in our lunchtime conversations. Lastly, I owe a great deal to Marc Lewis and the Westminster John Knox staff for keeping my writing alive. I cannot name them all here, but thank you to my editors, Daniel Braden, Tina Noll, Amy Plantinga Pauw, and Don McKim, who waited for kingdom come to receive this book. I am indebted to Emily Kiefer for marketing this book. David Dobson made this book manifest. As in the book of life, many more names need to be written here. I am confident that God, through the grace of time, will reveal these names and powers.

Introduction

Are We There Yet?

I am the Alpha and the Omega, the first and the last, the beginning
and the end.

—Revelation 22:13

Beginnings are perilous.

Such peril is familiar from family vacations. Often on family road
trips, I experience a painful question from the backseat: Are we there
yet? Barely out of the driveway, a youthful voice poses a question that
is really a complaint. Although the question is painful at the time, it
becomes humorous on reflection. Beginning our journey, we cannot
help but grumble for it to end. The book of Revelation not only ends
the Christian Bible, it also produces a great deal of complaints posed
as questions.

When traveling through the book of Revelation, one enters a world
of controversy and confusion. Without some clarity of context, such
controversy and confusion becomes all the more problematic. This is
not a family vacation in which the road trip entails a succession of sign-
posts and advertisements along the highway. The reader is set up to
enter a maze in which the final outcome is also the true beginning.
Similar to T. S. Eliot's wisdom, Revelation's end is really the beginning.
Events that occur in Revelation do not represent a succession of sequen-
tially occurring events. John writes as if dreaming, using a stream-of-
consciousness technique. The past and present occur at the same time,
as do the imminent and the transcendent. Such a methodology concurs
with my desire for the transcendent God to also be here and now.

In many ways this book you hold in your hand is a confessional
book, in the sense that I am a self-avowed Christian. I do not hide this

fact. My concern, however, is that I may contradict the aim of this
book if you, the reader, are not able to journey along with me, due
to feeling alienated by my particular identity or having already been
harmed by unhelpful interpretations of the book of Revelation. I am
reminded of my own alienation when I hear people co-opt blackness as
a negative image: black ice, dark soul, dark thoughts, film noir. Oftentimes, white people will use such language with no ill intent toward
me as a black and dark person. The parallel to Revelation is that we all
need to be educated as to how intent affects impact. John's intent is
to see the healing of the *ethnoi*, the
people. His impact, however, often
causes more nightmares.

> Discovering the Living One is dan-
> gerous, and we would know less of it
> without the fractured and disturbed lan-
> guages of people like John the Divine
> and their contemporary equivalents.
> —Rowan Williams, *A Ray of Darkness*

Rowan Williams is helpful in
solving the problem of the gap
between intent and impact. The
provocative title of his book *A Ray
of Darkness* is a paradox, he says,
but one that easily annoys those who suspect that paradox conceals
"muddle"—an intellectual or spiritual cowardice. We *need* paradox,
however. Of all people, John of Patmos helps us see this because "we
need to express some sense of this strange fact that our language doesn't
'keep up' with the multiplicity and interrelatedness and elusiveness of
truth."[1] Perhaps this is why I adhere to my context as a black Episcopal
priest and theologian who still sees himself in the black church. I hold
up the black church in a white church here because I still see myself in
a unified church. John encourages me in his Revelation when he says
that light and darkness as we know it will one day have a complete
paradigm shift (Rev. 21:23). So, before we begin, please know that my
intent is not to alienate anyone; rather, I seek to imagine in my particular Christian context how a view of heaven need not lead to culture
wars and further excuses for oppressing others. Heaven, as envisioned
by John of Patmos, has much greater purpose.

In our beginning it is important to understand that John does not
provide a linear narrative in which we know how many miles are left
until we reach Disney World; rather, he jumps back and forth, with
God's judgments and events happening at the same time. This way
of telling the story is important for so many of us using Revelation. I
mean it when I say we "use" the book. Too often Revelation is used
to wag God's judgmental finger. From the reader's perspective, however, much of God's judgments appear unintelligible due to conflicting

symbolism. For example, the seven broken seals seem to be obvious, and yet from another perspective they look like seven trumpets, and from a third angle they look like seven bowls of wrath.

John writes in medias res, in the midst of a messy world, to encourage the members in the backseat of his journey to resist the powers and principalities that keep making us turn in the wrong direction. Indeed, where is God and what is God doing in the midst of such confusion and haplessness? In short, God is already with us (even driving in the front seat), but like little children on a long road trip, we lose patience with God because we lose patience with the journey. It is better to create our own gods, idols, and powers. In other words, we want to stop our journey with God too soon. So, God reminds us with nightmares and visions that we haven't arrived yet—that the way we live now must become a more mature way to live. Similar to the need to grow out of the immaturity of treating heaven as some kind of pot of gold at the end of a rainbow, John's Revelation demands that we change our selfish paradigms of heaven that is separated from earth. This is so heavy a challenge that Revelation bursts our bubble of what heaven is like.

John takes this methodology seriously because he does not edit his stream of consciousness. He allows its own logic to imagine normative ethics through the story of a persecuted Christian community. This is why he uses superheroes and monsters to symbolize how Christians discern what is of God and how to behave on earth as it is in heaven. But what I love most about John's imagination is in how the main superhero is often galloping (or however lambs walk) behind the scenes as the greatest power. The Lamb is the greatest superhero—even more than the rider on the white horse. Although true to the indiscriminate nature of a lamb's pastoral presence, this greatest of superheroes causes the apocalyptic bang. In other words, the Lamb is more ferocious than the dragon and the beasts from the sea and land.

* * *

With this strange journey of ending before we begin and superheroes who are little lambs, I feel the obligation to tell you about our trip here before we get into the thick of things. In terms of my methodology, I rely on personal experience and use this genre—including vignettes from theologians, hymnody, literature, and popular culture—throughout the commentary to make the case for a sense of how to realize heaven on earth. I hope the reader will discover that I am passionate about this work, and I hope that my particular perspective will not hinder the reader from also pursuing heaven on earth. In fact, I hope such passion will reflect the creative bent to my work. Of course, such creativity will always have to be judged through the eye of the beholder—the reader. The commitment to a concretized view of heaven requires passion, given the state of our world: political deadlock, war, global warming, racial profiling, civil war among Abrahamic faiths (Islam, Christianity, and Judaism), increasing poverty, and a squandering of resources.

So, how will I make this book manageable to read? How do I map it out? I divide this book into three parts. First, in order to better see our own chaotic world and societies around us, we look at the nightmares and strange occurrences in the narrative of Revelation. I introduce my thesis here that the writer of Revelation creates the same parallel because he never allows heaven and earth's nightmares to separate. I adopt John's stream-of-consciousness technique of going back and forth between the nightmares and strange events in both heaven and earth.

These shocking nightmares and visions lead us to part 2—waking up to the problems in Christian faith today. Problems such as individualism often result from these nightmares; unfortunately, we would rather stay in our individualistic worlds than enter into the dreamscape again to envision better communities. Although in parts 1 and 2 we wrestle with John's strange world, it is important to note that visions like John's are not linear. A significant number of biblical scholars would even agree that it is wrong to force a chronological framework on the visions of Revelation.

This conundrum leads to part 3, in which we dream again, but this time with guides along the way who help us navigate the paralysis of our nightmares and idealism, guides such as Martin Luther King Jr. and Desmond Tutu. These two guides help us with our stream of consciousness in that we are now free to wrestle with nightmares and still remain hopeful that change and good dreams are possible. Even more, they remind us that dreams can become reality. Because we have these good guides, our nightmares, insomnia, and good dreams flow together in a more cyclical pattern.

Throughout the book the reader will experience my impatience in the midst of nightmares and insomnia, of not waiting until John's beautiful and redemptive ending. Even in the first two parts I try to find ways of pointing toward John's beautiful ending of redemption.

Although our goal in organizing the book in three parts is to finish a trip, John's trip toward a healing tree of the *ethnoi* (ethnicities and nations), we must also be mature enough to withstand the contemplation needed to complete such a long and seemingly impossible journey. Inevitably on this journey we will experience the effects caused by impatience for John's new heaven and earth. Mostly, these effects are lethargy and false dichotomies between heaven and earth. Instead of heaven providing a reference point from which to see how to live on earth, we use our individualistic concepts of heaven to obsess about who is in or out of our constructed heavens and earths. We need Christian exemplars who adhere to restorative justice rather than the retributive models of justice that create eternal barriers between heaven and earth.

> Although many Christians preferred to leave the book [of Revelation] behind, others chose to not give up these vivid and compelling visions. Instead they reinterpreted them, as Christians have done ever since.
>
> —Elaine Pagels, *Revelations: Visions, Prophecy, and Politics in the Book of Revelation*

There is great need to return to our visionaries like King and Tutu to inform how we may practice heaven by becoming more like God. We must practice the presence of God in order to find heaven in our midst. In order to practice heaven, I argue, we will need to become more like God—a deeply troubling notion for most of us to wrap our minds around. In order for us to exist in heaven without such reality becoming too overwhelming to us, we will have to become God's beloved community. In the minds of many Christian mystics, the human process of becoming like (or mutual to) God creates helpful social and political movements. King's concept of the beloved community is vital here. The blessing of seeing God, however, becomes a burden in the world because those who become visionaries can no longer stay silent in systems and structures that belittle God's image.

In the process we learn more about the concept of Ubuntu, in which the spirituality of community continues to take on deeper meanings and connections to the concept of heaven. Tutu is a champion of this concept of Ubuntu in which the goal is to be persons in community. The concept of Ubuntu also helps us solve the divisions between heaven and earth, which need not be mutually exclusive but in fact exist in order to provide the reference point for why we are here at all. Jesus sums up why we are here: we are to love God, self, and neighbor. As we will explore in this book, there are many reasons why it is difficult for Christians to really believe this. Perhaps we fail to take Jesus seriously because we often grow bored with his simplicity and focus. Perhaps our language betrays us as we use spiritual language. And perhaps we need to mature enough in our spiritual lives so that our individualistic tendencies no longer interpret apocalyptic discourse to meet our own needs.

PART ONE

Revelation's Nightmares

1

God, Are You There?

It opened its mouth to utter blasphemies against God, blaspheming his name and his dwelling, that is, those who dwell in heaven.
—Revelation 13:6

I know God is beyond us, but I need God here with me.

I am not the only one in this predicament, as you will hear me argue in this book. It is my hope that a down-to-earth conversation about why the book of Revelation remains important today can help with this predicament. Revelation is down-to-earth because it is not just for church folks to read—or preachers, or scholars, or students—but for anyone trying to understand the goal of what God creates. People riding subways, working on farms, and protesting in the streets are all wondering about this goal. The wonder is so profound that we often end in deep conflict as we struggle over whose interpretation is the true answer. The goal of God's creation, Revelation tells us, is to end in heaven, but it's not the kind of heaven you might have in mind.

The essential problem of heaven is that not many of us really want it. A friend told me that a Nazi once said, "You take care of the things of heaven and we'll take care of the earth." Thankfully, my friend had a witty response, "That's a bad division of real estate." Out of nothing, God makes human beings dream of and envision a community reflective of heaven on earth. Even through hopeless situations, God requires us to believe—even in heaven. One of the essential points I want to make is that many of us no longer know how to believe in heaven. We are caught between two extremes. On one hand, the concept of heaven is no longer taken seriously because of seeming irrelevancy to our earthly existence. On the other, some believe so strongly in their

3

personal versions of heaven that whole swaths of human communities are considered dispensable and left out.

I want to find a way to believe in heaven in which we can both take it seriously and leave no one behind. Whether we like it or not, heaven is important. Without a concept of heaven, we lack the basis for why we exist on earth. Lacking such vision, we wander in a wilderness and forget for whom we are made. Therefore, my vision of heaven does not assume anyone else is in hell. For this reason, I need to make sure that the reader receives a "map" so that one knows where one is going. In addition, we need to deal with biblical texts that seem to contradict me, suggesting that there indeed is a hell.

If one consistently argues that heaven is not otherworldly but a means to God's presence, then one needs to bring to life teachings of Scripture (for instance, Rom. 8:18–25; Rev. 21:1–7; 1 Cor. 15:20–29). The typical criticisms against my argument that heaven and earth are intrinsically related usually follow the same debates around pantheism in which perceived reality is inseparable from divine reality. Perceiving my argument as somehow against God's transcendence misses the mark, however. I am more iconoclastic than pantheistic. What many Western Christians perceive as "orthodox" Christianity is more aptly described as "individualistic" or "personal" Christianity. This kind of Christianity easily sees the apocalyptic only in individualistic terms: for example, if one does not accept Jesus as personal savior, then one goes to hell forever. I argue here, however, that there can be no individual salvation (understood as an afterlife) apart from communal transformation of communities and sociopolitical systems. In order to guard against Westernized, individualistic kinds of utopias, one must wrestle with how earth and heaven are interrelated. Heaven is not separated from earth, because by doing so we define earthly existence as somehow the same as heavenly existence. In other words, heaven is for those who deserve it and earth for those who deserve less than heaven. Heaven becomes the extrapolation of the good life for those who are underprivileged. What I argue here, however, is that the confluence between earth and heaven is not meant to make heaven simply a better earth. No, heaven provides the reference point of paradigm shifts and transformation rather than technical fixes such as making the poor a little less poor.

My method will be to travel toward heaven in light of its common problems of individualism, boredom, and delusion. Through these three pitfalls of heaven, I will ask how counterviews of heaven can facilitate a better life on earth. Be warned that I will not try to exhaust the historical thought on heaven nor try to trace all the factors that led to the current demise of heaven. Rather, I examine pivotal figures who offer explicit direction as to where (or where not) to look for heaven. I invite the reader to slow down and imagine with me how heaven and earth intersect.

We will have a wise cast of characters to help us imagine this intersection. It is also important to note the meaning of some of the terms used in this book. I use the ancient category of *soul* (the emotional center of life) that is distinct from *spirit* (conscious being). I understand spirit to be capable of the full presence of God, but few obtain such awareness. Those who do obtain consciousness of God's presence are called *mystics*. Mystics describe heaven as unmediated contact with the supernatural life of God. So those on earth can catch glimpses of heaven. I also see heaven as that place where our deep gladness meets the world's deep hunger, which is Frederick Buechner's beautiful definition of vocation. This *theology of proximity* also describes heaven, which also constitutes angels and the community of saints who always touch the world's deep hunger with deep gladness. Such a worldview of mystical community is increasingly strange for Westerners, whereas in the Southern Hemisphere angels and the communion of saints remain alive and vital in our earthly existence.

One way for Westerners to recover a healthy concept of heaven is to reintroduce the concept of *beatitude* as synonymous with heaven.

> Christianity is "permanent revolution" or *metanoia* which does not come to an end in this world, this life, or this time.
> —H. Richard Niebuhr,
> *The Meaning of Revelation*

Beatitude is essentially the knowledge and experience of God that, when possessed, leaves nothing to be desired. Beatitude enables imagination of how relationships among persons are healthy. Charles Williams has such imagination as he states, "So full of derivation and nourishment are these [relationships] that they may well be named the in-othering . . . and the in-Godding."[1] This in-othering and in-Godding too can happen on earth—the discovery of beatitude in the other.

Lastly, *earth* is used differently than *world*. *Earth* means the corporate life of empirical existence as we know it here and now—that is, our struggles as mammals and creatures, systems and structures. In this book, I do not intend heaven to mean a better earth, because such imagination forfeits the possibility of the paradigm shifts needed for us to solve seemingly irresolvable conflicts (i.e., war, poverty, disease).

What I suggest by *world* that is different from earth are those instinctual and structural struggles that are ambivalent toward participating in the full presence of God.

Many have used the language of transformation, spirituality, and empowerment to write about the apparent notion of heaven. Rather than putting forth a new interpretation of heaven, I intend to remember heaven as some of my Christian ancestors and contemporary Christian exemplars teach me. Even still, my concept of heaven will indeed be challenged by many who pursue discrete and exclusive worldviews within Christian communities. Eventually, in this book, I argue that there should be a common desire for heaven—otherwise, heaven will remain unintelligible. This common desire is the miracle we are all looking for. Without an interdependent vision of what perfects us all, no person can be ultimately happy—in heaven.

In large part, this down-to-earth approach is vital for us today because Revelation remains an authoritative document about what God's presence (i.e., heaven) looks like and who gets to live there in an uninhibited way. Instead of this world in which bad things happen to good people, many of us believe there will be a world of uninhibited goodness in which select citizens get to live. Such a controversial conversation, however, usually does not end well because select citizens presuppose others who are excluded. I argue here that the book of Revelation narrates this conversation about heavenly selection in a different manner. Human beings do not select heavenly citizens. God makes these determinations, which is fitting since the actual book of Revelation does have a "happily ever after" ending. So, why do we fuss and fight about who lives uninhibitedly with God?

In short, we fight because we are narrow-minded. I must apologize here for making insults in our very introductions to each other! Here is what I mean. Conversations concerning the book of Revelation fail to consider how the writer of this apocalyptic vision is also weighted in controversy and confusion. In other words, Revelation is a disorienting vision that naturally elicits controversy and, I would add, confusion. John's speech intentionally interrupts and throws us off course. This is so because John himself is disrupted by a vision any mortal person has difficulty recognizing—heaven on earth. His disorienting voice can speak for itself, "I turned to see whose voice it was that spoke to me" (Rev. 1:12). Only someone who is confused "sees" people's voices.

Any book on Revelation worth its salt contains controversial elements. This is so because Revelation is meant to be a controversial, provocative vision of what it looks like for God to be uninhibited with us. I write this book with such vision in mind so that spiritual leaders may know how to respond in healthy ways to the dreams and nightmares in Revelation. Throughout history most civilizations have contemplated their own end. In my writing, therefore, one will not find a great deal of debates between faith and history or how one applies the historical-critical method to Scripture. In short, my premise is that John's Apocalypse is a vision in which heaven and earth cannot be separated because God's presence cannot be inhibited. In fact, the term *apocalypse* means a veil lifted, disclosing something hidden from humanity.

An uninhibited God is what I think of as heaven. Such presence among creation is the reason for the design on the cover of this book. It displays the *mandorla* (an Italian word for almond). The mandorla, two circles overlapping one another to form an almond shape in the middle, symbolizes interaction between opposing worlds. In this book, these worlds may be taken to represent heaven and earth. Early Christians used the symbol of the mandorla to represent a merging of heaven and earth. This evolved into the symbol of God's merger through the incarnation in Jesus who becomes heaven and earth in microcosm. The deepening of the symbolism of the mandorla to mean Jesus himself was practiced by early Christians who revealed themselves to one another by scratching a small circle in a wall. Another Christian would come along and scratch another circle slightly overlapping the first one. In this clandestine activity, Christians could communicate during times of persecution and thus complete a mandorla, which also indicated the sign of the fish, an early symbol of Jesus.

The symbol of the mandorla is important in terms of understanding worlds torn apart. It is also an image that helps us understand Jesus. Rowan Williams explains Jesus' impact: "He has made an empty space in the world for God to come in. And so he does not any longer belong just to the world of human beings: he is a space in the world . . . the place where God is free to act and to suffer. He has made room for God."[2] It is as though Jesus becomes the ultimate mandorla, in which there are no divisions, no exclusions of race, politics, sex, economics, and power. Jesus is the space between worlds for all to move from desolation to consolation. And so I invite the reader to move with me theologically as I anticipate typical culture wars over what inhibits God's freedom to merge heaven and earth.

Here we struggle between heaven and earth to discover that place where God ultimately resides. In my speculative imagination, that place looks like ultimate reconciliation. At the heart of the drama of reconciliation in the book of Revelation is the war both in heaven and on earth in which good struggles against evil, consolation against desolation. My interpretation of the book of Revelation is ultimately not doom and gloom. The ultimate message that I discover in Revelation is one in which the times of desolation, when one surrenders in apocalyptic tensions, provoke God and us to move toward consolation. This is why God's angelic hosts show us a crystal clear river at the end. By the riverbank is a fruit tree—perhaps even an almond tree. Eating its fruit this time does not cast us out of paradise but welcomes us back in and even heals the *ethnoi*, the nations.

John's apocalyptic vision unconsciously invites God into our mandorla. The healing of the splits in creation begins. My spiritual director, Brother Curtis Almquist, SSJE, gave me a metaphor to help me see what is going on in Revelation. When I was going through specific tensions in my own life between desolation and consolation, he told me, "A Christian is called to live in between desolation and consolation, like a mandorla." As a spiritual leader I am called not to settle in consolation or desolation, because I will need to minister to those stuck in one or the other. Such claustrophobia will only wreak havoc and dysfunction.

"Michael," Brother Curtis said, "you must bushwhack a well-worn path between consolation and desolation. Remove the weeds and briers so that you can move easily between the two worlds and create your own mandorla."

The important point here, especially in light of our conservative, moderate, and liberal conflicts over Scripture, is that John's Apocalypse neither traps folks in hell nor makes us content in heaven knowing that others are weeping and gnashing their teeth forever. The book of Revelation instead invites an overlap between heaven and earth, generally very thin at first as John has a lot of nightmares and scary visions, but the well-worn path between heaven and earth that John describes eventually produces greater overlap. So great that a crystal river runs through. With greater overlap between heaven and earth, the healing of the nations is finally seen.

When we think better about heaven we think better about justice—especially restorative justice. Despite some readings of Revelation, God's presence is not vindictive. Such a narrow perspective of God justifies many power schemes in which our phobias and isms flourish. Racism, sexism, homophobia, and classism all flourish through a big story that says God smites those who live in darkness and blackness. In this metanarrative, God's retributive justice regains the power balance of the way things used to be. More and more, we are hearing a counter metanarrative in which God's power is not controlled by time and circumstance; rather, God's power is not what we often think it is, such as toppling chariots, gutting dragons, and building mass graves for sinners to weep and gnash their teeth. God's power is not like that. Instead, God's power is revealed through the vulnerability of love that does not coerce or demand unearned intimacy. Such a power is practical realizing that retribution's logic yields to anarchy. In Jesus, the power of restorative justice looks practical in its counternarrative against anarchy, cycles of violence, recidivism of the incarcerated, and so much more.

> The oppressed do not see any dichotomy between God's love and God's justice.
> —Allan Boesak, *Comfort and Protest: The Apocalypse from a South African Perspective*

We must remember that those who focused on reparation and retribution, like the liberation theologians in the 1960s and 1970s, were *all for* a collective vision of shared theology, humanity, and, yes, heaven on earth. Other American Christians like the Catholic convert Dorothy Day advocated for restorative justice and change, trying to bring heaven to the cities of the 1930s to 1950s. Although I focus in subsequent chapters on the thought and work of Archbishop Desmond Tutu and Martin Luther King Jr., there are many others who share a restorative justice vision for heaven on earth, including Latin American and Hispanic liberation theologians whose ideas overlap with my own. And yet, more work remains to discover how restorative justice is a vital concept to help us think toward ultimate solutions.

INTERDEPENDENT SALVATION

Especially in this twenty-first-century world, still dominated by Western culture, we need others to help us rethink justice outside the scope of personal salvation alone. The problem here is that in personal salvation no one else really matters. As long as I am saved, it doesn't matter if I hear others weeping and gnashing their teeth forever. My personal heaven is so titanic in its protective membrane that my existential happiness is not affected by others who suffer forever. In fact, I can be ultimately happy that people deserve their just punishment. This way of reading Revelation, however, is erroneous and dangerous.

The confluence of heavenly and earthly existence can only be imagined through a personal lifestyle that takes into account the fact that others exist. Logically speaking, I cannot even be happy unless I have a frame of reference that others are happy as well. For example, when I celebrate my birthday I do so only in the reality of others who help me practice the concept of celebration. In other words, celebration implies that others exist. The reward in this imagination is the discovery of what indeed is personal; namely, we cannot be personal without also being interpersonal. I'm sorry to say to the rugged individualists out there—that's just the way we are made.

So I invite the reader to guard against those heavens in which one is personally joyful while others suffer in hell. We need each other to know our own personal salvation. Even though we must first confess our broken reality, eventually we should all have a common quest for heaven. Without such a common vision we perpetuate war on earth, as individuals and groups think they can be whole at the other's expense. In philosophy, this is called solipsism—the individual's world is all that really matters.

It was only when I first traveled to Africa that I realized my own Western solipsism. I realized that I have amphibious identity as an African American. Because of the historical and sociological realities of the United States, I never really felt like an "American"—a description that is itself problematic and presumptuous (as if Canadians or Bolivians are not American also). But when I was in Africa, those who were African did not see me as African, but American. My accent, attire, and lack of rites of passage let them know right away that I was not really African. I found that those experiences have helped prepare me to write this commentary.

In this book about heaven and earth's communal approach to salvation, I have the daunting task of trying to show our amphibious identities as citizens of heaven and earth. My daunting task is that I must find a way to bridge my point of view with those who rightfully refuse to listen to me. A conservative Christian certainly can critique my universalism. Non-Western readers are right to critique my perspective as a Westerner who has the leisure to write a book. Unless I make this personal confession, many readers will feel as though they have embarked upon one long sermon—unclear as to whom I imagine is sitting in the church pews. As I have already indicated, I hope the church pews morph beyond affinity groups and into chairs and subways full of diverse people who want to figure out a better heaven than a personal one in which I can be happy while someone else is suffering. And yet the personal dimension of heaven is important because it creates a desire to reach ultimate fulfillment. What is counterintuitive (at least for many Western people) is that such personal fulfillment requires community. Trying to explain personal fulfillment in this way is a daunting task in Western culture.

I also think my task is daunting because of the social isolation of the United States in which many may say they want the planet to flourish while at the same time lacking a worldview that other people around the world are actually suffering because of how we live in the United States. In other words, my habits betray me by wasting the world's resources. My nation-state is a fraction of the world's population, and yet we control an outsize share of the global resources. Saying this and truly realizing this are two different realities.

One of the most important practices for citizens in the United States is to travel the world (yes, really the world, and not just southern France or Ireland). Such travel moves away from lavish vacations and into pilgrimage toward God. Responsibly seeking God in the world will not waste resources if such travel opens the eyes of US citizens to how we positively and negatively affect God's creation. As in the pilgrimage of Malcolm X and many others, when we travel we cannot help but be open to epiphany and the empowerment of others. Such travel is our responsibility, especially since many of us are capable of doing so. Such experience will let us know there really are worlds—heaven and earth—out there and not just in here. This is also important because not many Western people, especially through their belief in heaven, realize how narrow our worldview is. One piece of evidence of this was a national geography test in which a majority of high school students in the United States thought Nicaragua was in the Middle East. Again, it seems difficult to write a book with the intent of helping people to want to see heaven differently if the frame of reference is small. And so I even hope people will read this commentary without a church pew—perhaps in a subway or on a bench in a temple or on a mat in a mosque.

To make this book manageable, I have sought to narrow my mandorla pursuit of heaven on earth. If the reader seeks more analytical surveys of the concept of heaven, I suggest works such as Huston Smith's *Why Religion Matters* or Robert Orsi's *Between Heaven and Earth*, especially to address the challenges of studying religion. Also, Robert Wuthnow's *After Heaven* could give some sociological and theoretical context for concepts of heaven.[3] These works seriously entertain other perspectives of heaven (all the while trying to *understand* why these other perspectives have worked for so many people). These authors also show how American Christians have related to and imagined heaven, and they are models of sound and original scholarship. I provide more of a confessional work than these authors because I consciously write as a Christian theologian and practitioner of Christian faith.

I believe in heaven, but I do not want to go on a crusade or inquisition. Heaven is too dangerous for that. I do not want to use heaven on earth for those with power to justify their own political and personal favor. Because of this confession, my work on heaven is not analytical in the sense of tracing a theoretical concept. It is not my intention to analyze the notions of heaven by tracing its existence across long periods of time and diverse cultures. After all, heaven cannot be analyzed without recognizing how its subjective nuances might differ in varied cultural contexts. Therefore, I have provided this reference point to not only show the problem with heaven that I have located but also explain why it is a problem. In this way, I appreciate the candor of one reviewer who saw an early draft of this book and wrote that I "would do much better if [I] were to step down from [my] soapbox a bit." And so I look seriously at what others are saying about heaven—because after all, the Western, individualistic perspective of heaven and classical Christian eschatology has worked for so many people from a variety of ethnic backgrounds.

> Long before Mahatma Gandhi in India or Martin Luther King Jr. in the American South, John of Patmos asked his people to engage in a testimony . . . nonviolent resistance.
>
> —Brian Blount, *Revelation: A Commentary*

The same critic also reminded me that one's argument, however strong, is weakened by a failure to look at the other side's position. It is not enough to say the other perspective is wrong. By doing so, I would defeat the very purpose of writing this book—trying to imagine a heaven on earth for us all. I am in debt to reviewers of this book because they forced me to confess that I cannot write about heaven in an analytical way—that I am always standing on a soapbox as long as heaven comes out of my mouth. This is why I rely a great deal on King and Tutu. King contended with the shattering of hope as many in the civil rights movement began to view his utopian vision as unproductive and idealistic. King states: "Yes, I am personally the victim of deferred dreams, of blasted hopes, but in spite of that I close today by saying I still have a dream, because, you know, you can't give up in life. If you lose hope, somehow you lose that vitality that keeps life moving, you lose that courage to be, that quality that helps you to go on in spite of all, and so today I still have a dream."[4]

It is in the face of shattered hopes and dreams that recourse to heaven on earth is made all the more powerful. King states, "Let us be dissatisfied until rat-infested, vermin-filled slums will be a thing of a dark past and every family will have a decent sanitary house in which to live. Let us be dissatisfied until the empty stomachs of Mississippi are filled and the idle industries of Appalachia are revitalized. . . . Let us be dissatisfied until our brothers and sisters of the Third World—Asia, Africa and Latin America—will no longer be the victim of imperialist exploitation, but will be lifted from the long night of poverty, illiteracy and disease."[5] King is helpful here as we must pay historical attention to why the book of Revelation was written in the first place to address how hopes and dreams shatter.

2

Context Matters

Then I turned to see whose voice it was that spoke to me, and on turning I saw seven golden lampstands.

—Revelation 1:12

The book of Revelation is really a letter. Similar to the insight of the mandorla, it provides a message moving between despair and hope. Such apocalyptic literature provides such movement to warn us that there is a collision ahead. Ordinary language is not sufficient to describe this collision. There must be visions, poetry, and dreams. Apocalyptic imagery is odd for a reason—John sees voices for a reason—namely, because we lack a full reference point from which to describe the newer reality in our midst. Hence, as we will soon see in John's visions, strange things occur, like a lamb being the shepherd. In the case of Revelation, the historical setting is important—both in terms of why the book was written as well as the situations of the audience to whom the book is addressed.

To situate this historical setting in light of my theme of heaven on earth, John's vision is that the church should not flee from this world. John's focus is rather on changing the world through nonviolent resistance to evil powers and principalities.[1] On this point, Brian Blount engages the reader to think deeply about John's "mean book" of Revelation.[2] To understand why Revelation is a mean book, it serves us well to identify who it is that writes this apocalyptic text. But biblical scholars confess the impossible task in absolutely identifying the authorship of Revelation. What makes us call him John comes from the autobiographical approach of the writer who names himself (1:1). The question is not so much whether John wrote Revelation as it is which

John wrote it. We tend to settle on John the beloved disciple because early church authorities like Justin Martyr identified the writer of Revelation as the famous John, one of Jesus' twelve apostles.[3] There is no betrayal of trust, however, if the author is not actually John the beloved disciple of Jesus, because apocalyptic literature was often written under pseudonyms.

Until recently, biblical scholarship dated the book of Revelation to the times of systematic persecution of the early church, but recent studies conclude that Revelation was written at the end of Domitian's reign (81–96 CE), when there was no such systematic persecution. Most likely, John of Patmos put forth his vision in approximately 95 CE, during the time of colonial forces that did not go out of their way to hunt down the early church. Historical evidence suggests that John's apocalyptic vision was not about Christians fleeing from the world but more about proactive Christianity—that is, what happens when Christian commitments are lived out in the world. Such expectation will naturally produce persecution from corrupted powers and governments. Blount sums it up by saying that the problem lay with the imminent conflict John of Patmos knew would erupt if his audience lived out their Christian faith. This would be John's own kind of uncompromised Christianity that he refused to back away from and so expected from his churches in Asia Minor.[4]

That Christians during this time were not systematically persecuted also explains John's admonishing the seven churches in Asia Minor that they need to practice their faith. It was almost as if John wanted the churches to go on the offense rather than defense, a scenario that may seem counterintuitive. As we will see, however, with Martin Luther King Jr. and Desmond Tutu, such bold action is par for the course for Christian leaders who plan nonviolent resistance. Although John's Apocalypse will be interpreted differently by each of us, his historical and theological context safeguards against dysfunctional interpretations of the book of Revelation.

I aim here to recover such theological safeguards that can inspire common language for heaven—safeguards that provide a frame of reference beyond crusades or the exclusion of someone or some group. Without common language, there is no organization of our wants and needs. So I provide diverse images and voices in pursuit of heaven on earth. In so doing, my theological and social argument about heaven on earth is: We need heaven in order to see how to live on earth. Even more, we need each other to be in heaven. None of us can be in heaven unless we all are there. Any person's suffering disallows my own heaven. This perspective gives us better insight to improve our economics, politics, psychoanalysis, and social practices on earth. It also improves our religions and provides accountability to not make earthly matters worse.

John's Revelation provides apocalyptic opportunities—that is, we can learn new reference points in which to move out of constantly colliding worlds. Because our normal frame of reference entraps God, John uses weird and strange imagery to break our deadlock on God. John continues the narrative of monsters in combat scenes that he heard from prophets like Isaiah, Ezekiel, and Daniel. Like these prophets, John envisions the monsters in the stories to represent how human sin can run amok. Beasts represented corruption in human hearts as well as in colonial powers. Even though the early church may not have resembled the persecuted church of the Cecil B. DeMille movies, in John's context following his leadership was courageous in the sense that early Christians needed to know the consequences of their commitments to Jesus Christ as Lord. If they followed this Jesus, then they should not be surprised by how their commitments and habits would be in conflict with principalities and powers. This context continues to matter today because Christian commitments can have benign effects despite our historical contexts of crusades and witch hunts. A deterministic and often pessimistic view of history makes apocalyptic discourse distasteful to the contemporary believer who wants to believe that history is not planned out, that human behavior can effect positive changes in the course and direction of human living. In my commentary I aim for a view of Revelation that moves beyond dualisms and the rejection of the present world. I certainly do not want to favor an illusory future that never comes, but one that has already come in Jesus.

> So long as time lasts the apocalyptic reality impends upon each and every happening; in the very anarchy and futility that mark the fallen principalities and powers.
> —William Stringfellow, *Conscience & Obedience: The Politics of Romans 13 and Revelation 13 in Light of the Second Coming*

Christians who read Revelation should at least be acquainted with the historical context of John of Patmos; otherwise, we repeat a monstrous past in which human beings are unilaterally defined as means to a dictator's end. Revelation helps us see that we cannot escape apocalyptic worldviews, especially as I hear on the news of war beyond nation-states, pandemics, climate change, and unprecedented water shortages.

But in our present circumstances we can dream of a future in which human habits influence better outcomes than the end of the world.

Those of us who think we know who is going to hell or why John put certain words into the mouths of beasts and dragons would do well to learn from Jonah. He hated the Ninevites so much that he desired a pre-determined destruction for them all instead of God's universal redemption. Jonah's apocalyptic vision, however, was not God's vision. So in the course of time God used monsters like whales to actually save Jonah. God cannot be trapped into an apocalyptic predeterminism, because with mortals things are often impossible, but with God all things are possible, even using Jonah's obstinate behavior to change the course of an entire people's future. Even though John's Revelation of the Apocalypse is deeply problematic and scary, John believes that repentance is possible, even for the most egregious offenders (2:20–22).[5]

I hope that our conversation here raises theological questions as to how we can make heaven include not just those we like. As we delve into complex issues of who should be raptured or left behind, my hope is that we will join John's apocalyptic vision of clear water to wade through—eventually finding common understanding that we all will be healed (Rev. 21:1–4).

3

On Earth as in Heaven

So when the dragon saw that he had been thrown down to the earth, he pursued the woman who had given birth to the male child.

—Revelation 12:13

It might not be a surprise that with a name like Michael Battle I should be writing about the book of Revelation—especially given what is written in Revelation 12 about Michael battling the dragon. What should be surprising, however, is how I seek to describe the book of Revelation. We seem to receive mixed messages as to the confluence between earth and heaven. For example, the text from Revelation above seems to imply that earth is a place for the cursed. In this mixed message, the stereotype of biblical apocalyptic literature is such that many people (notably Hollywood producers and opportunistic writers) use it either to scare people into submission or to make as much money as possible from people seeking to escape this cursed existence. In fact, it is difficult even for me, a theologian, to find reliable perspectives on apocalyptic literature to help us think and feel closer to God and to each other on earth as it is in heaven. In short, these reflections on Revelation are summed up in the question: Should we desire heaven on earth? As we will see in John's vision, the answer is not so obvious.

On one hand, the return of Jesus is like a superhero movie—his hair like white wool, eyes like fire, and a voice "like the sound of many waters" (Rev. 1:14–15). Upon seeing this warrior holding stars and wielding a two-edged sword, one quickly concludes that not much heaven will be brought to earth—only destruction.

And war broke out in heaven; Michael and his angels fought against the dragon.
—Revelation 12:7a

And yet, as we will discover as we move through John's vision, Jesus as warrior becomes a lamb who ironically leads us to the healing of earth and, surprisingly, of heaven.

My simple definition of heaven is this: where God is present. After all, heaven is God's abode—where God hangs out. Should we desire heaven on earth? Yes, we should desire to hang out with God. This longing has special importance to me as a black theologian. So much of my work has been trying to get people to be aware of God's ways and peculiarities. For example, unlike the cliché about God, God is not color-blind. God does not want us all to be the same when we hang out together. Indeed, God took great delight in making us strange and peculiar. God wants us to be different, but different in the way God is by coupling difference and community together.

So I begin our journey with the quandary of heaven on earth. I perceive that our pursuits of various kinds of heavens (some inclusive of earth and some not) have exacerbated culture wars through individualistic pursuits of salvation. For many who focus on this apocalyptic book of Revelation, the existential reality is this: as long as I make it into heaven (to hell with earth), that is all that really matters. I seek, however, to answer this question about heaven through a different existential scope—one which sees that Revelation invites the reader to imagine beyond individual angst and aim toward aligning God's creation with God's intentions. How will God fix earthly things to contain heaven?

In this volume I will refer to the following simple chart by my fellow Anglican E. W. Bullinger that shows how he understands the pairing of heaven and earth.[1] I will reference work from older and more traditional scholars as well and provide my own contemporary theology from often-neglected sources such as African and black church leaders. All of these sages teach us that heaven is a communal pursuit and is inclusive of God's created universe, even earth.

It is in God's inclusive nature that we understand the structure of the book of Revelation, in which there are seven pairs of visions. These visions are symmetrical, so that in each John sees "in heaven" and also "on earth." Heaven's vision prepares John for his vision afterward on earth. Heaven and earth mutually form one another. This mutuality is key to understanding Revelation and is often difficult for those whose theology cannot tolerate synthesis and mutuality. Theological interpretation of Revelation favoring one's own perspective or affinity group can only lead to division and dangerous interpretations.

Symmetry of Heaven and Earth

1st	Rev. 4 and 5	In Heaven	(The Throne, the Book, and the Lamb)
	Rev. 6:1–7:8	On Earth	(The Six Seals and 144,000)
2nd	Rev. 7:9–8:6	In Heaven	(The Great Multitude and the Seventh Seal)
	Rev. 8:7–11:14	On Earth	(The Six Trumpets)
3rd	Rev. 11:15–19	In Heaven	(The Seventh Trumpet)
	Rev. 11:19	On Earth	(The Earthquake, etc.)
4th	Rev. 12:1–12	In Heaven	(Woman, Child, and Dragon)
	Rev. 12:13–13:18	On Earth	(The Dragon and Two Beasts)
5th	Rev. 14:1–5	In Heaven	(The Lamb and 144,000)
	Rev. 14:6–20	On Earth	(The Six Angels)
6th	Rev. 15:1–8	In Heaven	(The Seven Angels with Bowls)
	Rev. 16:1–18:24	On Earth	(The Seven Bowls)
7th	Rev. 19:1–16	In Heaven	(The Marriage of the Lamb, etc.)
	Rev. 19:17–20:15	On Earth	(The Final Five Judgments)

THE FAITHFUL WITNESS

Individualistic interpretations are misleading and often incite the Hollywood frenzy of a solipsistic apocalypse—one in which God's metanarrative of redemption is ignored. These heavenly and earthly visions are important in terms of framing our interpretations because they never allow us to separate what is going on in heaven from earth's activities. John's vision begins with Jesus, "the faithful witness," who provides the importance and significance to the whole book of Revelation. Jesus and his paradoxical imagery in John's visions is the key to all that follows and carries us forward through the muck and mire, the dreams and the nightmares. John says, "To him who loves us and freed us from our sins by his blood, and made us to be a kingdom" (Rev. 1:5). No words could be more important for fixing our minds on the great central principle of Revelation.

So my starting point is problematic, just as is Revelation. This apocalyptic book is a natural lightning rod for affinity groups trying to buttress their own concerns and worldviews. At the end of the day, however, they display only their self-interested outcomes. Naturally, a conservative political reading of Revelation will inevitably end up championing how heroes and heroines in Revelation look like conservatives. Likewise, liberally minded readings rearrange virtues to match liberal agendas. And so the numerous commentaries as well as the millions of people reading them are often abiding in self-fulfilling prophecies—preaching to the choir.

Many readers treat Revelation as an oracle in which to find who is in or out of favor with God. Who will go to hell? The whole Bible is for everyone, and in every age, and yet it must be read responsibly and particularly. The book of Revelation is no exception. Erroneous readings arise from our own natural selfishness. Those who interpret Revelation naturally want to be among the saved. On this system of interpretation the Bible is useless for the purposes of divine revelation. Instead it is only useful for warring human revelation. No wonder Revelation is usually neglected in mainline Christianity and obsessed upon in more conservative forms of Christianity.

It is in this problematic context of reading Revelation that I desire to understand this book of prophecy not out of the warring interpretations of the book but out of its purpose—to finally see heaven on earth. It will require patience and prayer as we test together how we can discover such an apocalyptic claim of heaven on earth. As a good seminary professor is prone to do, I invite you to forget those assumptions that keep us at war and be prepared and ready to unlearn anything that you may have received from self-interest alone, and learn afresh from the Word that is near you.

"Blessed is the one who reads aloud the words of the prophecy, and blessed are those who hear and who keep what is written in it; for the time is near" (Rev. 1:3). Not many of us really want what I describe as heaven—that state of God's presence in which *all* persons are made wholly complete. Some may disagree, but heaven is not ultimately about whether you or I get there as individuals. The ultimate reality of heaven is the joy derived from interdependent persons who adore someone greater than themselves—God. I argue for this definition of heaven because I cannot imagine being wholly complete unless everyone else is. In other words, how could I be completely happy and still be conscious of someone else weeping and gnashing their teeth forever in hell?

John's own quantum physics also invites us into this reality as he collapses space and time into one person. "'I am the Alpha and the Omega,' says the Lord God, who is and who was and who is to come, the Almighty. I, John, your brother who share with you in Jesus the persecution and the kingdom and the patient endurance, was on the island called Patmos because of the word of God and the testimony of Jesus" (Rev. 1:8–9).

How could I still be in heaven at the same time someone else is suffering in hell? Surely, in heaven as on earth, I would feel remorse for the other's suffering, thereby lessening the reality of my joy. Yet it seems to me that if one did a poll asking most Christians whether they personally hope and would like to go to heaven, there would be a mixed answer. For example, one could refer to a poll which found that among those Americans who believe in heaven, 82 percent expect to go there.[2] On the other hand, the poll mentioned that only 85 percent of Christians even believe in heaven.

Even in popular culture outside of Christian circles, personal expectation of going to heaven carries a mixed response. A 2014 poll of U.S. adults found that only 47% of non-Christian people of faith and 37% of nonbelievers even believe in the existence of heaven. This poll did not say what proportion of those people believe they are headed to heaven, but it sheds light on the ambiguity of heaven in the 21st century world.[3] In my work in prisons, I noticed that some of those who were on death row or who had committed violent crimes still find the faith that God can forgive them, allowing redemption to enter heaven one day. So most of us in the western world may find the concept of heaven ambiguous at best because as I argue here, heaven loses its existential fullness of joy in the logic that someone else is in hell. In addition, since much of religious discourse has been cast into the personal realm, I think it becomes all the harder to imagine heaven that includes those who are different from me. I argue here that most of us who consciously believe in heaven have not meditated deeply enough on the interpersonal dimension of heaven—that heaven is unintelligible as long as someone else is suffering.

How then can we talk intelligibly about heaven? According to most Christian conceptions, God's domicile is in heaven and not on earth. What is cloaked in this dualistic construct is the idea that the transcendent God is beyond the earth. This is a crude concept of God, however. God lodging in heaven is little more than an attempt to form the abstract idea of transcendence in space and time. This problem also leads to the confusion of terms like heaven, eschatology, the kingdom of God, or the kingdom of heaven.[4] God is imagined as being far away because how could Almighty God be on a suffering earth?

Although we have many questions about heaven and have difficulty talking about it, there is good news. We long so much for a different world from this one because the desire for a perfect world becomes the proper reaction to God's act in the crucified Christ. In other words, through the birth, life, death, and resurrection of Christ, God shows us that there is no once-removed reality between God and this earth. Christian theology does not delude itself into thinking that it is easy to imagine heaven, but it knows how to get there through the special revelation of Jesus.

Addiction to a delusory world is when heaven becomes a Land of Oz, some distant place, a fantasy land restricted to the medium of fantasy articulated by those in high socioeconomic positions capable of telling the story or those barely making it in life who desperately need to believe an alternative reality. In both states of being, it does not matter what happens in this life so long as I personally make it to heaven. So in forging the foundation of the United States, white people used heaven as a carrot and stick for African slaves. Many white Christian slaveholders did not see the discrepancy, that their behavior contradicted finding God's presence (Matt. 25:34–36). And today, Christians of financial means move to the suburbs in order to avoid bad school systems or urban blight and talk about heaven abstracted from the suffering that we may (inadvertently or not) be causing the rest of the world. We must wake up. Even though it may be overwhelming to imagine heaven for every living soul, it still remains the great commission to which Christians are called.

So when we talk about heaven, we must do more than talk about it only for our individual selves. And here a confession must be given—for the sake of world peace. Christians must confess a failure of language around heaven. Whether you are called a conservative, liberal, or moderate, our individual pursuits of heaven are making this earth even more vulnerable to our destruction. If our concept of heaven is really a subtext or euphemism in which we retreat from a suffering world in order to enjoy our own spoils of war, then we are not following Jesus.

Fundamentalists, whose language about heaven is certain, are often trapped in the idea that this temporal world is empty in the face of the transcendent God. Liberals, who discount supernatural reality on earth, are often trapped in a European Enlightenment view in which rationality and individualism are the only adjudicators of reality. And moderates, who try to live in these tensions, often end up only in a response mode with little to contribute to the conversation—outside of trying to be superficial peacemakers. All of this describes our insecure state of church in the twenty-first century.

We must talk about heaven differently. Instead of accepting the world as a domicile of particular evils in order to pursue our private heavens, we must discover how God is already in our midst helping human actions to form an atmosphere conducive for flourishing. As we will learn in this book, the solution of heaven is Ubuntu—communal existence. Ubuntu can be realized in Jesus' proclamation of justice for this world, to love your neighbor as you love yourself. Our call from heaven

> Our Father in heaven, Hallowed be your Name, your kingdom come, your will be done, on earth as in heaven.
> —*The Book of Common Prayer*

on earth is to become a person through other persons. We can no longer rely on self-references to know ultimate existence. I need someone else to know myself. In this way the premise of the European Enlightenment is wrong by positing that knowledge of God is given primarily to the individual alone. This premise ushers in both the negative of judgment and the positive of the kingdom of Heaven; but both the negative and positive are reconciled through the reality that I am inextricably known through my love for my neighbor. Through this kind of knowledge, perceived limitations of the earth are no longer seen in a shameful way, as something to escape. Rather, God's love for us makes us heavenly and infinite. In Jesus we learn the mystery that, by becoming someone for the other, we become eternal.

4

Keys to the Kingdom

I was dead, and see, I am alive forever and ever; and I have the keys of
Death and of Hades.

—Revelation 1:18

Revelation begins with John's vision of a spiritual figure who wears a
set of keys. But what doors do they open? In Matthew's Gospel Jesus
declares, "All authority in heaven and on earth has been given to me"
(28:18). What about hell? Does Jesus have authority there? John of
Patmos answers yes (Rev. 1:18). Jesus has authority through his suffering and divinity to be anywhere, even in hell. It seems a dangerous
thing to have the keys of death and hell. Whoever has such authority
will inevitably have enemies. Rowan Williams writes that "resurrection is not a resuscitation"; rather, it is a gift of a new kind of life that
exists counter to "death and hell," "destruction and disintegration."[1] In
short, our language about heaven can only be rescued from death and
hell if we can imagine Jesus' power and authority.

This is why I am so drawn to the apocalyptic vision of the Son of
Man seen by John.

I saw one like the Son of Man, clothed with a long robe and with
a golden sash across his chest. His head and his hair were white as
white wool, white as snow; his eyes were like a flame of fire, his feet
were like burnished bronze, refined as in a furnace, and his voice was
like the sound of many waters. In his right hand he held seven stars,
and from his mouth came a sharp, two-edged sword, and his face
was like the sun shining with full force.
When I saw him, I fell at his feet as though dead. But he placed
his right hand on me, saying, "Do not be afraid; I am the first and

25

the last, and the living one. I was dead, and see, I am alive forever and ever; and I have the keys of Death and of Hades." (Rev.
1:13–18)

Not only does the ethnicity of this divine figure (hair like wool and skin
like bronze) resemble so many of us, this Son of Man gives us permis-
sion to boldly go where no one likes to go.

> One of the things that St Francis has in
> common with the Buddhist and Hindu
> traditions is the understanding of death
> not simply as an enemy (as it is in some
> respects), but as friend and sister.
> —Brother Ramon, SSF,
> *Heaven on Earth*

Death no longer has dominion
over this Son of Man. He can no
longer be imprisoned and held hos-
tage. He is not a historical memory
nicely institutionalized. In Rowan
Williams's words, "From now on
he belongs to all people and all
times, he is available to all. He is
free." Williams goes on to say beau-
tifully that Jesus "is already empty, already poor, already nothing, for
God is everything in him; and so the inexhaustible life of God meets
death and eats it up and exhausts it."[2]

Heaven on earth is not a poetic imagining; rather, it is a matter
of authority and self-fulfilling prophecies that include the one who
holds the keys to death and hell. John knows this and so enters into a
trance, overwhelmingly concerned for an authentic Christian message
integrating spirituality and justice. Instead of the ultimate concern of
the personal journey, heaven on earth provides both concern and question for how those who suffer can be healed. And yet there is a particular Christian message. Heaven does not attach itself with earth in
such a way that the Christian message has no point of reference from
which to judge the world. Herein is the legitimate concern of conservative Christians who maintain the particular language from a biblical
and traditional worldview and then correctly wonder where Jesus is in
the latest humanitarian construct of civil religion. Where we all come
undone is in the legitimate liberal critique of what actually is the Christian message. The irony of its particularity is that the Christian message is ultimately about radical inclusion in which heaven can include
even disparate realities like earth. Herein liberal Christians rightfully
critique conservative Christians for not taking literally Jesus' Sermon
on the Mount—a sermon that tells listeners, forgive your enemies and
if anyone strikes you on one cheek, turn the other. Both conservative
and liberal Christians are having a mighty time figuring out whether

we are freeing the gospel from the world's fetters or amputating the gospel's limbs.

Developing language about heaven on earth is not a task to reject the Christian message or Scripture, rather it seeks to dispel the out-of-sync cosmology that many Western Christians have for God's communal nature. In many ways, this entire project of talking about heaven is an exercise in developing a Christian spirituality of community that does not call for a *sacrificium intellectus*; rather it is a proclamation to the individual hearer that individuality is unintelligible apart from community. In the same way, earthly existence is unintelligible apart from heaven. In an individualistic world, there is too much noise and too many distractions prohibiting the hearer to reckon with what is the essential message of Christianity. Trapped in ourselves, there is little incentive to strive for the joy beyond self. With community, however, the noise of otherness can become a symphony orchestra in which each particular part knows its uniqueness in relationship to each other. This is Ubuntu, and this can become heaven on earth.

Herein we see the crucial use of apophatic theology—a way of unknowing in order to know idol from reality. I bring up apophatic theology because a large part of my argument here is that what we call heaven really is not. No doubt, this will get me in trouble within the many folds of Christianity who may think they can say about heaven— "There it is." But I pray that I can hold the attention of people from diverse backgrounds, including the diverse backgrounds of those who call themselves Christian.

It is an unnecessary contradiction, however, to juxtapose conservative and liberal Christianity. Both are necessary to the other. As conservative Christians teach us, we all need to become aware that there is direct intervention by heaven in this world. In other words, I learn from my conservative friends that heaven really exists. And liberal Christians teach us that heaven is transforming earth to become a place capable of possessing the unusual nature of God's community. In other words, heaven must always be transforming our perceptions of where heaven exists; after all, in a new heaven and earth there will be no need of a sun or moon (Rev. 21:23). Apophatic theology provides the confession that both liberal and conservative Christians often ignore how God is completely revealed on earth.

Until we can see more clearly through our mirror dimly, apophatic theology is one of the best methodological ways of understanding heaven on earth. Although the evangelical Christian rightfully seeks to restore personal faith in the half believer of this age, she or he must also become aware of the inherent dangers of an individualistic cosmology, often representative of evangelical Christians. The shocking truth that personal salvation is not the ultimate goal must be revealed. Apophatic theology is such a methodology in which the ultimate goal of heaven is not personal salvation. The ultimate goal is always God, who is both subject and object. The danger for the liberal Christian also resides in individualism—striving for a privatism in which tolerance somehow becomes a virtue. God revealed in Christ, however, is not about tolerance. Jesus reveals shalom—a way of flourishing and not a way of being tolerant. With flashing neon-light persistence, the word of God shows liberals and conservatives alike that we must be saved together— the normal schism at the drop of a hat must stop. We must organize around a different reality than our Western individualism. How can we do this without being too scared?

Seeking first the kingdom of heaven frees us without amputation of ourselves (or God) because we are no longer bound to the vain attempt to hold onto personal security on this earth. For now we see the real scandal through a "heaven on earth" kind of faith that says nothing of God is visible to those who seek only personal security in the world. No one could see that Jesus is God from this perspective. For example, Pontius Pilate looked God in the face and still asked, "What is truth?" (John 18:38). Through Jesus, heaven come on earth, we can now recognize the truth in the apparent contradiction that genuine freedom is in human service but is not in human security. It is a freedom gained in responsibility and decision. For heaven on earth, freedom is found in insecurity. So if you are certain in your ideology and theology, this book may be unsettling for you.

Through the apophatic theology represented here, I intend to destroy the misconceptions surrounding the Christian message—especially those misinterpretations that condone perpetual violence, war, famine, sickness, slavery, and the poor always being with us. Most of these realities have been blessed with rhetoric of heaven or biding of time until things get better. As our teachers will show us, we must learn to interpret Scripture from its deeper sense, looking beyond misconceptions and thereby freeing the world of false gods that we are all inclined to make. My intention is not to decode the mystery of God—it is humorous to tell God such a plan anyway. Instead, we need to listen to the proper place in which to experience the mystery of God in heaven. Such a place is not necessarily the sphere of theoretical thought, nor is it the domicile of God existing fifty billion light-years away; rather, it is in this earthly existence. Heaven now becomes a place where God is not an individual satisfied within God's self but a place where God communally acts and communally is with us—here and now. We must all become concerned about each other's "personal" journey to God—that God's whereabouts need not be privately remote.

Friendship, love, and faithfulness can be understood only by genuinely understanding that they are a mystery that can only be received, thankfully, in a community. Without such community, these concepts are unintelligible. You receive them only in the open readiness to relational encounter. The friend who comes remains a mystery, and God's grace is like this. You ask for it as long as it does not come, accepting it thankfully when it does come. But God remains forever a mystery not because God performs in the irrational manner of breaking the causal nexus of nature. In other words, God breaks into us through radical generosity and community. Thus, when you seek God's whereabouts, you should no longer put God fifty billion light-years away; rather, you should understand that the more difficult place to discover God is actually where you are—a place that may lack generosity and community.

I think we need a deeper concept of heaven because such depth expands our communal perception. No longer can concepts of heaven that remain individualistic work in our need for a global community. Even more strongly put, some supposed Christian concepts of heaven are not helpful at all to healing the world. In fact, revenge is so sweet for some people who call themselves Christians that many seem to take delight in the victory over those enemies who will suffer forever. Revenge becomes heaven for some people. For these people, there seems to be no disconnect between personal completion and the other's demise. This has to change.

I articulate my own view about heaven on earth, drawing from several sources in order to argue that heaven (and therefore salvation) is indeed social and earthly. A more congruent heaven is one in which persons participate in the communal beatific vision of God's presence on earth. This does not mean, however, that heaven is finite and lacks

> Our worldviews determine to a large extent what we can believe about life, faith, and the very cosmos. If we are unaware of which worldviews claim our allegiance, they will continue to determine our behavior in ways to which we are simply blind.
> —Walter Wink, "The New Worldview: Spirit at the Core of Everything," in *Transforming the Powers: Peace, Justice, and the Domination System*

transcendence. Because heaven is foundationally God's presence, Christians have it in their theological DNA that heaven has already come to earth through both the incarnation and the Holy Spirit. Christians also strangely believe that Jesus takes earthly reality back into heaven, especially as witnessed by the bodily resurrection of Jesus. I believe this; therefore, what I see is that heaven and earth have become congruent and yet heaven remains much greater than earthly reality. I argue against the critics who say that heaven is delusional and unhelpful to human communities because we need heaven on earth to see where God is taking us.

I am aware that heavenly problems still remain—especially, will we ever agree about who should be in heaven? I am aware that my argument does not resonate with the experiences and worldviews of some readers. One such group, I imagine, would be those who see heaven and earth as separate states of being (these persons see no contradiction between personal satisfaction in heaven at the same time as being aware of someone else suffering in hell). They quote Scripture references about hell and say to me, "Just look at Matthew 23:33; see, it says it right there that some people will be in hell."

I am also aware of another group who represent the other extreme perspective from those who quote Scripture. This other group may think my whole enterprise of thinking about heaven is silly in the first place. After all, these persons would think it impossible to prove the existence of God. They, too, have a good argument: those who think they have God figured out, they say, are the same lot who are leading crusades, inquisitions, and slavery. As we have already discussed, most talk of heaven carries an internal virus that seeks to wreak havoc on earth.

For both of these groups of detractors, I hope that they will at least hear me out. Both are faithful to their own worldviews in which one seeks either fidelity to Scripture or fidelity to world peace. I guess, as an Episcopalian, I want to have my cake and eat it too. I do not see these arguments as mutually exclusive. Therefore, my burden is to figure out how religious discourse around heaven (specifically, the Christian perspective) can actually not make matters worse for the world. How will I do this?

I seek first to convince the reader that the theological problem I suggest truly exists—how can I be in heaven while someone else is in hell? To this day, religious leaders in Jewish and Christian communities debate this question of heaven as well as the nature of an afterlife. It seems a bit unrealistic, according to this ongoing debate, to want humanity to desire a common heaven. In this way, I begin with the problem of heaven—and I know this is a great irony. After all, one would think that we would all want to pursue my model of a communal and interdependent heaven. A Christian spirituality of reconciliation, however, teaches us that there must first be confession of what currently exists before there can be anything held in common. In other words, we must first admit to ourselves that our view of heaven is currently broken.

For many, if not all, Christians, heaven as the final destination and reward for the righteous and those who act faithfully on earth is a given. My idea is a bit different—namely, heaven can only be imagined as *everyone's* final destination and reward. If anyone is left out or suffers, none of us are in heaven. Because this goes so sharply against commonly held beliefs and perceptions, it is not enough to just begin with the notion that the concept of heaven is a problem; one must take the time and care to demonstrate why this is the case in the face of such weighty evidence to the contrary.

Although Christian thought on the concept of heaven is fond of separating heaven and earth, an argument that heaven must be confluent with earthly existence is not unique. From the late eighteenth century, Christian communities such as the Shakers had communal visions of heaven that they sought to re-create and live out on earth. Beyond Christianity as well, many communal concepts of heaven are tied to phenomenological knowledge of earth (e.g., Native American traditions intertwine spirituality with the land). Theologically, I believe the worldviews of the Shakers and Native Americans are closer to the kingdom God has in mind. I believe this simply because heaven is God's presence. If God's presence abandons us, we become the walking dead—zombies.

5

The Church of Zombies

And to the angel of the church in Sardis write: These are the words of him who has the seven spirits of God and the seven stars: "I know your works; you have a name of being alive, but you are dead."
—Revelation 3:1

In my Christian faith and life experience as an African American shaped profoundly through my experiences with Desmond Tutu in South Africa, I have come to the conclusion that God has not abandoned the church—a church that some may consider the walking dead. This conclusion may seem very difficult at times, especially given how the church has behaved through history—often making matters worse in the world through infighting and scapegoating (e.g., of gentiles, Jews, women, slaves, gay people). Like zombies, the historic church often preyed on others, in the name of doing God's will. It was my great privilege, however, to witness a different kind of church when I lived for two years with Archbishop Tutu in 1993 and 1994. There and then a church made matters better. The church led by Tutu, in my view, was one of the most relevant witnesses to how to be in the world. Instead of the walking dead, here was a church singing, dancing, and alive with forgiveness.

John dreamed of such a living church. Although his dreams included horrible nightmares, John dreamed like a symphony conductor leading disparate instruments in crescendo toward a counterintuitive climax. Instead of the retributive justice that peppered many of his visions, John's counter intuition struggles out of retribution to end Revelation with restorative justice. Similar to Samuel Barber's famous Adagio for Strings, John conducts a symphony, trying to lead a seemingly lifeless and hopeless state of being to the climax that God desires—the pairing of a new heaven and a new earth. John's vision of the church is similar to mine. In each of the seven churches he envisions (Ephesus, Smyrna, Pergamum, Thyatira, Sardis, Philadelphia, and Laodicea) there is great room for improvement. The very structure of Revelation invites transformation of us all rather than the often-used condemnation of us all. He cannot help but write this vision.

It is vital to understand, however, to whom John is writing. In this section of Revelation we find out—to the church. The command to write in Revelation 1:11 refers to all that John envisioned, and not merely what he had seen with his eyes. In other words, the divine commander seems to understand John's conundrum of seeing only what John is capable of seeing. But there is so much more than what John can truly see. It is as if John wants the reader to know the good news that there is a divine commander who knows much more than he does. This is important because John warns us that he is about to enter impossible situations and face horrendous nightmares but will prevail in the end. Structurally, this is true as well in the stream of conscious technique of writing in which John's introduction to Revelation could just as easily be his conclusion For example, the first chapter contains much of the same language of beginning and end as the final chapter.

The structure of Revelation is divided into natural pairs of connecting events between heaven and earth. Contrary to this apocalyptic literature's reputation for being divisive, in fact the structure is such that harmonious pairing and coupling continuously take place—seven pairs constitute Revelation, with the contrast between events taking place first "in heaven" and later "on earth." In this instance we have seven churches. We discover that the scene in heaven is preliminary to the subsequent events on earth. Revelation offers a simple arrangement of things seen first in heaven and then immediately taking place on earth. This is done seven consecutive times. Our guide through Revelation is marked clearly by the repetitive perspectives "in heaven" and "on earth." I adhere to this structure in order to understand this book as a whole.

The reader may be aware that many books on the Apocalypse base their whole system of interpretation on far-reaching worldviews fueled by affinity groups whose desires are not necessarily the will of God. Hence John's vision of seven churches, each seemingly out of joint with God's will, that need to align their own visions for how God is in both heaven and earth. They need not behave like zombies waiting only for heaven to know where God's abode lies. Interpretations of God's presence for the seven churches ought to have a firmer foundation on which to rest than their own desires. When we desire our own outcomes outside of God's will, we adopt an interpretation of Revelation that rests on hypothetical grounds at best and anarchy at worst.

The problem of dealing with apocalyptic literature is the same problem of dealing with the diverse contexts of the church. The difference in human contexts may be so great that one wonders how it is possible for them to ever be reconciled. Christian contexts are no exception.[1] When Christians fight and kill each other while blaming other religions for doing the same, it is difficult to believe anyone's apocalyptic interpretations. If we had not all been brought up believing in a common identity given to us through baptism in Christ, we could never take John's vision as having anything in common with those addressed in the first and second centuries. In our fundamentalistic and narrow interpretations of John's vision, it is easier to think we know better than John what is his revelation.

The beauty of John's revelation is that everything points to a different order of things altogether. Herein lies the tension. It is God's order of things that truly matters. This is why the alpha males and females often run around harried and distraught, full of warning and reproof. Promises are made only to the "overcomer," but the one who really overcomes is a lamb—a paradox too difficult to fathom. It is a paradise paradox, as Martin Luther states: "The only trouble with heaven is that you have to go through hell to get there."[2] Pondering the Lamb sitting on a throne is vital lest we think John's vision is for those who are under a covenant of achieving heaven by human will alone and not for those who are under the covenant of grace. The lamb paradox confuses our neural pathways entrenched in certain interpretations, especially when such interpretations are only about the destruction of the "other." Therefore, such confusion is a good thing.

The paradox of who is in and who is out of God's grace is not easily fathomed. In John's revelation, the messages to the seven churches each conclude with Christ's command that anyone who has an ear should listen to what is being proclaimed. Also in the Gospels, Jesus uses this formula—"Let anyone with ears listen!" On fourteen occasions Jesus uses it—always when he is speaking of great change about to take place. It is connected therefore with the problem of diverse contexts and how one seeks consensus of interpretation. Great and awful change exemplifies the entire book of Revelation, but there is a happy and restorative ending, an ending similar to the Day of the Lord in Isaiah's vision (66:18): "For I know their works and their thoughts, and I am coming to gather all nations and tongues; and they shall come and shall see my glory." So the premise of my theological analysis is that of restorative justice.

What do we do, however, with John's dreams of retributive justice? John has nightmares throughout Revelation that make me shiver. There are visions of blood flowing down streets. Heads roll. John provides a voice I do not want to hear: "I have this against you, that you have abandoned the love you had at first" (2:4). This voice is emphatic—similar to a powerful exchange between Nathan and David. With indignation David says to Nathan, "As the LORD lives, the man who has done this deserves to die" (2 Sam. 12:5). Nathan responds simply but powerfully to King David's stupidity—"You are the man!" (12:7).

Similar to David's epiphany of justice, John's Apocalypse is about God's justice—something that we cannot deny. Retributive justice is undeniable—at least without the central tenet of Christian faith, love, something just as fierce as retributive justice. God established the criteria of how we know love in the first place. God loved the people, but not because they were all that lovable. The people learned—perhaps even better to say, evolved—to love. Such evolution occurred through the imprinting process of following God. We evolved to love because God first loved us (Deut. 7:7–9; 1 John 4:19). Love is essentially God's doing, something that I think major prophets also knew about God: "I passed by you again and looked on you; you were at the age for love. I spread the edge of my cloak over you, and covered your nakedness: I pledged myself to you and entered into a covenant with you, says the Lord GOD, and you became mine. Then I bathed you with water and washed off the blood from you, and anointed you with oil" (Ezek. 16:8–9). God does not wait for our repentance.

Repentance is important language because it helps us understand what it means to overcome a world of violence. The members of Christ's body, however, have already overcome such a world. They are already more than conquerors because of love—something not vapid but powerful (Rom. 8:37). But how do you love while living in the days of the beast, in the midst of the great tribulations? How do you endure to the end? We read in Revelation that the beast will make war and shall overcome the members of Christ's body and kill them (11:7). We also read that those who overcame the beast did it by the blood of the Lamb (12:11).

Revelation is full of overcoming. At least sixteen times it uses the verb *nikao* (Gk., overcome). These overcomers are foreseen in Matthew 24:13, but what we must not miss is the good news of Jesus' Sermon on the Mount (Matthew 5 and following) that precedes this passage. God will give the fruit of the tree of life to heal even those who do not overcome. The tree mentioned (Rev. 22:2 and Ezek. 47:12) is intended "for the healing of the nations" (*ethnoi*). The promise here refers to the new earth, when the curse will be removed and the whole earth restored as the paradise of God. Jesus speaks of this paradise of the new earth to the dying thief who says at the crucifixion, "Jesus, remember me when you come into your kingdom." Jesus provides a curious response, one that helps me write this book, "Truly I tell you, today you will be with me in Paradise" (Luke 23:42–43). The good news is that God's love lingers in such a way that those who overcome are saved, just as are those dying on a cross.

SUFFERING

What is disturbing in Revelation is not the hybrid of animal or human monsters manifesting at will in John's vision. What troubles most is suffering. Even more troubling are those among us who use the book to argue that God inflicts suffering. This is troubling to me because of the revelation of God made known in Jesus. Those who argue against my "progressive theology"—that God sees to it that both overcomer and the one striving to overcome are healed—argue that such theology maintains that God means something quite different from what "He" says.[3] My interlocutor usually concludes, ". . . for we do insist on believing that God means what He says." The contradiction occurs when I engage my sister or brother Christian with suffering itself; after all, suffering does not depend on our faithfulness to God. No, suffering hits anyone like a tractor-trailer run amok. No one is immune from suffering in this life—even our Lord Jesus Christ. As a Christian, I believe that what God ultimately says is Jesus, the very Word of God. Yes, God speaks a person. Although this may sound grammatically incorrect, it is accurate to the inner and outer workings of the life of God.

> Do not fear what you are about suffer.
> —Revelation 2:10

Labels of conservative and liberal theologies only obfuscate arguments. Suffering goes beyond such affinity groups. There will be many martyrs in those days, but no one should long for such a designation. These are the days specially referred to in Revelation in which there are no easy answers because many of us have forgotten the true question:

What do we love most? Suffering makes us do this—makes us more competitive and survivalist. So John poses dilemmas to the seven churches, ending with this greatest indictment: "I have this against you, that you have abandoned the love you had at first. Remember . . ." (Rev. 2:4–5).

It is as if John has a vision akin to a pearl born from suffering. God will give a white stone, and on the stone a new name written. What that new name will be is not yet revealed, but with their new name they will be distinguished in a most emphatic way from those who will worship the beast and receive a mark on their forehead. Those who will be on the earth in those days will thus be divided into two opposing parties: the party of the beast, and that of the Lamb; each having its own distinctive mark or brand.

The two parties of theology are similar. Liberal and conservative theologies are fond of saying the other does not belong. What must be remembered, however, is that the one giving judgment is the Son of God, who has eyes like fire—the only one who can be truly angry. This is why the attribute of eyes "like a flame of fire" is important, because God is the only one who can see through mitigating circumstances surrounding human judgment. In other words, God's perspective is not influenced by human biases or affinity groups. As the Christian mystics teach us, God's judgment is unmediated and direct. This tells of God's judgment against the wicked that many other troubling apocalyptic prophecies foretold (Isa. 14:25; 41:25; 63:1–6; Mal. 4:3; Dan. 7:19; 8:7, 10; Mic. 4:13; Deut. 33:25; Job 40:18).

The problem with apocalyptic prophecies, however, is that they are mediated—that is, someone is doing the interpretation. They are what they say they are—prophecies, visions. Words that come out of God's mouth in the Scripture passages above must be filtered through Israel and the very definition of that name—one who struggles with God (Gen. 32:28). Prophecy is tricky. We have to be careful in imposing human prophecies on God's prophecies. For example, there are many references to false prophets in the apocalypse that point to suffering in the coming days, especially the infamous prophet known as Jezebel (2 Kgs. 9:22, 30; Jer. 4:30; Nah. 3:4). We need only read the history in the book of Kings to see how prophecy is connected with suffering (1 Kgs. 18:13, 14). In this regard, Jezebel also seems to be the reference to the woman of Revelation 17:1–4 and to the violent scenes then going on in the earth. "Beware, I am throwing her on a bed, and those who commit adultery with her I am throwing into great distress, unless they repent of her doings; and I will strike her children dead. And all the churches will know that I am the one who searches minds and hearts, and I will give to each of you as your works deserve" (Rev. 2:22, 23)

Jezebel is problematic in the profound sense of the apocalypse or the great tribulation (Rom. 2:8, 9, 16). The casting into a bed, here, is in contrast with Jezebel's being cast out of a window (2 Kgs. 9:33). And it refers to a bed of anguish and of judgment. But when Christians try to perceive the things of God, we are greatly perplexed by this imagery of Jezebel. We often get lost in a tangle of theological interpretation, such as: "I will give to each of you as your works deserve" (Rev. 2:23). Jesus' revelation proclaimed a different word—namely, we do not get what we deserve. Apocalyptic discourse is troubling to discern, especially in misogynistic narratives in Revelation like this one and elsewhere (e.g., the great whore in chap. 17). It does not help Christians when, for example, Craig Hicks, claiming to be an atheist, commits multiple murders of Muslims and then allegedly writes on his Facebook page a critique of religion, particularly Christianity: "If you plan to be enjoying heaven while multitudes are tortured . . . then you are as much a sociopath as the god that you worship."[4]

A suffering world obfuscates judgment, and, I suggest, tempts us to put our own prophecies into God's mouth. Most troubling is that the sociopath Craig Hicks may be correct in his critique of Christianity. The perspective of so many who think they know who is in and out of God's grace cannot lead to a healthy worldview. Perspectives within Scripture itself struggle with the dilemma of who is in and out of God's grace, as expressly told in 1 Thessalonians 5:2: "For you yourselves know very well that the day of the Lord will come like a thief in the night."

Those who overcome do not get what they deserve because they serve God and follow the Lamb wherever it goes (Rev. 7:14–17; 14:1–5; 15:1–4). Instead of rushing to human judgment as to who is in or out of God's kingdom, a better interpretation through which to see the structure of Revelation exhibits the kinds of promises in which all may overcome suffering eventually. The time of trial may sift and separate the people for various dispensations, but there will come a day when time will no longer be measured by natural standards. In that day all will be seen in the light of God who needs no limitation, suffering, or death.

6

Heaven in Beast Mode

And the beast that I saw was like a leopard, its feet were like a bear's, and its mouth was like a lion's mouth. And the dragon gave it his power and his throne and great authority.

—Revelation 13:2

The phrase "beast mode" became well known as a result of the 2015 Super Bowl. It is a fond nickname for the enigmatic running back Marshawn Lynch of the National Football League's Seattle Seahawks, who with an aggressive running style often pulverized defensive backs and linebackers on his way to a touchdown. (It is interesting that the nickname Beast Mode has become so popular for an African American athlete, given that so much work has taken place to move beyond the stereotypes of black players being like animals. White players, meanwhile, are more likely to be assigned words like "cerebral" or "tactical" and called "generals on the field.") In John's vision in Revelation and elsewhere in the Bible, Beast Mode has no such fond association. When Paul wrote that we struggle not against enemies of blood and flesh but against the devil (Eph. 6:10–17), he was clueing us in to the visions and nightmares of Revelation.

Many of the visions in John's Apocalypse include wild beasts. For example, in seven passages we read of the image of the beast (13:15; 14:9, 11; 15:2; 16:2; 19:20; 20:4). The greatest beast is the dragon who even gains sovereignty over the world but cannot arise before its time. Here in this section of Revelation we are told why and how this is. We have here the penultimate events involving beasts and dragons that lead up to conclusion of Revelation. The beast climbs out of the abyss and makes war (chap. 13). Strangely enough, however, the war first takes place in heaven (12:7). Did you know there could be war in heaven? Michael battles Satan and casts him onto earth. Then John sees awful beasts coming up from the sea, and others from the earth. These visions in heaven correspond to a great sign seen in heaven. The Greek word for sign is *semeion*. It is interesting here that we are warned from the very beginning not to take this literally, although so many of us go straight to numerology and literal signs like 666 in order to know who the monsters are. We are warned in the narrative that when John even tries to gaze upon what and who is revealed, he can barely keep his eyes open: "When I saw him, I fell at his feet as though dead. But he placed his right hand on me, saying, 'Do not be afraid; I am the first and the last'" (1:17). John's visions are impossible to see without "one like the Son of Man" enabling such vision (1:13).

Instead of looking around for signs for whom to blame or typecast, it proves more beneficial to see Beast Mode in the vision of John as the cause of suffering—instead of a jungle full of literal wild beasts. Instead of trying to fix a number on the chancellor of Germany or the president of the United States, it is better to desire a garden in which the lion would lie down with the lamb. This is a better reading of Revelation.

The psalmist refers to troubled times when people are at their wits' end, "Whom have I in heaven but you? And there is nothing on earth that I desire other than you" (Ps. 73:25). The longing is for God to break us out of Beast Mode. The better wisdom is for us to cooperate with God in moving out of Beast Mode. Instead of watching the NFL or Hollywood movies, or any other entertainment, we would do well to simply look around at how and why Beast Mode comes into being through the systematic injustice in which we participate. Instead of looking for stigmata or signs of the number 666 on the body, we would do well to look for how injustice anywhere is a threat to justice everywhere—something Martin Luther King Jr. tried to teach us.

Our search for heaven need not be for a heaven for individuals in their private homes—such results are inevitably catastrophic. We end up bored with heaven.

The potential for danger still remains, however—even if one accepts my premise that community is crucial for an individual's understanding of heaven. More specifically, how is it that different kinds of communities trying to go to heaven also contribute to Beast Mode? And are these communal perceptions of heaven mutually exclusive? These questions seem to imply that warring communities are just as bad as warring individuals. These are important questions in light of my critique of a Western culture that places the individual at the center of the universe. However, how does my argument about the intelligibility of heaven through community hold up in non-Western communities—and how do they make sense of the individual's pursuit of salvation? The primary aim of this chapter is to see how to answer these questions with some kind of lucid response. In short, my answer is that varying communal concepts of heaven need not lead to relativism or vapid understandings of heaven but may provide a richer reference point for why we need each other to see heaven, especially on earth.

Indeed, there are many frames of reference for heaven. Many communities see heaven differently. Although religious thought has always been diverse in its approach to existence, it is generally agreed among Buddhism, Hinduism, Christianity, Judaism, and Islam that ultimate happiness is found through a larger reference point. The problem of my argument, however, is that Jesus constantly pushed for the "co-natural" existence of heaven and earthly existence. For example, the kingdom of heaven is already among us. When the Pharisees asked when God's kingdom was coming, Jesus answered that it was already here (Luke 17:21). In other words, Christians are taught to look for heaven on earth, but this may not be the case for other communities who seek heaven in other places and states of being.

THE LION IS THE LAMB!

We learn from Beast Mode that heaven is dangerous. John is told to write in dangerous times, especially to the angel of the church in Pergamum. It is so dangerous that John records the threat to this church from him who grips a sharp two-edged sword. The threat is this: I know where you live (Rev. 2:13). Heaven is dangerous in several ways, but perhaps its greatest danger is in how our longing for our own kind of heaven means that heaven is easy to generalize, politicize, and reduce to simplistic terms. So John records particular warnings for the seven churches struggling to maintain life in dangerous times. To each of the seven churches (Ephesus, Smyrna, Pergamum, Thyatira, Sardis, Philadelphia, and Laodicea) John records a job evaluation as he first describes what they do well and then drops the hammer on their failings. John writes, "I have a few things against you" (2:14). If they do not improve in their performance evaluation, "I will come to you soon and make war against them with the sword of my mouth" (2:16).

So, besides Beast Mode, what is this danger all about? To answer
this question John makes us first aware of his surroundings in heaven.
There is a rainbow around the throne. It speaks of promise and deliverance for those suffering in the world. The rainbow also tells of mercy
in the midst of judgment (Hab. 3:3; Ps. 101:1). Along with the one in
judgment (sitting on a throne), four creatures (*zoa*) full of eyes stood
around. These are creatures, not beasts, which we will explore later
(Rev. 12, 13, and 17). The first time the *zoa* are mentioned in the
Bible (Gen. 3:24; Ezek. 10:20) they are called cherubim. They offer
worship but are never worshiped themselves (Isa. 6). They are no ordinary angels, since they are distinguished from the angels (Rev. 5, 8,
11). They are attached to the throne of God and are never seen apart
from it. We first see these authoritative creatures in connection with
Adam and Eve being forced out of the garden of Eden; but here we
see something new occurring. These *zoa* are no longer casting out but
welcoming in. In fact, no muscles are flexed by these powerful creatures
in heaven; instead, they flex their vocal cords as they sing the doxology,
"Holy, holy, holy, the Lord God the Almighty, who was and is and is
to come" (4:8).

POWER OF THE LAMB

When it seems there could be nothing weirder, a stranger thing occurs.
No one in heaven and earth has the power to open the scroll, which I
am led to believe includes the one sitting on the throne. The only one
capable of doing so is the Lamb. The *zoa*, ferocious-looking monsters,
sing again, but this time to a Lamb. How strange is that? They sing a
new song, "You are worthy to take the scroll and to open its seals, for
you were slaughtered and by your blood you ransomed for God saints
from every tribe and language and people and nation; you have made
them to be a kingdom" (5:9–10).

The power to open the scroll was monumental because others could
not open it in the great tribulation (Dan. 12:1–3). Because no one had
the authority to open the scroll or the book, even great prophets like
Daniel were not permitted to prophesy the end: "But you, Daniel, keep
the words secret and the book sealed until the time of the end. Many
shall be running back and forth, and evil shall increase" (Dan. 12:4).
But there is more to the mystery of opening the scroll. There is also the
object of all judgment of the scroll. That object is the redemption of

the world by an odd entity capable of doing such a thing, the Lamb. What is beautiful about John's vision here is that this disconcerting image of the Lamb saving us guards against anthropomorphic tendencies to keep needing sacrifices. The contradiction of a Lamb with power concedes the need for a sacrificial victim. Here we discover a dangerous heaven—namely, there is a disturbing figure in power who looks like a sacrifice. John of Patmos must have been afraid in such a vision. Am I next? Jesus, however, explodes this sacrificial nature of needing a victim.

The Lamb represents nothing less than the redemption of creation, accomplished by one who was altogether worthy. Although Jesus may be compared to "the Lion of the tribe of Judah" (5:5), the prevailing metaphor for Jesus' saving power is a Lamb slain. Hence, when John in his vision looks for the powerful Lion able to open the scroll, what he sees is not a Lion, as the elder announced (5:5), but a Lamb. The Lamb is now seen at the throne—an embarrassing sight. The Lamb dripping with blood now occupies the place of power. It alone is entitled to enter and approach the throne, for it alone is "worthy." Of course this discourse is reminiscent of the apocalyptic vision of the judgment of the nations in Matthew 25:31–46. The lamb is the one with power and salvation—not the goat, the wolf, or the lion. Redemption has already occurred, and that is why John assents to a Lamb "slaughtered." The power of the gospel is in how Jesus' sacrifice is the basis of our power (Col. 2:15; Heb. 2:14). This is the theme of the new song; and now the worthiness of the Lamb controls the interpretation of the book of Revelation.[1]

The French anthropologist René Girard provides renewed self-esteem to Christians by showing how Jesus explodes the sacrificial, violent nature of human community. Jesus explodes the mechanism in human beings that requires another victim. Girard brilliantly articulates how human beings are entirely dependent on the re-establishment of order after cycles of victimary bloodletting. Girardians like James Alison conclude that Jesus offers "an ongoing set of words and acted-out stories which always serve as ways to detect how sacrificial mechanisms operate in any human group, how we must not accept them, and what the consequences are of refusing to accept them."[2] I think this Girardian voice is important because it articulates a corrective for how many read the book of Revelation—that God has bloodlust, wanting to kill God's only Son. But God does not want sacrifice, rather redemption. Jesus even says, "Go and learn what this means, 'I desire mercy, not sacrifice.'"[3] Redemption is key to reading Revelation. Those who are entertained or enticed with bloodlust and horror stories are not reading Revelation correctly. This is why I think John has the vision of the Lamb with power, to throw us all off our Pavlovian association of power with blood.

What specifically needs to be redeemed? The word "redemption" is mentioned in Exodus 15:13: "In your steadfast love you led the people whom you redeemed; you guided them by your strength to your holy abode."[4] But the people continued to scatter and separate from God. They could not actually separate from God, since God's mercy is everlasting, but the people's stubborn will resisted God's mercy. The psalmist warns, "Do not be like a horse or a mule, without understanding, whose temper must be curbed with bit and bridle, else it will not stay near you" (Ps. 32:9). It was only the Lamb who brought back together the scattered people (Rev. 5:9). The price has been paid in the sacrifice of the Lamb who now deserves our authority in heaven as on earth. It is in the life, death, and resurrection of the Lamb of God that redemption of the earth takes place. The Lamb creates a space of freedom, as Williams states: "This life and death and empty grave are the mercy-seat, the space of God's freedom."[5] So how should the resulting power of the Lamb be used? With this question the nightmares and horror movies begin in Revelation. Because the Lamb is not understood by many as having power, which even John initially did not understand as he looked first to the Lion, the paradox of power erodes to a nightmare. Here we enter into John's nightmares of evil monsters who try to wield power they do not rightfully own. John's nightmares result because he tries to see the redemption of the Lamb in Heaven but struggles to hold the same vision on earth. For example, how does John's vision for redemption work for Israel?

> Some primitive societies avoid striking out at the true guilty party because it might awaken the spirit of vengeance. Channeling violence toward a sacrificial victim as if toward a lightning rod doubtless stops violence, but it's not very pretty.
> —René Girard, *When These Things Begin: Conversations with Michel Treguer*

Few Scriptures have suffered more at the hands of Christians than those having to do with Jews, women, sexual orientation, and slaves. The example of the sealing of the 144,000 (7:1–8) is no exception. Notwithstanding the fact that many Christians commit the heresy of supersessionism, popular interpretations of Revelation insist on God's wrath on earth smiting everyone except those of the particular socioeconomic and religious perspective envisioning the smiting. Any system of interpretation which has this for its foundation only makes apocalyptic discourse worse. Such a faulty system of interpretation is described by Richard Hooker as one "which changeth the meaning of words as alchemy doth, or would do, the substance of metals, making anything of what it listeth; and bringeth, in the end, all truth to nothing."[6] This is why strong voices like Allan Boesak and Miroslav Volf coming out of violent settings like South Africa and the war-devastated Balkans provide a strong caution not to place a nice suburban theological interpretation on Revelation. Volf writes, "One can smell a bit too much of the sweet aroma of a suburban ideology, entertained often by people who are neither courageous nor honest enough to reflect on the implications of terror taking place right in the middle of their living rooms!"[7]

Those who misinterpret Revelation, from both the political left and right, often fail to feel the gravity of matters that John describes. Even though I am a self-confessed theologian of nonviolence, I understand how many grow impatient with dysfunctional interpretations of the book of Revelation. From the political right, often there is a skewed vision of who is included in heaven, with little regard for who goes to hell. On the left, there is often little belief in God's literal acts of judgment and justice. Those who dismiss John's apocalyptic vision altogether often lack "the cultural lens of a people who have been raped and pillaged by the bestial power of a force like the one John fights against in Rome."[8] We would be wise to pay attention to the parabolic nature of John's visions as, however, we see the description of power given to a Lamb.

This is the same parabolic wisdom of Jesus when he gives us the parable of the Judgment of the Nations. Just like Jesus in Matthew, John in Revelation tells the same parable. "They will hunger no more, and thirst no more; the sun will not strike them, nor any scorching heat; for the Lamb at the center of the throne will be their shepherd, and he will guide them to springs of the water of life, and God will wipe away every tear from their eyes" (Rev. 7:16–17). How strange! The Lamb will be the shepherd. In the wisdom of the parables, Christians must realize God's reversal of human biases and hierarchies. This is why Jesus used parables to illustrate how the lost are found and the last are first.

Western Christianity would do well to study such parables, especially in light of how rhetoric is often used to replace Israel with the church as the one which is chosen first by God. And in the wars among the Abrahamic faiths (Christianity, Islam, and Judaism) we would all do well to keep a humility that reflects Scripture's unusual perspective that God's ways are often not the ways of biased human beings. If white slave masters had understood this, they would have been more reticent in their white interpretations of God's power. In addition, the tensions in the Holy Land could loosen theologically if the Abrahamic faiths understood the parabolic nature of how God chooses people and leaders. This discussion is especially important as international violence has increased among Muslims, Christians, and Jews. The Lamb will be the shepherd.[9] Revelation invites us first to be open to a very strange narrative, one where, if we are open, we may understand the way toward the healing of all people. In Holy Scripture, whether it be the Torah, the Koran, or the Christian Bible, we must not literalize the salvation of any people based upon the slaughter of another (Rev. 21:3, 4; 22:1; and Ezek. 47).

MISUNDERSTANDING THE PARADOX

Then the four horsemen of the apocalypse appear, stereotypically described as Pestilence, War, Famine, and Death (6:1–8). Some interpret the rider of the white horse to be the anti-Christ, citing differences between this white horse and what appears to be Jesus on the white horse in Revelation 19. Some interpreters disagree, saying that the white horse represents Jesus Christ coming in justice because white is seen as a symbol of holiness. The rider of the red horse is generally held to represent war, the red symbolizing blood spilled on the battlefield. He wields a sword striking peace from the earth. The third horseman, riding the black horse, is called Famine, although the black color is stereotypically described as a symbol of death. And the fourth horseman rides on a pale horse. Since the Greek word *chloros* can mean both green and pale, the fourth horseman symbolizes the carrier of plague and sickness that explicitly brings death.

One must not miss the paradox in this section. These four horsemen may have swagger, but they are controlled by the Lamb who has the power to keep them in the barn or release them. In fact, the paradox becomes all the more stark when John writes that the kings of the earth, magnates, generals, the rich and powerful all hide "from the wrath of the Lamb" (Rev. 6:16). Why would they hide from a lamb, much less imagine that it had a wrath? This paradox is all about Jesus. No doubt our misunderstanding the paradox has something to do with how he died or that he did not reenact a Hollywood superhero blockbuster where heads roll and bombs explode. Although some would like to see such a Jesus in Revelation (the one riding the white horse), Jesus the lamb and the shepherd never makes heads roll. I think many people subconsciously do not have patience for paradoxes between heaven and earth because of the problem of boredom. In our minds, heaven is like going on vacation. But vacations often become boring. For many of us, the book by the beach can be satisfying for only so long. Putting up with fat white babies on clouds playing harps forever is a scary thought. In this section of Revelation, however, we learn further that the problem is not really boredom; rather, it is our individualism that prevents paradox and causes contradiction. The following humor sent to me by a church member illustrates that we will indeed be bored to death through an individualistic construct of heaven.

> One day God was looking down at Earth and saw all of the rascally behavior that was going on. God decided to send an angel down to earth to check it out. So God called out an angel and sent the angel to earth for a time. When he returned, he told God, "Yes, it is bad on earth; 95 percent are misbehaving and 5 percent are not."
>
> God thought for a moment and said, "Maybe I had better send down a second angel to get another opinion." So God called out another angel and sent her to earth for a time too.
>
> When the angel returned she went to God and said, "Yes, the earth is in decline; 95 percent are misbehaving and 5 percent are being good."
>
> God was not pleased. So God decided to e-mail the 5 percent that were good because God wanted to encourage them. Give them a little something to help them keep going.
>
> Do you know what the e-mail said?
> No?
> I didn't get one either.

This joke illustrates that we can be so trapped in our individualistic worlds that we lose sight of that which brings ultimate worth. Therefore, heaven extrapolated as a personal heaven inevitably leads to boredom. In such boredom we either take God for granted or do not believe such existence at all, thereby becoming oblivious to God's presence. Heaven is grossly misunderstood by Western Christians. Heaven is not a static existence—and most of all not an imprisoning vacation. If we knew what some of the early Christians thought about heaven, we would not conclude that the Christian story has a boring ending.

For the early writers, like Origen, it seemed as though a Christian had two options for finding heaven, either to go backward or to look forward—back to the garden of Eden or forward to the apocalyptic writer's vision of heaven. In going backward, we have the opportunity to lament our forfeiture of paradise in the garden of Eden. On the other hand, the advantage of the apocalyptic writer of Revelation's vision is that we have the goal of riding in tow with Christ toward a future heaven—a new heaven and earth.

Through the history of Christian thought on heaven, writers have traveled in these two different directions to heaven—backward toward the garden or forward toward heaven. Origen wants us to go all the way back to preexistent souls to analyze the relationship between heaven and earth. Others like Thomas Aquinas want us to make a forward journey to heaven, guided by beatific vision capable of one day contemplating God completely. And Dante seems to look in both directions (backward and forward) as he spirals upward to the empyrean.

By no means is heaven boring or the Christian story intolerably tedious. The problem here is again the lesson Jesus was trying to teach the disciples about our limited definitions of what is possible for God and our pride to think that we can fully define what God can reconcile by ourselves. Even if Origen was deemed a heretic by some for having such a vivid imagination (and, more painfully, for allegedly castrating himself), the great lesson he teaches us is that all of us are heretics if we pursue a heaven that does not contain paradox. Origen teaches us a most humbling lesson: our individual importance is derived only from God. In fact, Origen teaches us that our individualism and boredom are signs of our fall from God. Knowing this should make us behave differently—our habits should look more communal. Habits like forgiveness should manifest. Now forgiveness can be experienced not only as a gift given but as a gift received. The very term "forgiveness" is built on the root "give." Forgiveness is a symbol, a sacrament of one's conviction of the givenness of life. In the act of forgiving, believers imitate God's heaven. Forgiveness is a creative act that changes us from prisoners of the past to guests at a festival banquet. The problem with a boring heaven is the problem of memory, how we recall that which lives and moves and has being. Human memory tends to make history static and manageable. We do this to God as well.

Our boring heavens are nothing more than bad imaginations derived from being alone. These kinds of imaginations have gotten us all in trouble. It is easier to create a caricature of someone else if we actually do not relate to them. The beauty of heaven is that it invites fuller imaginations in which we know from the outset that we will fail to define heaven if there is no community—after all, how can a person know she is beautiful and intelligent if there is no community in which the concepts become intelligible? Counterintuitively, community does not lessen our personhood; rather, it accentuates our individuality and personality. I have written about this through Archbishop Desmond Tutu's concept of Ubuntu.[10]

Heaven helps us see how ridiculous it is to think we can define (label) another human being, much less define God's ultimate presence. Heaven helps us see this because of the paradox that we are and we are not yet. Although Origen tried to describe this paradox, he readily admitted that heaven is ineffable because of its diverse and united community; and this is why his concept of heaven is not boring. He leaves a lot of room for us to continue in this beatific vision. We must learn from Origen's concept of heaven that the genius of heaven is in how we flourish and are not bored through communal existence. We are not simple individuals. There are no static definitions of the self. He knew that once we make definitions of the living and try to remember them, those definitions inevitably change.

So if community is the stimulus to keep us from being bored in heaven, how do we practice heaven on earth when heaven's inhabitants are so diverse (e.g., Native Americans, African Americans, Jews, gays, and lesbians)? Even listing such diversity may do more harm than good due to my limitations and context. Listing those "other" than myself can easily lead to a patronizing posture or lead to the invisibility of those not on my list. It is as though some religious groups need to update their VIP list to heaven's banquet. Those who *once* were not on the list may now be. Many Christian groups in the short history of the United States have even changed their guest lists. Such a guest list to heaven is politically important because it reflects our contemporary scene and often our lack of imagination as to who is in and who is out of heaven. Former Episcopal Presiding Bishop Frank Griswold provides a better imagination of heaven in his opening comments of the Spring 2002 House of Bishops Meeting at Camp Allen: "The ultimate work of reconciliation has already been done by God. Our task is the living into, re-calling, God's work of reconciliation."

We misunderstand God's paradoxical heaven through community in our selfish needs to control the nature and scope of God's accomplishment in Jesus, who reconciled us back into God. Such control gets folks into trouble reading the book of Revelation, because they will cast groups of people into the roles of monsters or those left out. The need to control John's stream of consciousness in Revelation is an indicator of the lack of imagination needed to understand the God paradoxes thrown our way. Any lack of training and understanding of the parameters of divine reconciliation often leads to vapid understandings of reconciliation—this is what Origen warns against. For example, the need to control the divine work of reconciliation from the Lamb that is the shepherd leads to static concepts of heaven and hell that inform similar mutually exclusive earthly realities. In other words, we think we have an idea of who God has ultimately reconciled based on our individualistic perceptions.

PART TWO

Staying Awake

7

Yawning in Heaven

Then he came to the disciples and found them sleeping; and he said to
Peter, "So, could you not stay awake with me one hour?"
—Matthew 26:40

Misunderstanding the paradox in John's Revelation produces a boring
church and idealistic rhetoric that wreaks havoc on applying heaven
on earth. In fact, those outside the church often seem to make heaven
work better on earth. I will explain this phenomenon further through
the wisdom of an Anglican psychoanalyst. In 1970, the British child
psychoanalyst D. W. Winnicott was approached with this question:
How does one distinguish between parishioners who could be helped
by pastoral conversation alone and those who need to be referred to a
psychiatrist for assistance? Winnicott was caught off guard by "the awesome simplicity" of this question. He paused for a while and then said
to the ministers asking the question, "If a person comes and talks to
you and, listening to him, you feel he is boring you, then he is sick and
needs psychiatric treatment. But if he sustains your interest, no matter
how grave his distress or conflict, then you can help him alright."[1]

Winnicott's answer to the complex question of pastoral care or psy-
choanalytic care was about being boring. It is kind of like watching
an athletic event and seeing an athlete fall to the ground with what
could be a severe injury. The crowd, upon seeing the athlete writh-
ing in pain, moving all of her limbs, should, ironically, sigh in relief
that the athlete will recover, but upon seeing the athlete lying still,
not moving, they should then assume the worst. Likewise, if someone
who comes for counseling is deeply intriguing—even as they articulate
their struggle and pain—then there is a sign that the individual will

recover. If someone comes in need of counseling, however, and the spiritual director discovers deep depression or acedia, as was articulated in the spirituality of the desert tradition, then a professional counselor is needed.

Winnicott was trying to teach Anglican clergy that some people are like the still athlete who may be paralyzed, unconscious, or dead. They have lost hope for life, only performing life as a routine. Many caught in depression or physical and mental illness cannot display signs of life. (To understand Winnicott's wisdom fully, a further qualification will be made momentarily.) Winnicott sharply distinguishes between a person who is boring and one who is bored. To bore others is to betray an intensity of psychological distress, whereas to be bored is instead an ordinary, even necessary and oddly desirable, part of everyday life.[2] For Winnicott, a young child's capacity to be bored—closely linked to the child's capacity to play contentedly alone while in the benign presence of a parent, or what Winnicott called the capacity to be alone—reflects a welcome developmental achievement and a sign of psychological health. Robert Dykstra writes: "Indeed, the capacity to be bored may serve as something of an antidote to the emotional terror hidden in the act of being boring. Put differently, preachers whose sermons are found to be boring may well be those very preachers, often through circumstances beyond their choosing, sadly incapable of being bored."[3]

Child psychoanalyst Adam Phillips explains further: "Boredom is actually a precarious process in which the child is, as it were, both waiting for something and looking for something, in which hope is being secretly negotiated. . . . In the muffled, sometimes irritable confusion of boredom the child is reaching to a recurrent sense of emptiness out of which his real desire can crystallize." Caretakers err in rushing to alleviate rather than simply acknowledge a child's boredom: a "premature flight from uncertainty" circumvents the negotiation of hope and condemns the child to a life that "must be, or be seen to be, endlessly interesting."[4]

The qualification is this—we must not short-circuit people's boredom, nor circumvent their secret negotiation of hope in boredom, nor condemn them to reactionary lives that must be, or be seen to be, endlessly interesting. I am afraid, however, that the church does a poor job of this as it often gives in to entertaining models for liturgy and education. By this I do not mean that the church should shy away from contemporary worship or the use of technology in worship or Christian education. It is more how a Christian community governs itself in acknowledging how easily we all are seduced into spiritualities of convenience and the diminishing returns of overstimulating church members to show up on Sundays. Dykstra concludes:

> The most public expression of all this, at least in those mainline churches most familiar to me, is the petrified and predictable sermon where nothing is allowed to happen. The preacher overly controls the language of the sermon, seeking to limit any surprising eruption of emotion or spirit or any challenges to familiar patterns of belief or practice. Monotonous words and metaphors ringing of inauthenticity paralyze rather than elaborate or change human experience.[5]

Dykstra's intention here is to plead not for heresy in preaching, nor for indifference to the gospel of Christ, nor for a rejection of the institutional church, but for an increasing playfulness, honesty, confidence, and courage as preachers approach a given biblical text. Dykstra believes that unless the preacher and text alike first become vulnerable to the other while holding at bay outside authorities that include ecclesiastical doctrines and traditions, there can be little hope that preacher or text will inspire anyone else. If the minister refuses to be changed by and, more provocatively, to "change" the biblical text through dynamic encounter, the resulting sermon will almost invariably paralyze and bore rather than touch and transform. If play is akin to recreation, and recreation to re-creation, then Winnicott's vision for psychological health calls for a willingness to create and to be re-created again in relation to God. Playing alone with the text, finding and creating truth, is the first and foremost task, although not the last, in effective pastoral preaching.[6]

Joyful and or playful existence helps us to reflect on how our attention to heaven provides the proper vision of how to live on earth. A Christian's joy and playfulness, even in the midst of suffering, witnesses to God's power to save us all. I do not write this to engage in debate over universalism, conservatism, and liberalism—isms that still fuel and entertain Western Christian audiences. I want us rather to focus on Jesus' concern, "Seeing they do not perceive" (Matt. 13:13). I especially want us to obtain such focus pertaining to the problem of imaging heaven on earth. I argue here that the central problem is that we lack imagination because we have failed to develop sufficient practices of contemplation that sustain us through our boredom. Our imaginations, at least in the Western world, are too individualistic to understand the grammar of heaven. And we lack sufficient spiritual skills to help others see the possibility that there can be heaven on earth.

We do a better job imagining hell. The Hollywood movie *Constan-tine* (starring Keanu Reeves) illustrates how vivid our imagination is for hell on earth.[7] When we imagine heaven, however, we tend to lose our audience with vapid displays of one-dimensional characters who lack dynamic existence. Among younger Western audiences, comic book characters like Spawn excite better imaginations of hell than heaven because the character ambivalently presents a perspective beyond the typical Neoplatonic dualisms of good and evil. In short, heaven does not entertain us, but hell does. Unfortunately, imaginative writers find little use for heaven.

The best theologians today are also not thinking or writing about heaven. The most exciting work is being done by those concentrating more on hellish existence, those who display the dire circumstances of the poor and the incommensurate existence of God alongside a suffer-ing creation. Their mantra being: any theology that remains abstract becomes of no earthly good. Their weakness, however, is in never imagining sustainable solutions to the problem of which Jesus spoke, "You always have the poor with you" (Matt. 26:11). It is as if good theologians these days are caught in the trap of Hollywood and comic book writers of making hell the most exciting existence.

In many ways, this book seeks to challenge the assumption that heaven is boring and irrelevant. I argue that the concept of heaven is no longer taken seriously because of its seeming irrelevancy to our earthly existence. Without a concept of heaven, however, we lack perspective for why we exist. We also lack awareness of for whom we are made. Spiritual and theological work often leaves out the joy of heaven or imagines it in a self-confining way through personal salvation only. So, inevitably heaven becomes boring—fat white babies sitting on fluffy clouds. Individualism has entrapped our spirituality into a privatistic religion. By doing so, heaven cannot help but become a boring concept as scores of individuals are left alone trying to figure out ultimate exis-tence only in terms of self-fulfillment. This misses the point of heaven, however. Western Christians love to ask, "Do you have a personal rela-tionship with Jesus?" And so, the question, "Do you have a communal relationship with Jesus?" becomes unintelligible and so does the joy of heaven. Personal gods lead to an idolism in which the living God is constantly shattering into pieces. Even the practice of God's com-munal and living presence in a seminary environment is often left out these days. Seminarians imprint on a religious life in which they jockey for the world's power and prestige rather than the kingdom of heaven.

Theological vocations then become jobs in which clergy lose their passion for God and only long for a paycheck or early retirement. This lapse into boredom, I suppose, is caused by many factors, including the critical prowess of thinkers like Karl Marx and Sigmund Freud who led many to believe that heaven is a delusion, bad both for the individual's well-being and for the health of the corporate whole.

As a result, many Western religious people have capitulated the supernatural to antisupernatural schools of thought that are empirically oriented. They do this, I believe, to the detriment of the Christian life. As a result of Freudian critique, we find seminarians confused between sickness and faith or prayer and delusion (as was illustrated in the cafeteria at Yale Divinity School when a fellow student mistook my bowed head over a meal for a sign of illness). If the Christian faith is to be maintained, even in the tensions of academic criticism, we must turn our attention back to heaven. But how can we do so without resorting to vapid thinking as Freud and Marx so valiantly tried to warn us against?

Even though the reflection on heaven may open Pandora's box—full of delusion, self-righteousness, and racism—those who are trained to imagine a better world (i.e., theologians, psychologists, economists, and ethicists) need not throw all that proceeds from this box into the trash can. They need not do so because our imagination of heaven can provide meaningful practices of how to behave on earth. Even if it merely means our living into a self-fulfilling prophecy of peace and justice for all—that's a good thing! Such reductionism, however, is not my goal.

My assumption is that heaven on earth provides the needed vision in which those on earth become more than they are, and those in heaven become mutual with creation. In other words, heaven then becomes a model for human existence—rather than a pie in the sky. Heaven on earth produces a responsible environment suitable to encourage life not simply to survive but to flourish. God is both at the end of earth's journey and at its beginning—coaxing human nature to realize its potential. And yet God is already interacting with this earth in such a way as not to allow the delusion of God to devolve into an old, white human male (with a beard). It is in these delusions that we grow bored, and more fatally become boring. In the end, I seek to restore the view that the effects of heaven on earth provide the light onto our path to move toward flourishing existence now, and always.

My justification for how heaven is not boring can be seen through the ever-growing interest in spirituality (not religion) that addresses the possibilities of God inbreaking into our world and our potential to experience and participate in God. Such interest is a good thing, but I also worry about how spirituality currently construed in the Western world is so personal that it lacks communal coherence. This is why I believe the concept of heaven needs to be recovered from its misuse.

Instead of heaven being a battle cry to enact war through self-interested nation-states and individuals, I argue that heaven as a concept should help us change the paradigm altogether—there should be no war. It is not only some Muslims who use heaven as incentive to die in war; some Christians do as well. These kinds of justifications support my assumption that the essential purpose of Christian faith in particular must be reconciliation with God; otherwise, our self-interests will believe only in gods at war. Such a concept of heaven may be entertaining, preventing boredom; but such a concept that produces violence or estrangement cannot be Christian in character. Thus my aim toward heaven will mean taking the reader from ancient thought of heaven to the contemporary theologian's irritation with heaven. I have such aim in order to show that attention to heaven is integral to practicing a better earthly existence. Studying the concept of heaven is not an exercise in studying a delusion; instead, increasing our attention span for the heavenly allows better vision of our potential on earth. Without a concept of what transcends our existence, there will be no movement beyond the ordinary.

One of the crucial problems of heaven is whether or not we will get bored. If you think about it, most goals of our happiness can only be experienced for so long before our attention fades. Going to heaven is like going on vacation; we get tired of watching television, reading that book, and simply doing nothing. The following story illustrates our dilemma.

> A man trying to understand the nature of God asked God, "God, how long is a million years to you?"
> God answered, "A million years is like a minute:"
> The man then asked, "God, how much is a million dollars to you?"
> God answered, "A million dollars is like a penny."
> Finally the man asked: "God, could you give me a penny?"
> God said, "In a minute."

Heaven on earth will not occur overnight; time and patience are involved. Both kinds of time are needed: *chronos* and *kairos*. *Chronos* refers to chronological time that can feel overwhelming at times. *Kairos*

is the kind of moment of indeterminate consequence in which everything seems to happen at once, making all time to stop. The effects of
chronological and indeterminate kinds of time in imagining heaven on
earth have already begun, and have even been celebrated around the
world. For example, the civil rights movement, spawned in the black
church, has been replicated in many world movements. And the miracle of the Truth and Reconciliation Commission in South Africa has
inspired numerous nation-states to imagine more creative ways to solve
earthly conflicts. The problem remains, however: How can we be content in the realization of heaven on earth? In many ways, this question
makes us deal with the theological concept of time and space—how
can we be content with God's kind of time?

8

God's Time

And the city has no need of sun or moon to shine on it, for the glory of
God is its light, and its lamp is the Lamb.

—Revelation 21:23

Revelation provides a different frame of reference in terms of telling what time it is according to God. Too many people who predict
end times have no clue that God's time is different; so different that
we cannot stay conscious of this new time or we make up our own
sequence of events. My contention is that this is why Jesus more than
preached a realized eschatology, he embodied this eschatology. The
very incarnation is heaven on earth. The problem for us is this different frame of reference for time: How do we see the *future* coming of
Jesus alluded to in Revelation? This is a special problem since we get
so easily bored with heaven and the establishment of the kingdom that
Jesus had preached. Getting bored can have disastrous consequences.
An account in Acts illustrates this. "A young man named Eutychus,
who was sitting in the window, began to sink off into a deep sleep while
Paul talked still longer. Overcome by sleep, he fell to the ground three
floors below and was picked up dead" (Acts 20:9). The most ardent
proponents for Jesus' kingdom still find it difficult to stay awake to
its presence on earth. This was even true for the disciples in the very
presence of the incarnation, because Peter, James, and John kept falling asleep. "Then [Jesus] came to the disciples and found them sleeping; and he said to Peter, 'So, could you not stay awake with me one
hour?'" (Matt. 26:40).

So there was a crisis of attention span even in the presence of Jesus.
This seems counterintuitive since one would imagine great excitement

in the presence of God. The crisis deepens, however. The Christian story continues with Jesus crucified and resurrected. This brings us into the crisis of the delay of Jesus' return, which caused the earliest members of the Jesus movement to grow idle—a constant problem for the apostle Paul, who writes, "And we urge you, beloved, to admonish the idlers, encourage the fainthearted, help the weak, be patient with all of them" (1 Thess. 5:14). Paul also provides constant exhortation about "those who have died" in Thessalonica, already in the first-century church (1 Thess. 4:13–5:11). Later, responding to the crisis in Corinth, Paul provides a detailed description of the events of the end time (*eschaton*), when the Lord would have returned, including the resurrection of the dead (1 Cor. 15:20–57). The expectation of a future end time and the preoccupation with the afterlife became central concepts, but like the disciples trying to stay awake in the presence of Jesus, we have difficulty staying focused on such concepts. It is like the question, why would anyone want to stay focused on death? Christian salvation is involved at the most profound level with the perennial human problem of a deficient attention span.

Jesus knew this and required his disciples to stay awake to the connatural existence of heaven and earthly existence. One could witness an example of this in the transfiguration, to which the disciples had a difficult time staying present (Luke 9:32). After the spectacle of Jesus' transfiguration, the disciples experienced a drastic mood change. "Suddenly when they looked around, they saw no one with them anymore, but only Jesus" (Mark 9:8). Jesus did not look the same way. There was no glory in his face anymore. Such diminished attention to Jesus is the plight of this world. Our familiarity with Jesus breeds contempt. Like the Zealots, we expect Christ to turn the world on its head with violent force. Once Christianity became a part of civil governance, we expected a familiar Christ to bless our wars, slave trades, and other horrible political practices. We have become like the disciples after Christ's transfiguration—surprised to find "only" Jesus. Our domesticated perspectives of Jesus can lead to similar plight of the disciples who think the miracle is gone when Jesus looks normal again. There is no clearer example of our mood changes with Jesus than when we encounter Jesus' nonviolence. After all, as you can tell from the success of the movie and gaming industries, violence is more attractive to us.

Thinking that we have figured out Jesus, we make God familiar—our "buddy," "copilot," or "the Man upstairs." We figure we can go to the mild and meek Jesus if need be, but by and large we need not waste our ordinary time with Jesus' wishful thinking. Here, it is interesting to note how our culture wars over biblical interpretation seem hypocritical when it comes to literal interpretation. We seem more eager to argue over passages of Scripture pertaining to sexuality than passages such as Matthew 5:38–45, when Jesus says:

> You have heard that it was said, "An eye for an eye and a tooth for a tooth." But I say to you, Do not resist an evildoer. But if anyone strikes you on the right cheek, turn the other also; and if anyone wants to sue you and take your coat, give your cloak as well; and if anyone forces you to go one mile, go also the second mile. Give to everyone who begs from you, and do not refuse anyone who wants to borrow from you.
>
> You have heard that it was said, "You shall love your neighbor and hate your enemy." But I say to you, Love your enemies and pray for those who persecute you, so that you may be children of your Father in heaven.

We play a game of hide-and-seek with Jesus. We are with him when it is convenient and proves our point, and away from him if he offends us and oversteps our personal boundary. The thing with Jesus, however, is that we cannot hide from him.

And so, counterintuitively, Jesus talks too much. We cannot get away from him. This is counterintuitive because our usual complaint in prayer is: God, where are you when I need you? Like the disciples, we are frustrated with Jesus. Yet again, they think, Jesus is telling us another parable? Or here he goes again with some extreme expectation of us to be good. Jesus tells the disciples, "There is nothing outside that can desecrate you. That which desecrates comes from the heart" (Mark 7:15, paraphrased). To hear Jesus like this all the time would be akin to a woman who invited some people to dinner. At the table, she turned to her six-year-old daughter and said, "Would you like to say the blessing?"

"I wouldn't know what to say," the girl replied.

"Just say what you hear Mommy say," the woman answered.

The daughter bowed her head and said, "Lord, why on earth did I invite all these people to dinner?"

The reason it is difficult to follow Jesus is the same reason it is so easy to become irritated with Jesus—namely, there is no off switch with Jesus. Jesus time is both *chronos* and *kairos*. At the end of a long day— of fighting the crowds on the subway, doing the boss's bidding, taxiing the kids around—the last thing you want to hear is a teacher's voice: "Now class, take out your assignments and let us begin to do more work." The disciples could not turn Jesus off—even when he died.

When I do sermon preparation and meditate on Jesus' relationship with the disciples, I often imagine Jesus constantly turning to Peter to explain the Sunday school lesson. I imagine Jesus needing to say to Peter, "No one outside of you really makes you angry, Peter. Your anger is made by you." I imagine Peter looking at Jesus and laughing to himself, feeling like Kevin in the following joke:

A mother was preparing pancakes for her sons, Kevin, five years old, and Ryan, three. The boys began to argue over who would get the first pancake. Their mother saw this as a time for a moral lesson.

"If Jesus were sitting here," the mother said, "Jesus would say, 'Let my brother have the first pancake.'"

Kevin turned to his younger brother and said, "Ryan, you be Jesus!"

Like Kevin, we all reach our limitations with Jesus. We yawn in heaven. I think this is why the disciples had a hard time staying awake with Jesus. Their consciousness could only receive so much truth, and being unable to turn Jesus off, they developed their own circadian rhythm to cope with Jesus' incessant ways. Knowing they could not control their external encounter with Jesus, they did the next best thing—they learned to turn themselves off in the presence of Jesus.

How does all of this relate to heaven? And to whose heaven does it relate? In our effort to cope with the living God, who could easily overwhelm us, we pick and choose lesser forms of heaven. Settling on the wrong form of heaven is a most dangerous state of being. Such danger happens on many levels. A group of people may decide that heaven is made only for them, as was the case for many European Christians as they encountered African people. For example, it is only within the last forty years (1977) that a council within the Church of Jesus Christ of Latter-day Saints approved a resolution that black people make it fully into heaven. A revised Book of Mormon (2004) still includes embarrassing passages such as these:

> "And their curse was taken from them, and their skin became white like unto the Nephites; . . . and they were numbered among the Nephites, and were called Nephites." (3 Nephi 2:15–16)

> "And the skins of the Lamanites were dark, according to the mark which was set upon their fathers, which was a curse upon them because of their transgression." (Alma 3:6)

Of course, personal and convenient heavens are not simply a Mormon problem. Systemically, the concept of race determined different kinds of heaven for white and black Christians as the nation-state of America was being formed. Milton Sernett describes the difficult work of the Rev. Francis Le Jau, an Anglican priest in 1709 in South Carolina. Le Jau's "reports of the difficulties of an Anglican minister in an outpost of the British empire often touch upon efforts to convert the native American and African populations. A few slaves did become Christians, often against the wishes or will of planters who feared that baptism would lead to social revolution."[1] Such fear points to the disciples' frustration with Jesus, who is always pushing us beyond our worldviews and limitations.

Not only is this a danger on the large scale of racial politics, it is also a most difficult state of being in an individual's spiritual life. This is known as *acedia*—the devil in the noonday sun. Acedia is a dreariness or a stupor that separates our heart from our passion. Our desert fathers and mothers saw acedia as our most difficult challenge in this life. Acedia clouds our vision and, more fatally, deletes our desire for God. Jesus knows that this is our greatest challenge. And so he comes to us as a doctor would come to someone with certain kinds of head wounds—he does not let us sleep because to sleep would be fatal. Jesus constantly expands our worldview through his hyperboles and parables. We cannot turn Jesus off because he is keeping us alive. In this endeavor, he is constant—sometimes even irritating. Just when we think we have figured out the spiritual life, Jesus comes along and makes us work harder—explodes our paradigms.

Medgar Evers was like Jesus in this way. A sleepy racist society had settled on convenient and compromised truths. Those in power, no doubt, already thought they had given up enough concessions to keep the society stable, but here comes yet another demand—to allow black people into their universities. Those who killed Medgar Evers thought they could turn him off. When he was getting out of his car at his home on June 12, 1963, particular white people killed him—their hope being that the 1950s TV life of *Leave It to Beaver* and the stability of the white America of the 1950s would return. But it did not. Jesus knows that all of us have this same problem of wanting to turn off the truth and settle on our own version of truth. But Jesus refuses to allow us to truncate self, to disconnect our heart's passion from the most worthy of desires—the living God. Jesus doesn't allow us to settle on convenient arrangements of truth but instead always reveals God. Such revelation can be irritating in the least and dangerous in its constancy—but ultimately saving of our whole selves: bodies, souls, and minds.

The pursuit of individualistic heavens puts us in the drastic dilemma of pledging our allegiance to the flag or to God's presence. We must resist individualistic, boring heavens, just as Jesus teaches us to be in the world but not of the world. Henri Nouwen is correct in his conclusion that to live in the world without belonging to it summarizes the essence of the spiritual life.[2] This way of living in the world without belonging to it is represented by detachment and passion, two important concepts in Christian spirituality that keep us awake and aware of our true home, not of individualistic heavens in which God's love becomes a platitude. God's love becomes a platitude only when we forget our paradox of being here and there. As long as we are on the earth, and far away from heaven in the demeaning systems of the world, Christians should be asking the question: How should we be reflective of heaven on earth? The answer seems to aim toward our learning the contexts of detachment without falling asleep.

Detachment allows the perspective that much of life is like the game of hide-and-seek. The very things of God that are perceived to be absent often, ironically, appear to be lucid. In other words, we usually are most aware of what is valuable to us only when we lose it (Luke 15:8). Strangely enough, to admit that we cannot find God is the beginning of wisdom, especially if the god we seek is no God at all. God is absent in a world in which some pray like the Pharisee, "God, I thank you that I am not like other people: thieves, rogues, adulterers, or even like this tax collector" (Luke 18:11). Instead of praying to a superficial god, made by human hands, it is better to detach from dehumanizing behaviors and violent systems of the world. Detachment is the means in which we remain open to the living God who seeks to redeem what we have made finite. Through detachment we learn how to stay awake to God. The discipline of detachment helps us to imagine heaven as more than a reward. Because of Christ's passion we are compelled to end the self-entertainment of existing without God. We no longer have an excuse to say that God is absent because the genius of Christianity articulates how God is most real in suffering (passion).

Detachment and passion show us how to live on earth. Detachment allows us to see that worldly success no longer becomes the absolute good. And yet identification with Christ's passion allows no one to define spiritual success outside the limits of earthly realities. The disciple Thomas shows us this success when Jesus proves the resurrection to him

through continuity of earthly existence. In other words, Thomas believed
Jesus was resurrected only because he saw Jesus' body, wounds and all
(John 20:27–28). Through detachment and passion, Christ teaches us
that spiritual success may mean failure. This is strange, I know. Jesus
concludes, "Many who are first will be last, and the last will be first"
(Matt. 19:30). As Christ reorients our vision by not being attached to
the violent systems of the world, we are better able to see how God is
with us always so that the game of hide-and-seek may finally end.

When you are with someone you love, writes Frederick Buechner,
the fullest sense of having "a good time" is realized. Here is an example
in which detachment and passion unite. Buechner continues that when
you are with God, something like the same experience of "a good time"
is achieved. The biblical term for this experience is *heaven*. For Buechner, being "with God" does not necessarily mean being religious. Being
"with God" is more like the idiom of being "with it." Someone who
is "with it" is so caught up in the presence of the other that, strangely,
none of the self is left. Whatever it is that everyone else is looking for,
this person is already experiencing it. And if this "being with it" is not
God, it is close enough to be kin to God.[3]

Our experience of heaven, describes Buechner, is like the experience
you get at night when a fast train approaches a city. He explains, "Even
the saints see only an occasional light go whipping by, hear only a sound
or two over the clatter of the rails. The rest of us aren't usually awake
enough to see as much as that, or we're mumbling over our nightcaps
in the club car." Examples of these glimpses of light are found in a
birth, death, marriage, and graduation. Through these events we often
catch a glimpse of what life is for and even what life itself is. The day
will break and the train will pull into full view, and the ones who have
managed to stay with it will see where to get off. Buechner writes, "The
whole purpose of God's slogging around through the muck of history
and our own individual histories is somehow to prod us, jolly us, worry
us, cajole us, and if need be bludgeon us into reaching [maturity] . . .
the measure of the stature of the fullness of Christ." To live in heaven
means in the final sense to be with God as Christ is with God, and to
be with each other as Christ is with us.[4]

Buechner's description of heaven helps our search for heaven not
become self-aggrandizement. This takes us back to the problem of
boredom. If the ultimate reward is for the self, I can easily be deluded
into thinking that my presence is really what constitutes heaven. When
I cannot find this kind of heaven, I become apocalyptic and look for

revelation that deals with an end time and "victory" (1 Thess. 4:15–17; 1 Cor. 15:51–52; Mark 13:3–37; Matt. 24:3–44; Luke 21:7–36). Most of us would rather have the apocalyptic tone in order to stay awake to Jesus. Similar to the idea that one must lose what is valuable to truly know its worth, many of us need competition and conflict to know that God is present. As I argue throughout this book, on the whole this is an unsatisfactory solution to how heaven can be realized and yet longed for. If heaven is only the individual's complete fulfillment, how could you not help but be bored? We need to think about heaven as more than an individual reward if we are going to get there.

9

Individualism

Hell on Earth as in Heaven

> And the smoke of their torment goes up forever and ever. There is no
> rest day or night for those who worship the beast and its image and for
> anyone who receives the mark of its name.
> —Revelation 14:11

John's second vision in heaven is repeated in his second vision on earth.
The Lamb has opened the seventh seal that accelerates a new series of
judgments—trumpets blasting and vials spilling horror. The paradox
here, however, is that the fire thrown to earth is the same fire and
smoke used to bless people in the church's liturgy. This fire of blessing may feel like hell, however. As hell breaks loose on earth, a voice
from heaven speaks to John, "Go, take the scroll that is open in the
hand of the angel who is standing on the sea and on the land" (Rev.
10:8). More stream of consciousness takes place in John's vision now
occurring between heaven and earth. It has to be stream of consciousness because, just like the paradox of the scroll revealing a blessing but
feeling like a curse, another paradox occurs. John takes the scroll and
eats it. Yes, eats it.

It is sweet as honey in his mouth but becomes bitter in his stomach.
And then what I think is the essence of the prophecies in Revelation
occurs through John: "You must prophesy again about many peoples
and nations and languages and kings" (10:11). The eating of the scroll
has its counterpart in Ezekiel 2:9 and 3:3. Ezekiel also ate the roll of
the book given to him, and it also was as sweet as honey in his mouth.
The paradox here is in how eating words is a Hebrew idiom for receiving knowledge, just as many Christians speak of digesting the word.
Just as Ezekiel ate so that he could speak God's words (Ezek. 3:4), now
John is doing so as well. This idiom also helps us with the enigmatic

expressions in John in which Christians eat and drink Christ's body and blood (John 6:53). Rowan Williams states, "The author of the fourth gospel puts it with characteristically blunt and shocking imagery: Jesus has made himself our food. His flesh is the bread of God's goodness; eat him and live."[1] Williams is helpful because we often talk about the Eucharist without a larger context of social violence. James Alison states, "The Eucharist is always in a sacrificial context as the antidote to that context."[2] Here again is caution about taking John's stream-of-consciousness visions literally.

John's visions of fire and brimstone, heaven and hell, are not meant for an individual or affinity group to interpret in ways that only benefit their perspective and interests. If this were the case, such individuals and interest groups would become like the Pharisee who prayed, "God, I thank you that I am not like other people: thieves, rogues, adulterers, or even like this tax collector" (Luke 18:11). Jesus constantly taught his disciples to change their narrow vision from seeking good outcomes for self alone and to increase vision for how goodness is interdependent in unexpected ways. If I want good outcomes for myself, I have to learn to seek good outcomes for others. Jesus wants us to live in the paradox of community: "For those who want to save their life will lose it, and those who lose their life for my sake, and for the sake of the gospel, will save it" (Mark 8:35). So what do we do for the sake of Jesus and his gospel? We live in community.

Revelation allows me to advocate in this book that a communal concept of heaven rather than an individualistic one provides a needed corrective on earth to the nearsighted vision of Western religious persons. Heaven cannot be known through individualism. For many of us this raises a new way of thinking of heaven. Perhaps what we thought was heaven really was not. What should encourage us here is what Paul teaches us, "But if we hope for what we do not see, we wait for it with patience" (Rom. 8:25). The insight here is that we need a reference point to see something so much greater than we could ever see alone. Revelation seeks equilibrium between heaven and earth capable of providing us with greater reference points beyond individualism and conflict.

How can we recognize the heavenly without retreating to our instinctual havens (segregated homes) that retaliate against the strange and foreign? John's revelation tries to expand our vision to see—even more, to see in a manner that is not threatened by God's strange presence and actions among us. Perhaps this is why the strange actions

occur next in John's vision. "And the smoke of the incense, with the
prayers of the saints, rose before God from the hand of the angel. Then
the angel took the censer and filled it with fire from the altar and threw
it on the earth" (Rev. 8:4–5). Now on the surface of this event one
might think, "Here we go, another act from a vengeful god." But no,
this is not what is occurring. The fire and smoke from the censer is
meant to bless, not curse. One can experience this in High Church
services in which incense is used. The acolyte waves the censer full of
fire and smoke to bless the people. This is why I think heaven is using
fire to meld a bridge of equilibrium to earth.

Whether we like it or not, much of our Western theology causes
dualisms in which incarnation and heaven on earth remain unintelligible. One can, and should, avoid Western individualism because of
how it abandons communal salvation, but how did we gain this perspective in the first place? Many argue that it is because of Platonism.
Significant among these ideas is Christian Platonism, which shifted
Christian anthropology from a communal conception of the human
person that characterized traditional Jewish (and most of New Testament) thought to a dualistic conception of the human person as a
(rational) soul trapped in a material body. This kind of Platonic dualism accentuated Christian thought to attribute an intrinsic, immortal
element to the human person, an element which, at death, is capable of
survival into heaven.

Although orthodox Christianity rejected extreme dualism—such as
the idea that the spiritual world is good while the material word is
evil—in much of Christian thinking, the human person is still defined
by its distinctive soul. It is by the soul's intelligibility that it most
approaches the divine life. It follows that we enter heaven not through
what happens on earth but rather in the introspective contemplation of
the distinct soul. The problem, however, is that our distinct souls alone
can only know so much about God (e.g., the story of the blind men
knowing the elephant). We will need more than our individuality to
know that we are in heaven.

In light of this problem of insufficient knowledge of God in and
of ourselves, Christian thought matured to include the concept of
"beatific vision" in which the presence of God may encounter the soul
fully after death when the soul departs from the body in resurrection
and rejoins the intelligible divine essence of God. Christian thought
struggled, however, with Jesus' resurrected body. And so this beatific

vision became problematic if soul somehow was removed from the resurrection of the body and the transformation of the earth.

One of the best theological minds struggling with all of this was the African theologian Augustine of Hippo. Augustine taught us to compartmentalize an interior life (as if interior and exterior could somehow be separate). Kim Paffenroth helps us see this in Augustine, for whom "the soul must turn inward and then look upward, shifting its attention from the bottom of the ontological hierarchy to the top: Augustine thus turns away from external worlds of bodily things, enters the inner world of his own soul, and finally gazes above his soul at the light of Truth, which is his unchanging Creator."[3] And so there can really be no heaven on earth for Augustine, whose earthly and heavenly cities are perpetual rivals. Augustine's logic takes us to our typical way of thinking: you can only know you are on earth if you are not in heaven. This leads us to the crucial problem of heaven—how could anyone be in heaven while knowing someone else was in hell?

My experience with Archbishop Rowan Williams illustrates this problem. In 1990 I was Rowan Williams's student at Yale University. At one point in his lecture he was discussing a Russian theologian, Nikolai Berdyaev (1874–1948), and his thoughts on the problem of heaven in the Western world. Berdyaev (an Eastern theologian) wrestled alongside Jacob Boehme (a Western theologian) with how one could be in heaven while knowing someone else is in hell.[4] To his credit, Boehme was tormented by this question. Berdyaev states:

> The East is always more cosmic than the West. The West is anthropocentric; in this is its strength and meaning, but also its limitation. The spiritual basis of Orthodoxy engenders a desire for universal salvation. Salvation is understood not only as an individual one but a collective one, along with the whole world. Such words of Thomas Aquinas could not have emanated from Orthodoxy's bosom, who said that the righteous person in paradise will delight himself with the suffering of sinners in hell.[5]

Berdyaev in conversation with Jacob Boehme presents the conundrum of how anyone could be truly in heaven while also conscious of someone in hell. Berdyaev goes on to say, "There can be no individual salvation or salvation of the elect" because "everyone is responsible for everyone else and [individualism] rejects the essential oneness of the created world."[6] There can be no eternity to hell, although any experience of it may seem like eternity. In other words, how could you be perfectly content while knowing others are weeping and gnashing their teeth forever?

I remember raising my hand in Williams's class. As many people are wont to do when feigning to ask a question while really making a statement, I said, "You know, many people's concept of heaven is based upon others being in hell. In other words, for many people, revenge is so sweet that they would enjoy being conscious of their enemies weeping and gnashing their teeth forever." As we have already seen with Augustine's interior spirituality, Western Christians seem to have no conundrum whatsoever with the pleasures of heaven and the concept of hell alongside one another. The goal for many Western Christians is personal salvation. In such a compartmental worldview, no conundrum exists between my personal heaven and the rest of the world going to hell. The conundrum of heaven points to the Western obsession with personal salvation. Such knowing of heaven on earth is very difficult, especially for individualistic societies. We have lost the art of relational or communal knowing. I have written about such relational knowing (e.g., Desmond Tutu's Ubuntu) but we must clarify that such a way of knowing ultimate things can never be separated from what is mundane—just as the universal cannot be separated from the local.[7] In other words, for me to know my ultimate identity I need you as a reference point to make what is ultimate beyond myself. I cannot know my potential self—by myself. This is why the concept of the triune God is so important. As triune persons, God displays the interpersonal dance, *perichoresis*, of knowing self to the fullest. Jesus prays "that they may all be one. As you, Father, are in me and I am in you, may they also be in us, so that the world may believe that you have sent me. The glory that you have given me I have given them, so that they may be one, as we are one, I in them and you in me, that they may become completely one, so that the world may know that you have sent me and have loved them even as you have loved me" (John 17:21–23). God made us so interdependent that we end up looking like the *imago Dei* (the image of God). As a person made in the image of God, I need other persons to know my own identity. For example, I am not conscious of what I am thinking without a reference point or an external stimulus that makes me speak or write down what I'm thinking. Like Diego who encounters the overwhelming sea, we need others to help us know anything at all. Most of all, we need others to know ourselves.

The conundrum of heaven is still not solved, however. This world-view of needing others to know self makes us all vulnerable, as the great African American intellectual W. E. B. Du Bois writes:

> The Negro is a sort of seventh son, born with a veil, and gifted with second-sight in this American world, a world which yields him no true self-consciousness, but only lets him see himself through the revelation of the other world. It is a peculiar sensation, this double consciousness, this sense of always looking at one's self through the eyes of others, of measuring one's self through the eyes of others, of measuring one's soul by the tape of a world that looks on in amused contempt and pity. One ever feels his twoness, an American, a Negro; two souls, two thoughts, two unreconciled strivings; two warring ideals in one dark body, whose dogged strength alone keeps it from being torn asunder.[8]

Du Bois makes us realize that interdependence is a dangerous reality. If I depend on others to know myself, then what happens when the other wants to define me as inferior or worthy of hell? Du Bois's two unreconciled strivings remind me of the Cherokee tale of Two Wolves. The story begins one evening with an old Cherokee chief. He tells his grandson about a battle that goes on inside people.

"What kind of battle?" the grandson asks.

"My son, the battle is between two 'wolves' inside us all. One is Evil. It is anger, envy, jealousy, sorrow, regret, greed, arrogance, self-pity, guilt, resentment, inferiority, lies, false pride, superiority, and ego."

"Who will battle this creature?" the grandson asks.

"Well, the other wolf is Good. It is joy, peace, love, hope, serenity, humility, kindness, benevolence, empathy, generosity, truth, compassion, and faith."

The grandson thinks about it for a minute and then asks his grandfather, "Which wolf wins?"

The old Cherokee simply replies, "The one you feed."

It is hard to envision a reconciled reality by one's self because our desires may prevent our seeing what we have become. If we are constantly feeding one identity, that same identity can easily become the whole worldview. The other becomes irrelevant or, worse, the enemy. This kind of world is overwhelming and violent. And so it may seem to some who are victimized in this world that I am naive to believe what I am saying about interdependent identity—that I need someone else to know myself. It is an irresponsible leap of faith, they would say, to believe in heaven when we actually exist in a violent world. Such faith is irresponsible, they add, even subversive of whatever may be called justice. When we imagine heaven that is not separated from earth, however, what is imagined is the presence of God interacting positively in the world. Hence, a new heaven and earth come to mind, both of which we need not be ashamed to see. For example, Isaiah sees heaven and earth differently:

> The wolf shall live with the lamb,
>   the leopard shall lie down with the kid,
> the calf and the lion and the fatling together,
>   and a little child shall lead them.
> The cow and the bear shall graze,
>   their young shall lie down together;
>   and the lion shall eat straw like the ox.
>   (Isa. 11:6–7)

These are some of my favorite words of Scripture, for they expand my imagination to see instincts and natures changed to exist as more than predators and victims . . . more than eat or be eaten . . . more than a violent reality we call life. Sure, it is really hard to believe in heaven on earth, but it does not mean it cannot exist. A friend sent me the following parody and wrote, "Thought you . . . would get a kick out of this. It is so true. It's entitled, 'Food for Thought.'"

And God populated the earth with broccoli and cauliflower and spinach, green and yellow vegetables of all kinds, so Man and Woman would live long and healthy lives.

And Satan created McDonald's. And McDonald's brought forth the 99-cent double cheeseburger. And Satan said to Man, "You want fries with that?"

And Man said, "Super-size them," and Man gained pounds.

And God created the healthful yogurt, that Woman might keep her figure that Man found so fair. And Satan froze the yogurt, and he brought forth chocolate, nuts, and brightly colored sprinkle candy to put on the yogurt.

And Woman gained pounds.

And God said, "Try my crispy fresh salad." And Satan brought forth creamy dressings, bacon bits, and shredded cheese. And there was ice cream for dessert.

And Woman gained pounds.

And God said, "I have sent you heart-healthy vegetables and olive oil with which to cook them."

And Satan brought forth chicken-fried steak so big it needed its own platter. And Man gained pounds and his bad cholesterol went through the roof.

And God brought forth running shoes and Man resolved to lose those extra pounds. And Satan brought forth cable TV with remote control so Man would not have to toil to change the channels between ESPN and ESPN2.

And Man gained pounds.

And God said, "You're running up the score, Satan."

And God brought forth the potato, a vegetable naturally low in fat and brimming with nutrition.

And Satan peeled off the healthful skin and sliced the starchy center into chips and deep-fried them. And he created sour cream dip also. And Man clutched his remote control and ate potato chips swaddled in cholesterol. And Satan saw and said, "It is good."

And Man went into cardiac arrest.

And God sighed and created quadruple bypass surgery.

And Satan chuckled and created HMOs.

My friend, who sent me this story, said that it "is so true." Something about it resonates with a deep belly laugh and yet touches a deep pathos in us that knows we feed the wrong animal with the wrong food. Our lack of faith can produce its own realism, which makes it hard for God, even though God's love remains persistent, seeking the reality of vegetarian wolves.

Some of us have fully received God's vision of the wolf lying down with the lamb. Mary did, and Gabriel told her that she would bear a son whose kingdom (the kind where wolves and sheep are not eternal enemies) would never end (Luke 1:31–33). And even though this kingdom will be strange for us, à la vegetarian lions, we can rest in the fact that it is Jesus' kingdom and not ours. I am the Lord's servant, Mary answered. May it be to me as you have said. Then the angel left her (Luke 1:38, paraphrased).

Like blessed Mary, to see the world as God intends the world to be is to inhabit others who feed the good wolf in us. We feed the good wolf by practicing joy, peace, love, hope, serenity, humility, kindness, benevolence, empathy, generosity, truth, compassion, and faith. These practices make us see a different kind of wolf—a vegetarian wolf. After all, most urologists will tell you that a wolf (especially the male wolf) would be much better off becoming a vegetarian. Going back to the Cherokee story, it teaches us how to reconcile the identity crises that lurk within us all by practicing a better reality. In order to solve the problem of heaven, we will need certain practices to see heaven in our midst. These are communal practices that move us beyond individualism. Without such practices, we naturally lapse into solipsism, our own personal worlds. Besides the violence they breed, personal worlds can get boring very quickly.

10

Learning a New Language

And it was allowed to give breath to the image of the beast so that the image of the beast could even speak and cause those who would not worship the image of the beast to be killed. Also it causes all, both small and great, both rich and poor, both free and slave, to be marked on the right hand or the forehead, so that no one can buy or sell who does not have the mark, that is, the name of the beast or the number of its name. This calls for wisdom: let anyone with understanding calculate the number of the beast, for it is the number of a person. Its number is six hundred sixty-six.

—Revelation 13:15–18

Language is essential for human beings; however, in many circumstances our language or lack thereof facilitates dangerous realities. The way that certain Christians obsess about "the image of the beast" or postulate who bears the mark of the beast demonstrates how our spiritual language often betrays the reality of God. Proper language about God's presence (i.e., heaven) always needs a larger frame of reference than one's own. Let me illustrate with the protagonist from the movie *Akeelah and the Bee*. I am a stoic, so what happened while I watched the movie was unusual—my eyes watered and tears rolled down my face at the ending. For most of the movie, Akeelah had a hard time in school and at home. She was an inner-city black kid competing in a spelling bee against rich suburban white kids. Her rebellion grew out of her suffering of being disadvantaged, with her only agency of control being to withdraw from school and her family.

Then she had an epiphany that led to the climax of the movie. At the end of the movie, Akeelah won the spelling bee because the images of loved ones came to mind—loved ones who had tried to encourage her even as she rebelled against them. That helped her realize that the spelling bee was not an individualistic exercise and that she was not winning for herself, but for all those who invested in her. And so she worked harder and succeeded. At the end of the movie, these remembered faces became a kaleidoscope on the movie screen—a village of support. In many ways Akeelah was spelling the language of heaven.

Heaven should teach Christians that the essential project for the church is to learn to do a strange thing—to be not for itself. After all, Archbishop William Temple was right: the church is the only organization not made for itself. The world saw a glimpse of this kind of community in a pre-Constantinian era in which paradigm shifts were constantly occurring in that disparate people were learning to call themselves the church. Through the phenomenon of the church, we saw marginalized people from distant lands, including enemies, create a common language of faith. The beauty of it all was that God's Spirit leavened our particularities into a whole community. A strange new church realized that community was not for itself—it was made to glimpse the kingdom of heaven. This mystery of becoming more than who we are has always been God's project of birthing heaven.

Heaven entreats us to find more of one's self in the other. This interchange happens most notably in how identity becomes communally dependent. The communal image of God helps us with this. The Spirit that names Jesus also names the world as worthy of heaven. In this regard, Rowan Williams proposes that our identity is further formed in Christ through the resurrection, which becomes a means of restoring earth's identity and a means of restoring language about whole and interdependent identity. The community of the resurrection finds within itself not only a vision of humanity before and with God, "but a vision capable of being articulated in word and image, communicated, debated and extended."[1] Williams sees that the resurrection leads to a "rebirth of images" capable of going beyond the dissolution of vision. Through Jesus, grace is given to return to speaking of heaven.

The language of heaven then speaks for the inarticulate. Those frozen in the fear of the impossible are made to be courageous enough to believe the impossible. If someone gives bread to a beggar, that person has participated in a heavenly ethic both inside and outside of this world. Those formed in Christ offer a perspective beyond individualism and domination. Such a perspective, formed by following Jesus, gives us insight that those who imprint on following Jesus learn how to process how heaven and earth are interdependent instead of contradictory. For example, a Christian is formed to see how one can no longer wait for the beggar to die to find paradise. Unless we participate in heaven now by offering bread, we lose the vision of the real presence of God. Just as someone who describes two opposite sides of a mountain has visited the summit, so does someone display heaven who acts justly in the world. It is impossible to love our enemies except from that place outside the world and in the world where God dwells—heaven on earth.

The language of heaven on earth is difficult to speak. Talk of cheek-turning, coat-sharing, and second-mile love that heaven communicates often falls on deaf ears. Perhaps that is why Jesus constantly said, Those who have ears to hear, let them hear. The language of heaven intends for us all to flourish and for us not to settle for a realism that condones violent existence. Gabriel Fackre explains, "The Law of Heaven embodied and taught by Jesus Christ is the lure and judge of all lesser conduct that is too ready to settle for less. This ethic judges and condemns manifestly self-serving agendas. This ethic exposes us as sinners and marks our world as fallen."[2] Although we are not where we should be, it doesn't mean we cannot get there. In other words, attention to this world as fallen can be a healthy corrective to those who view human nature and history as sufficient unto themselves. If our existence on earth is seen in light of heaven, then we may know the bounds of goodness and the out of bounds of sin and evil. Admitting that this world is fallen guards against a reductionism of existence that leads to legalism.

The language of heaven refers to a beatitude in which love is perfectly reciprocated so that in heaven there is no evil or sin. The difficult question remains—how can there be heaven on earth? It seems that other languages of violence drown out this language of beatitude. In the world, this difficulty is further complicated in how perfect love ends up on a cross. Who would want to speak such a language of heaven if it is only an accident waiting to happen? These questions must be raised because too sanguine a view of human nature and history makes us ineffective communicators of heaven on earth—we end up being called idealists or those heavenly minded people of no earthly worth. To rearticulate the language of heaven, we must talk about justice.

Heaven's language makes earth speak about filling every need with justice—but it is God's justice. This is a vital qualification because our forms of justice usually compete against one another. With God, justice is embedded in love. In other words, Jesus is God's justice. Heaven shown by Jesus converts objects into subjects. Marginalized others (prostitutes, tax collectors, liars, betrayers, zealots, or terrorists) are transformed into siblings—growing to be more intimate to each other than was once imagined. "Someone told [Jesus], 'Look, your mother and your brothers are standing outside, wanting to speak to you.' But to the one who had told him this, Jesus replied, 'Who is my mother, and who are my brothers?' And pointing to his disciples, he said, 'Here are my mother and my brothers! For whoever does the will of my Father in heaven is my brother and sister and mother" (Matt. 12:47–50). This is the work of heaven, to embed justice with God's love that transforms natural relationships into supernatural ones. This vision of shalom predisposes us on earth to be better equipped to travel through this earth to heaven. Instead of being formed only as self-interested human beings, God's love makes us into communal beings who grow exponentially through our love for one another.

Heaven brings morality and the spiritual life into intimate accord. But our world would rather keep natural relationships instead of finding ways for relating us to God. In our natural relationships, nonwhite people discover discrimination. Underdeveloped countries scream for equal distribution of goods and resources. Drug lords are able to oppress whole communities through the accumulation of ill-gotten profits. Medical issues such as abortion, technological innovations such as in vitro fertilization, and ethical issues such as euthanasia all pit individual rights against the good of the society. Innovations such as genetics threaten how we will view humanity—will we shop for embryos like we shop for our favorite perfume?

Heaven shows us different relationality by showing us that there is no contradiction between the individual and the community. In heaven, Fackre states, "Selflessness evokes selflessness and its fruit is mutuality."[3] Dante tries to understand this mutuality as he asks those in heaven: "Do you envy the happiness of others?"[4] What Dante discovers is that heaven provides a new perspective in which individual happiness is dependent on the whole organism's happiness. We no longer compete for happiness but are given God's perspective that happiness is always interdependent. A friend on Facebook sent me the following story that helps me explain how happiness is interdependent.

An anthropologist proposed a game to children of an African tribe. He put a basket of fruit near a tree and told the kids that the first one to reach the fruit would win them all. When he told them to run they all took each other's hands and ran together, then sat together enjoying the fruit.

When asked why they ran like that, as one could have taken all the fruit for oneself, they said, "Because of Ubuntu."

"What does that mean?" he asked.

One child responded, "Well, how can one of us be happy if all the others are sad?"

We learn from heaven that quality of life is known in listening to others. Heaven makes us desire the presence of others. We are to thirst for nothing more. If we wished to be more than we were, our desire would be the residual effect of the world. Instead, what we will look like in heaven will look more like a being for others. For our very form (both corporeal and spiritual) will be held in composite unity within the divine will. From the threshold of what we will be, back to the threshold of what we are, God embeds us with God's kind of love in an appropriate atmosphere like heaven, a sea in which we will move and have our being. Our best attempt at naming this atmosphere is when we find ourselves caught up in the imagination of love. In such a state, envy and boredom become nonsense because there is no other beatitude to envy than the present and there is nothing more to anticipate in which to be bored.

In heaven, says Charles Williams, it seems there is no hierarchy at all. What the worldly pilgrim finds in heaven is a different law—passion. Do not expect to find a heaven that is like the world, but rather look in this earth for what is like heaven. As Williams writes, "Anything else is democracy intoxicated with itself."[5] As strange as it may seem, we find in heaven that there is no longer a scandal of particularity. One finds that existence is equal in heaven—that function is nonhierarchical—and at every moment, what we perceive as hierarchy alters into mutuality. Here we experience perfect freedom because we have found and have been found by God. It is the fulfillment of the self to be the self for others. It is freedom from sin.

We have now imagined heaven in which mediated contact with God may be experienced without us having to cast people into hell on behalf of God. This is not our responsibility because human beings only mediate God's ultimate truths, and too much is on the line for us to make ultimate judgments with our mediated truths. Instead of solitary individuals judging other human souls to damnation, I believe God would prefer a much different path: mutuality. The desire to go on such a journey is no delusion; instead, it is the proper desire of every human being to realize what it means to be mutually human in the presence of the living God. Heaven is this place where my words end and yours begin. The danger of heaven is in how complex issues get interpreted by those who think they are closer to heaven than others. I think this is why Jesus continuously taught through parables that those who think they are close to the kingdom of heaven may in fact be far away; and those who think they are far away may actually be very close, if not already there. I am mindful, however, to practice what I preach. That is, I must be open to those who have different perspectives of Jesus' parables than I have. For example, many would argue with the claim that Jesus preached "realized eschatology." Others would agree with me, but for different reasons. Those who adhere to the historical-critical method would say that Jesus did not expect a future inbreaking of the kingdom of God but rather saw its establishment in his own (present) work. This was proposed a while ago by such authors as C. H. Dodd. Dodd based his claim on a redating of the Gospel material, such that the (noneschatological) Gospel of John gained priority over the (clearly eschatological) material in the Synoptic Gospels.

Realized eschatology has gained some currency among biblical scholars in the United States. These tend to base their arguments, again, on the reordering of the Gospel material which then can be made to show that Jesus was a sort of Cynic teacher of social reform. My view, however, is based more on the notion that I attribute to Cate Waynick, the Episcopal bishop of Indianapolis. Bishop Waynick heard that I was writing this book and offered me this insight: "[Jesus] said repeatedly that 'the kingdom is among you.'" A critic could easily say that neither the bishop nor I seem to be aware that the passage we are referring to is unique in the Synoptic Gospels, occurring only in Luke 17:20–21: "The kingdom of God is not coming with things that can be observed; nor will they say, 'Look, here it is!' or 'There it is!' For, in fact, the kingdom of God is among you [within you; *entos hymon*]." This passage has been much controverted, especially in the context of saying that Luke constructed his own version of realized eschatology. The sharp criticism comes: If one were to assume that Jesus made the statement in this passage and meant by it that there was no future coming of the kingdom, then how is the material that follows (Luke 17:22–37) to be read? Did Jesus also make the other, numerous, futuristic statements in the Gospels?

In any event, I am one of those people like Bishop Waynick who believe that Jesus did more than say the kingdom is among us—he actually came among us. In addition, not only did he come among us, he is still here. Those like Bishop Waynick and myself practice this presence regularly through the Eucharist and caring for the least in society.

11

Redemption Song

They sing a new song before the throne and before the four living creatures and before the elders. No one could learn that song except the one hundred forty-four thousand who have been redeemed from the earth.
—Revelation 14:3

Let us now look at a much deeper perception of heaven, one better than those boring views of heaven. My inspiration for doing so comes again from the paradox of the powerful Lamb. The paradox deepens as inhabitants of heaven in John's vision follow the Lamb (again a paradox, because lambs are supposed to follow the shepherd). As they follow they get so overwhelmed that they have to fall down in worship of the Lamb and commence to sing a new song (Rev. 5:9). Something very deep is going on here.

No one in the early Christian tradition speculated on heaven more than Origen. Origen is important to our discussion because his imagination of heaven has greatly affected most Christians who imagine heaven on earth. Many Christians may not even be aware of how much Origen has filled in the gaps of John's apocalyptic vision of heaven and hell. Even more important to my argument, Origen fills in the gaps of biblical interpretation of heaven and tells the story of heaven as one of redemption, in which the final reconciliation of all creatures will include even the devil, through what he called the *apokatastasis*. In other words, God's love is so relentless that even the devil will eventually acquiesce to such love and thereby cooperate with the salvation continuously offered by God.

So how does Origen tell the story of the *apokatastasis* or ultimate redemption? As an old sage reflects upon his youthful days, Origen meditates upon an individual's existence where the soul was once a passionate spirit living in God. Before individual existence, however, there was God, good and just, who generated everything we know and seem to know into existence.[1] This cosmology is similar to the Gospel of John: "In the beginning was the Word, and the Word was with God, and the Word was God. He was in the beginning with God. All things came into being through him, and without him not one thing came into being" (1:1–3). In heaven, no disparity existed between the individual and community. There was no dialectic between existence and nonexistence because there was neither time nor space. We were innocent and eternal spirits living in complete communal existence. So before there was earthly or creaturely existence there was the community of God.

From the Middle Platonic belief of preexistence, Origen imagined that without an existing realm, God is rendered inactive and not omnipotent. In other words, Platonic thinkers surmised that a reference point was always needed to know God. Similar to a king needing a kingdom, Platonic thinkers thought God needed a community of heaven. Therefore, in this way of thinking God has always generated created beings. Some of the earliest Christian speculation of heaven had to deal with this Platonic worldview. Inevitably, this constant generation by God creates a contradiction. The metaphor of generation implies a temporal process, but there can be no temporality in heaven. Thus, eternal generation becomes a contradiction. Even though much of Origen's life is deemed controversial, Christians still owe a great deal to him as his brilliant imagination turns this Middle Platonic contradiction into a paradox by describing eternal generation as eternal relationship. We are no longer bound to a contradiction if we understand God through how God relates to us communally.

By meditating on God, every created spirit in heaven attended to the community (*koinonia*) of the Trinity. This meditation or prayer was vital to heaven because such contemplation on the Trinity alone, who is the author of all things, made the spirits aware of goodness. For Origen, all spirits once participated in such Community, also known as God who always burns purely without defect. In this heaven, there was no problem of good and evil, only peaceful coexistence in pure Goodness; therefore, no theodicy existed—the discrepancy between God's goodness and a suffering world. Also, there was a natural humility in knowing that goodness only came from the community of God. It was vital, however, to stay close to God's goodness and to meditate continuously.

So it was not so much that we are innately good, went this way of thinking, rather that we possessed goodness as an accidental and perishable quality and enjoyed blessedness only in the participation of God's holiness, wisdom, and divinity. Heaven was that place that kept spirits good and pure. We burned purely for God in the spiritual paradox of being one with God. This is a paradox of remaining created spirits and yet being transformed to be capable of being good like God. This paradox is available through the imagery of the burning bush that is not consumed (Exod. 3:2). Created spirits were like little still fires in heaven, but then tragedy occurred—some created spirits became individuals by wanting to leave heaven. Keep in mind, before this desire to leave, there really was no concept of individuality, only interdependence.[2]

Why would anyone want to leave heaven, though? Origen answers by saying that God indulged the spirits with the power of free will by which the good that was in them might become their own.[3] In other words, there was no desire for goodness because there was natural participation in God's goodness; and there was no need to desire what God was already feeding them. But for a strange reason, spirits decided not to desire God and in doing so became evil. A conundrum presented itself—individual spirits no longer desired God but wanted their individual rewards apart from goodness. Thus, Origen thinks that the proportion of one's fall from goodness is the same proportion that one delves into evil. In other words, *being apart from God is to be evil.* Perhaps Origen was reminded of this conundrum in Mark, when someone came up to Jesus as he was setting out on a journey: "A man ran up and knelt before him, and asked him, 'Good Teacher, what must I do to inherit eternal life?' Jesus said to him, 'Why do you call me good? No one is good but God alone'" (Mark 10:17–18).

So how does all of this relate to the problem set forth earlier in this book—that is, how could anyone be in heaven while still conscious that someone else is suffering? Well, Origen's speculative theology helps us see where the deep tragedy occurs—when we fell out of the paradox of community of being unique persons while still being in community. Instead of this beautiful paradox, spirits fell into the ugliness of individual compulsion and obsession. Strangely enough, spirits became individuals when their desire for goodness became separated from their desire for God. In other words, individualism is the sign of the fall for Origen. Naturally, this supports my argument that heaven is unintelligible apart from community. I cannot be in heaven unless you are also there. This is where I think the paradox of the Lamb who is also the shepherd is trying to guide us.

In Origen's expansive spiritual imagination, he had the audacity to speculate about what he describes as preexistence. Origen's imagination may appear to be audacious to us in the twenty-first century, but not so much for him in his Neoplatonic context in which the creator and created always existed conterminously. In other words, there never existed the creator without the created; and there never existed the created without the creator. So, before there was time as we know it today, God created our souls in God's image. Our souls' attention span for God decreased and our minds wandered from the meditating Word (Jesus, the second person of the Trinity) who made our desire for goodness and God symmetrical or connatural. Because of this disconnect between individual desires and the corporate presence of God, our full participation in God became infrequent and, conversely, we began what is now our present individuated motion leading to our downfall into souls and bodies. From our once completely still existence of contemplating the divine life of God, spirits fell into souls and bodies that now move like animals. Our individual movements are also signs of the fall because our intended state of being is contemplation and stillness.

Origen's imagination of heaven is instructive for our essential problem with the book of Revelation—that is, individualistic perspectives on who deserves to be in heaven and who deserves to be the victims of the beast and the devil (and even God). Heaven is essentially the mystery of community defined by the presence of God. God is the one who makes us holy and good. Also, Origen is one of the major Christian writers who gives us the language we now use, words like *spirit* and *soul*—terms that seem to be forever misunderstood. For Origen, the soul is the middle place between spirit and body where the creature inevitably decides to be either fleshly or spiritual. The soul is that liminal state in which choices are made to attain transformation back into spirit, otherwise there is further decline into obsessive-compulsive ways of individuation. The soul must choose lest it remain fleshly or obsessive through habitual choice of the material things. It is as though the movement that classifies us as animals is a sign that we are lost.[4]

Origen teaches us through his imagination of heaven that we are in a struggle to find God as individual souls, whereas before we knew God only as a symphony of spirits. In fact, that is the only way to know God—in the symphony of community. Not only have individual spirits fallen into souls "but the creation itself groans together, and is in pain until now" (*De principiis* 1.7.5, quoting Rom. 8:22). In a very Platonic fashion, Origen wants to show that from visible things we may by way of consequence see what is also invisible. The discrepancies that now exist in the universe between good and evil—for example, bad things happening to good people—are not due to God's absence at the wheel but due to the chain of cause and effect produced by individualistic beings. This chain is marked either with greater earnestness or with indifference according to the degree of their individualism. We are lost by our own individualistic ways.

Origen shapes our vision to see that the secret of heaven's final redemption is community. He instructs us as a parent instructs her child. As a screaming child disdains its mother's arms while struggling to be put down in order to play, we eagerly neglected God's embrace, thereby departing from our source of truly knowing our ultimate purpose and desire. The child's scream shatters the stillness, demonstrating that we abused our Godlike freedom, falling into animation and snuffing out our contemplative fire. Our full attention to God is now impossible because we mistakenly believe we can muster up enough attention as individual souls to know God when God can only be known in community. This is why prayer is difficult and God is so distant, because we try to reach ultimate existence through an individualistic nature.

Souls fell by creating individualistic motion which propelled them away from symphonic participation in God. Such motion indicates time and space, and therefore finiteness. Perhaps Origen might say here that the reason we have such a difficult time understanding

> If you don't believe I've been redeemed, God's a-gonna trouble the water. Just follow me down to Jordan's stream, God's a-gonna trouble the water.
> —"Wade in the Water," African American spiritual

evil in relation to an all good, wise, and powerful God is because of our individualistic being that has little patience for anyone else except for the self. It is not until we seek God communally (without contradictory motion) that we may return to God. It is hard to be communal, however, when you are already body and soul—when you are already socialized to see ultimate existence as a self. In the same way physically, you cannot simply be healthy by wishing for health. The longing must coincide with long-term practices.

Our longing back to the community called God is the same longing back to union with God, just like the longing for peace is a longing for stillness and serenity. Rowan Williams describes this longing well:

"Origen gives voice to the longing which has never been quenched in any religious tradition, the passion, not for 'intellectual' ecstasy or even for a mystical absorption, but for direct, palpable assurance and experience of the sweetness of a God who enters into intimacy with his creatures."[5] Our innate longing for communal existence indicates our inmost need for complete relationship with God.

The paradox of eternal relation to God became a contradiction when spirits lost their attention to God. This is the incongruity that forced the spirits toward sensibility and motion. Thus Origen defined the soul as *sensibilis et mobilis* (*De principiis* 2.8.1. We slowly became cooled-off minds (i.e., souls) in need of bodies,[6] and consequently, creation as we know it came about. Now the soul needs the body to move between the sensible and spiritual world to rediscover God. At this point Origen provides some of the most beautiful imagery of God's grace, namely, as catching falling souls. God creates this existence, this earth, to rescue our fallen being in an environment in which it would not be totally destroyed. Grace is why we exist on earth. What we see as the contradiction between God's goodness and the evils of this world is none other than grace catching and pulling us from complete nonexistence.

Grace creates an atmosphere within which to reach God again. Origen warns us that a seeming hierarchy forms because some souls have moved further along back to God than others.[7] Again, Origen's imagination helps us talk about the problem of heaven, in that some people seem to deserve to be there while others do not. This is not the case, however. The soul is the middle place between spirit and body where the creature inevitably decides to be communal again. *God has given us earth to practice heaven again.* On earth we are given a soul which is the "sliding middle" in which choices are made.[8] If we wish to attain transformation back into spirit, the soul must choose communal existence as opposed to individualism. By stoking the fire of individualism we remain fleshly or carnal through habitual choice of material things. We have direct responsibility in deciding whether to be continually delinquent toward God or restored completely through Christ. The Word comes from heaven to earth to get us to meditate on community again.

Just as Jesus is the communal image of the good to the degree that he participates in God the Father, so are creatures good to the degree in which they participate in Christ. In the incarnation Christ is the revealer of God to humanity, and, one might say, the revealer of humanity to God. Full participation in God's community through Christ allows for no individualistic existence; instead, it allows the soul to rediscover spiritual union with God where the distinction of subject and object are done away. The mystery of community returns. Our very uniqueness as distinct spirits is determined precisely from such communal participation. Therefore, only in the soul's communal orientation back toward God on earth is the soul immortal. Hans Urs von Balthasar writes: "Thus everything the soul has is 'grace' and every relationship of righteousness is encompassed by a relationship such as mercy. Thus the soul must strive for this participation with the most absolute of commitments, and build its life on the foundation of unmerited grace."[9]

In summary, heaven has come to earth to save us back into the community of God. The soul desperately needs relationship with God in order not to fall further into individualism and oblivion. With a childish attention span, spirits fell from a contemplative place into a longing to return to God. The transcendent state from which we fell now becomes our ironic future goal; and our messy end of things now becomes a beginning through God's grace. Here is the gospel for Origen, namely, we can indeed return to God on earth. Through the incarnation, Christ has untangled us from our trap and we may go back to symphonic existence in God.

Often when I teach or speak I encounter the following question: How can the sign of our individuality be seen as evil? Usually, the question is followed by discussion about the need for a personal relationship with God. Many people who hear me speak or read my writing become worried by my emphasis on communal salvation. Origen's speculation, however, teaches us the complexity of our Western worldview that there can be war in heaven (Rev. 12:7) just as there can be war on earth. We can easily misplace our individual desires in those things that do not warrant our ultimate needs—and this can lead to war. I want to be clear that *our individuality or personhood is not lessened through a communal emphasis, rather, our uniqueness is accentuated.* After all, how could you know you are beautiful unless a community existed to inform you of your beauty?

Perhaps, my emphasis on communal salvation is a result of my own social location as an African American. I will refer later to this through my analysis of how Martin Luther King Jr. and Desmond Tutu see heaven and hell. For now, this can be illustrated by the problem of racism. For example, in racism a power dynamic exists in which people live out a self-fulfilling prophecy of discovering identity over and against others rather than in concert with others. Racism is an individualistic power dynamic because it has the capricious ability to destroy what

Origen defines as the original human state of symphonic existence. All of us behave differently when we are in such symphonic community. Discovering community in which our gifts and talents are celebrated lessens our introversion and brings out our uniqueness. For example, a seminary professor, Dale Andrews, writes that "black preachers preach quite different sermons in exclusively black gatherings from those in the company of white congregations."[10] The black preacher feels at home among those who become his or her community. In an alien environment, enthusiasm takes longer to catch fire or never does. This relates to the problem of heaven on earth in the seeming oceanic divides among individuals, communities, and nation-states that lack habits and sensibilities of wanting to be in community in order to find salvation for self and this planet. Although many will say that Origen's speculation is either heretical or fantastical, I think his genius is to show us that heaven can only be found in community.

Heavenly vision occurs when we step outside of our solipsistic worlds and practice what I call a theology of proximity. This means simply behaving like God in seeking to be symphonically present to others—especially those different from ourselves. A theology of proximity requires us to listen and speak with others who are different from ourselves. Our very lives depend on such habits. In so doing, we discover self. This theology of proximity occurred when the famous German theologian Dietrich Bonhoeffer visited Harlem. Through black folk, Bonhoeffer learned who he really was and thereby crafted beautiful theology in which Christ is always for the other. This theology of proximity also happened with Malcolm X, when he left the United States and made his pilgrimage to Mecca. Through those different from himself, he learned who he truly was and thereby espoused a more reconciliatory politics.

12

A Theology of Proximity

> Nothing accursed will be found there any more. But the throne of God
> and of the Lamb will be in it, and his servants will worship him; they
> will see his face, and his name will be on their foreheads.
> —Revelation 22:3–4

Origen teaches us that we need to be in proximity to God to be in
heaven. In order to do this we also need to be closer to each other.
When I was growing up in Raleigh, North Carolina, I attended Ath-
ens Drive High School. Even though this was in the 1980s, I would
argue this reality remains the same today: If you walk in the cafeteria
at lunchtime, you'll see black kids sitting with black kids. The nerds
sit with nerds, jocks with jocks, rich with rich, and poor with poor.
Although I am dating myself with some of these descriptions (e.g., now
there are categories like goths), the reality remains the same. We lack
the ability truly to be in proximity beyond our natural tribalisms. It is
understandable, however. After all, who wants to sit and eat with someone different—it makes it difficult to digest your food if you're ner-
vously trying to make conversation with a stranger. But it is precisely
around a meal that Jesus is most present—he is in closest proximity to
us in the Eucharist.

Unfortunately, we do not naturally gather in proximity with those
who are different from us. This should give us strong theological pause
to consider how this is all the more problematic given how the one
most different from us is God. In other words, a theology of proximity
gives us language for how we easily worship idols of God rather than
the living God whose ways are not always our ways. Left to our own
devices we may not even realize we have settled for the counterfeit god
rather than the authentic one. Again, strange notions like the Trinity

and how even Jesus' own disciples struggled to understand Jesus' birth, life, death, resurrection, and ascension should help us see the difficulty of a theology of proximity. We will need visionaries to help us navigate our way through such a theology.

In 2007, when I lived in Alexandria, Virginia, near Washington, DC (and I suspect the same will be true in other communities), I often heard the questions: Why are there no visionaries like Mother Teresa and Martin Luther King Jr. anymore? Will we ever have them again? Indeed, Teresa and King were special people who embodied supernatural vision, but I believe the questions are really not about two individuals. I believe these constant questions point to deeper crises of faith—will human beings continue to dream of and envision a world reflective of heaven on earth?

> "Yeah, I just found out that Cleopatra was actually a Black woman."
> "What?"
> The first student went on to explain her newly learned information. The second student exclaimed in disbelief, "That can't be true. Cleopatra was beautiful!"
> —Beverly Daniel Tatum,
> *Why Are All the Black Kids Sitting Together in the Cafeteria? And Other Conversations about Race*

This crisis is a religious one in which our competitive religious worldviews often make for more trouble rather than presenting solutions to a desperate world. We get in trouble because oftentimes our theology of proximity only points to what is infinitely best for our individual selves or for a particular group of people. As the Christian Crusades illustrate, people can do horrible things in the seeming best interest of a certain group. Look at what happened to Jesus—well-intentioned folk thought they were doing a good service by having Jesus crucified. With a lack of vision, those who often have good intentions use horrible means to reach their nearsighted goal.

We continue to long for visionaries like Teresa and King because they are signifiers of a deeper reality among us. Their theology of proximity always points to how our personal salvation must be in proximity to those different from ourselves. Their dreams and actions tell us that if the Christian faith is to be maintained and expressed authentically, we must turn our attention to the new heaven imagined by God and meant for everyone (not just for those we think deserve it). So Jesus teaches his disciples:

> Two men went up to the temple to pray, one a Pharisee and the other a tax collector. The Pharisee, standing by himself, was praying

thus, "God, I thank you that I am not like other people: thieves, rogues, adulterers, or even like this tax collector. I fast twice a week; I give a tenth of all my income." But the tax collector, standing far off, would not even look up to heaven, but was beating his breast and saying, "God, be merciful to me, a sinner!" I tell you, this man went down to his home justified rather than the other; for all who exalt themselves will be humbled, but all who humble themselves will be exalted. (Luke 18:10–14)

Much of our own religiosity resembles that Pharisee. For example, I think we can see this with the problem of Western Christianity.

The Western and European idea of heaven has been expressed in opposition to life on earth (as a place our spirits will go when our bodies die, a place away from here). This vision of heaven, I argue, has contributed to individualistic understandings of Christianity that value the good of the individual over the good of the world. Through Origen's theology, I have tried to show a more Eastern approach to Christianity in which our earthly existence is not simply a place to escape but is instead a place of grace. Origen's understanding of heaven comes to earth through the incarnation and helps us make sense of the interconnection between earth and heaven. There are others who dream of heaven on earth like Origen.

These other visions of heaven can be seen through the spirituality of Martin Luther King Jr. and Desmond Tutu. Like Origen, both King and Tutu teach us that heaven is embodied among diverse community that learns to rely solely on God. For example, we all need to be constantly reminded of King's vision for a "beloved community," a global vision for peace, justice, and mutual care for each other and the world. In King's dream of heaven, different kinds of people are constantly in proximity one to the other. We also need living examples like Tutu, who facilitates diverse community in South Africa while remaining faithful to his Christian faith. King and Tutu provide a profound understanding for a theology of proximity. For example, they teach us that we cannot minister to the distressed without first becoming distressed. Such a teaching should be deeply convicting to Western Christians who often believe in disconnected salvation—as long as I make it to heaven, everything will be OK. Tutu and King challenge this kind of theology by instructing us that injustice anywhere is a threat to justice everywhere.

As we will learn later in this book, King and Tutu help us imagine and then practice heaven here on earth—experiencing beatitude *now*. This is revolutionary, and I seek to draw upon such examples of groundbreaking work like that of Tutu and King to illustrate how heaven is already proximate to us. I also want us to wrestle with the serious challenges to my argument. For example, I remember being jubilant upon meeting Mother Teresa in Calcutta when I was a seminarian. I conveyed my enthusiasm to one of my professors back in the United States. He quickly deflated my idealism when he told me that he would prefer the work of a rich individual (someone like Bill Gates) who could effect systemic change for poor people rather than the work of a Mother Teresa who simply helps individuals in an ad hoc manner. As I look back on that touchstone experience, I am all the more inspired to expand my theology of proximity beyond our either-or mentality of Mother Teresa or Bill Gates.

Making a significant difference in bettering the world is not a matter of choosing between the work of Mother Teresa and Bill Gates, however. Rather, it is about garnering an imagination capable of seeing communal existence beyond the violent and contradictory ways and means we set for ourselves. In other words, without the extraordinary example of Mother Teresa, my seminary professor would have lacked his subsequent vision for a Christian Bill Gates. A reference point was first needed to know the deep need before a systemic solution could be put in place. Visionaries like Tutu, King, and Teresa provide this kind of vision to see that my salvation is dependent upon yours. Even though a visionary like Mother Teresa did not have the complete means to care for those in her charge, she tried anyway. Her exemplary Christian practice provides the framework and reference point to imagine how those with means can now eradicate poverty and many diseases. Mother Teresa made us think about Millennium Development Goals before they were ever announced by the United Nations. I remember arguing with my professor that the altruism of Bill Gates could not exist without the incredible practices of folk like Mother Teresa. He needed Mother Teresa to help him see the need for a Bill Gates, with good stewardship of his resources. Again, we need a theology of proximity.

Because most of us are limited by time and socioeconomic resources, we all need help in knowing what in fact we are supposed to do to help ourselves and others. We need to be in proximity to others to imagine a better world. Instead of preferring one set of talents and gifts over another, we need visionaries who imagine and see how all talents and gifts fit together. We need each other to create an environment in which we all can become more than we are alone. Visionaries like Tutu show us how Christian spirituality is a ready resource that enables the impossible vision for heaven on earth. Christian spirituality offers a revolutionary worldview meant always to resist violence and division, and, more importantly, a proactive vision to move toward heaven on earth. Christians have a responsibility to become visionaries; as the biblical prophets remind us, without vision, people inevitably perish (Prov. 29:18).

This is an important discussion because, increasingly, religion (and Christianity in particular) has acquired a bad rap for dividing rather than uniting diverse people and communities. Yet I present a different and, to some, *controversial* version of Christianity—one concerned less with personal salvation in isolation and more with the salvation of whole communities engaged in lifelong process of nonviolence and community building. In fact, I argue that personal salvation is unintelligible apart from communal salvation. In so doing, I present a new understanding of heaven—not as some ethereal or otherworldly end of the individual in isolation but as a vision of God's communal presence continually wrapping us up in God's midst.

More particularly, heaven is found in our relationships with God and our neighbor. Jesus taught through his parables that the kingdom of heaven is recognized within how we form relationships with one another. Jesus coached his disciples to see and hear how God is already acting in our relationships and communities. We see such activity today among those who intentionally live among the poor to empower them. We see such activity in South Africa's Truth and Reconciliation Commission. These are only a few examples, but they give us vision and hope.

Jesus said: "To you it has been given to know the secrets of the kingdom of heaven, but to them it has not been given. For to those who have, more will be given, and they will have an abundance; but from those who have nothing, even what they have will be taken away. The reason I speak to them in parables is that 'seeing they do not perceive, and hearing they do not listen, nor do they understand'" (Matt. 13:11–13). Jesus is teaching here that many of us lack sufficient community to see the mystery of heaven. Good interpretations of these Scriptures do not imply that Jesus is trying to further divide us with talk of heaven. So Jesus is not speaking in parables to confuse us; rather, the parable is the judgment against our tribal gods always at war to protect our self-interests. Jesus is trying to coax us away from our limited way of understanding reality.

There is complexity, however, in Matthew's account of Jesus' parables of the kingdom of heaven. A reader wishing to take vengeance against an enemy or an individualistic kind of heaven can easily be inferred. It appears as though Jesus sanctions a separation of those not going to heaven—those separated by God's angels will be routed to "the furnace of fire" and the place "where there will be weeping and gnashing of teeth" (Matt. 13:41–42). The problem here is that looks are deceiving, and so is what appears to be Jesus' sanction of sending the unfaithful to hell.

The complexity of Mathew's kingdom of heaven can be noticed in the inextricable link between heaven and earth. Jesus gives Peter the keys to the kingdom of heaven and says to him, "'Whatever you bind on earth will be bound in heaven, and whatever you loose on earth will be loosed in heaven.' Then he sternly ordered the disciples not to tell anyone that he was the Messiah. From that time on, Jesus began to show his disciples" that he must suffer at the hands of those who appear to be righteous, "and on the third day be raised. And Peter took him aside and began to rebuke him, saying, 'God forbid it, Lord! This must never happen to you.'" But Jesus turned and said a very interesting thing to Peter, "'Get behind me, Satan! You are a stumbling block to me; for you are setting your mind not on divine things but on human things'" (Matt. 16:19–23). Within this brief narrative we are invited into a theology of proximity and a lesson in why Jesus uses parables. The thin space between heaven and earth is illustrated through Jesus' simultaneous rebuke of Peter and Satan. This thin space is also illustrative of how Peter also contains the keys to heaven and can bind and loose the connections between heaven and earth. In other words, Peter simultaneously acts in heaven, earth, and hell. These worlds seem to be contiguous based on one's connection to the suffering Jesus.

Just as Jesus does not advocate for Peter to become Satan, so he does not advocate for any to go to hell or be separated from heaven. Those who think Jesus wants some to go to hell do not understand how Jesus teaches through parable; and such exegesis or biblical interpretation misses Jesus' point about the kingdom of heaven. Jesus' essential point is this: "Seeing they do not perceive." Religious folk need to actively imagine and practice a more rich and flourishing existence than is readily perceived, not only for particular individuals but for all people. After all, those in Matthew's context who were supposed to be going to heaven—the righteous—were reinterpreted by Jesus as being the furthest from heaven. "For I tell you," Jesus says, "unless your righteousness exceeds that of the scribes and Pharisees, you will never enter the kingdom of heaven" (Matt. 5:20). Sinners like thieves, prostitutes, and tax collectors were closer to heaven.

Jesus makes us see differently. Those who are supposed to go to heaven are now seen as getting in the way of heaven come here on earth. The Gospel of Luke picks up on Matthew's insight into the complexity of seeing heaven. Luke recounts how Jesus "told this parable to some who trusted in themselves that they were righteous and regarded others with contempt: '. . . The Pharisee, standing by himself, was praying thus, "God, I thank you that I am not like other people [those going to hell]: thieves, rogues, adulterers, or even like this tax collector"'" (Luke 18:11). It is vital that we understand Jesus' crucial point: "Seeing they do not perceive." This insight of Jesus not only redeems the image of Christianity in the world, but it also allows Christianity to do genuine good, to grow into its global purpose of facilitating diversity and unity. In a theology of proximity, I hold on to Jesus' call that we both see and perceive to illustrate how we can create communities that envision and embody heaven for everyone.

I am aware, however, that this vision of heaven for everyone may cause great concern for some. My emphasis on how a Christian concept of heaven impacts practical social action toward diversity and communal spirituality leaves many in the lurch. They would rather talk about personal salvation. I realize, however, the audacity of making a claim that the Christian concept of heaven impacts social action toward diversity and communal spirituality. For others, my argument may seem to be the typical overstatement of religion, as others argue against me that while the focus on social justice may be distinctive, there are many books that address the interaction between heaven and earth or the communal nature of heaven. Indeed, the notion that heaven and earth are intertwined seems to be widespread among religious thinkers.[1]

However, only a few current books on heaven share my concerns that one's personal fulfillment is unintelligible apart from communal fulfillment.[2] The genre of books on heaven are helpful in their rearticulation of the problem of Christian imagination and how the goals of the Christian life are seldom reflected in daily and political life. If Christianity is to be relevant in helping to solve global problems, it will have to respond to the problem of being otherworldly and for no earthly good.

PART THREE

Good Dreams

13

A New Ethic

On either side of the river is the tree of life with its twelve kinds of fruit, producing its fruit each month; and the leaves of the tree are for the healing of the nations.

—Revelation 22:2

The psalmist prays, "LORD, let me know my end" (Ps. 39:4). This, too, should be our prayer as we aim toward being better persons in community. How does our purpose toward heaven shape our life on earth? In order to answer this question we must discover the humility mentioned before to know that we are not in heaven and that heaven is not a construct of tribal or personal salvation. Much of the work of this theological commentary is to remind us of our tendency to define heaven in our own self-interested images—especially, who has to go to hell. Heaven is God's doing, however. And what God does often is strange to us mortals.

> For three and a half days members of the peoples and tribes and languages and nations will gaze at their dead bodies [of the two witnesses] and refuse to let them be placed in a tomb; and the inhabitants of the earth will gloat over them and celebrate and exchange presents, because these two prophets had been a torment to the inhabitants of the earth.
>
> But after the three and a half days, the breath of life from God entered them, and they stood on their feet, and those who saw them were terrified. (Rev. 11:9–11)

The gospel is that even though none of us deserve to be in heaven, especially with how we treat each other, God is graciously bringing heaven and earth together—even if God has to raise the dead. God's movement of us, however, is not deterministic. God moves us through the deepest desires of our being. For example, unlike the mob frenzy in the above passage from Revelation, our very demand for justice is but a ray of light from God. Justice, flowing out from the inmost being of God, demands that the will of heaven be brought to earth. And for that demand to turn back upon its own source in protest keeps us in perpetual conflict. Herein, we find the predicament of heaven versus earth.

Although God moves us along toward heaven, we are still free. God created us with God's image, which includes freedom; and God will not encroach upon such freedom lest we become automatic in a great, deterministic scheme. God takes no delight in such robots. Therefore, our freedom is exercised wisely when our deep desires meet the earth's deep hunger. It is at this point that one begins to see how heaven and earth interact, namely, by our acting in concert with God-given desire and earthly needs.

With this perspective of heaven, we participate in a self-fulfilling prophecy to become more than we would naturally become (or want to be) on earth. We can no longer settle for all-white churches, violence against those who have a same-sex orientation, a revisited crusade against Muslims, or all-male leadership. God's image in us helps us to see differently and creatively. All creatures are ordered to God as their ultimate purpose. But all creatures attain this last end in the measure in which they share in its likeness. As human beings we obtain our ultimate purpose in the manner peculiar to us, namely, by being held to higher standards than the behavior of a jaguar in a jungle. Such a creature lives simply by instinct and survival. Human beings, on the other hand, have the ability to suspend instinct and survival for higher purposes. Such higher callings are illustrated as Mother Teresa voluntarily becomes poor and prone to disease and violence or as Martin Luther King receives threatening phone calls and still carries on the civil rights movement. Human beings must *know* God in a higher manner than other creatures know God. It is in this knowledge of God that we are driven to heaven. On our way, all our intermediate ends are gathered up in heaven, including each particular happiness on earth.

We know our purpose because God orders human life to heaven through our very freedom. To conclude the above passage from Revelation 11, we would do well to read what God does next: "Then [the two witnesses] heard a loud voice from heaven saying to them, 'Come up here!' And they went up to heaven in a cloud while their enemies watched them" (11:12). Having heaven as our cause, we experience freedom toward the ultimate end. Christians believe that our lives are subject to God and that ultimate meaning exists above our particular ends—not to make the end justify the means but to make us see how our end in God gives us our beginning. God's judgment does not discount our particularity or personality. As the mystery of the Trinity suggests, our particularity is made sense of through the interdependence that God offers us.

Because of God's challenge to us that earth contain heaven (e.g., the incarnation of God in Jesus), we are forever changed. We cannot settle upon anything less than our ultimate existence. So Jesus teaches the disciples that earth can contain heaven: "As you go, proclaim the good news, 'The kingdom of heaven has come near.' Cure the sick, raise the dead, cleanse the lepers, cast out demons. You received without payment; give without payment" (Matt. 10:7–8). This ultimate purpose inspires human desire in the same way that the first mover moves all movable things. If there is no matching response to ultimate existence, we find the following drama unfolding, Peter Kreeft writes:

> Why do we keep repeating the mistake? Why do many people go through an endless succession of earthly loves (of persons or even of things) even after repeated experience tells them they are always disappointed? Pascal says, "A test which has gone on so long, without pause or change, really ought to convince us that . . . the infinite abyss can be filled only with an infinite and immutable object, in other words with God himself." We keep trying despite repeated failures because we're looking for God. We can't help it; we have to have him. But we look in the wrong places. "Seek what you seek but not where you seek it," advises Saint Augustine.[1]

We react properly to God if we realize that our particular ends are completely fulfilled only in God.

Delight in God requires the quiescence of the human will to stop seeking ultimate existence in temporal things. And yet heaven is manifest on earth. We need a deep spirituality in order to figure out this puzzle. Through our daily prayer of seeking God we develop a spirituality to know that life on earth is not the end. And even when those joys and celebrations come to us, we must not ultimately delight in them. In other words, since we may find heaven in earth, many mistakenly seek ultimate purpose in riches, health, power, sex, and any other corporeal good. But our ultimate purpose is none of these things. Our ultimate end is heaven—where God is. And though a person longs for heaven, one need not substitute short-term pleasures for ultimate existence. On the contrary, God entices us to always withdraw from things that addict us, seducing us to separate heaven from earth.

We become heavenly minded persons who are of earthly good. A communal perception of heaven changes the cliché that heavenly minded people are of no earthly good. Christians now help to imagine and see ideal existence as communal existence by helping the world to see that no person can be seen as an object. In God's mysterious being we have received the gift of being like God—never an object but a subject. We know the other as we are known by the other. Paul articulates this mystery of heaven: "For now we see in a mirror, dimly, but then we will see face to face. Now I know only in part; then I will know fully, even as I have been fully known" (1 Cor. 13:12). We come to know our ultimate place by knowing the ultimate person, God.

Heaven naturally accompanies our knowledge of how then to live on earth. Though the human person is not the last end of the universe, she or he is a particular being ordered toward the last end, which is heaven. Therefore, neither the satisfying of the body nor its conservation can be constituted as ultimate purpose. Even if we concede that the end of human reason and will is to conserve the human body, it still does not follow that our last end consists in a corporeal good. We can only find true delight in God.

Christian spirituality is crucial in helping persons see that our ultimate purpose cannot be defined by us. Heaven is not a good that belongs to the soul but subsists outside the soul and infinitely above it. As Thomas states, "Beatitude pertains to the soul, but consists in something outside the soul."[2] Heaven on earth helps us see that we are only our potential selves. Anything potential bespeaks of something more complete. It is clear that there can be no movement where there is no potentiality to something else, for movement is the act of that which is in potentiality. Thomas believes "that the human soul exists in view of something else; it is not its last end."[3] Human beatitude cannot ultimately consist in any created good. It can only reside in a perfect good that fully satisfies the appetite, for it could not be the last end if one still has a craving.

Since a created good never quenches our desire, then human beatitude resides in God alone.[4] What confuses us, however, is that upon arriving more fully into the life of God in heaven, one still does not cease to wonder and dream. This wonderment, however, does not mean dissatisfaction. It helps us to solve the complaint we started with—a boring heaven. Where there is eternal wonder, how can there be stagnation? This goes against all who think heaven is boring. Instead, heaven is the eternal now that Buddhists speak of, not a shallow succession of experiences that eventually bore us to death.

John's apocalyptic vision is not meant to make us obsess with who belongs in heaven and who in hell. Instead, his vision points to our desire for ultimate life, not a fragmented one. John's vision is so intense that he seems to have little patience for editing his stream of consciousness in terms of good dreams and nightmares. He leaves them all mingled together so that we who are also mingled together may find a common ground on which to long for heaven on earth. As for pleasure involved in desiring heaven, it only surges in us because the object sought is already present. In other words, we delight in heaven because God's presence was already in us. John's apocalyptic vision, therefore, is not meant to be taken literally. His is a speculative theology akin to the patristic figure Origen, who also dreamed about the content of heaven. The most perfect power of John's vision is the one whose object is the most perfect, that is, whose object is the essence of God. John's vision of heaven and earth constituting beatitude must therefore be of a speculative nature, and this amounts to saying that it must be an act of contemplation.

What we are ultimately looking for is both here and not here, because what we are looking for is in heaven. We are called to look for heaven on earth. It is as though God requires of us to live in a self-fulfilling prophecy—look for heaven on earth, be an agent of heaven on earth. This is a logical conclusion. The more a thing is desired and loved, says Aquinas, the more does its loss bring sorrow and pain. Christians are to be contemplative and mindful that an existence on earth that is painful and tragic is not to be accepted as natural. We are to be aware that something is missing. Heaven is often missing. Therefore its loss brings the greatest sorrow. But we are called to be mindful and contemplative also that death is natural. If we indeed discover God's beatitude in this life, it will certainly be lost, at least by death. Also, it is possible for everyone in this life to encounter sickness, which debilitates the operation of comprehension—for example, mental illness, which hinders the use of reason. Our heaven on earth, therefore, always has sorrow naturally connected with it, and consequently it will not be perfect until God breaks the paradigm altogether (Rev. 21:1).[5]

The human intellect knows no other essence than those of the sensible world. From this we come to know that God exists, but we never

attain the essence of the first cause in this present state. Therefore
we experience the natural desire to know fully and to see directly the
essence of God in heaven. So if we naturally desire heaven, we cannot
know it as human beings, without the light of God's revelation. But we
can at least know it in the measure that God can be known as human
beings can know God. Thus it is only through union with God that the
ultimate end is attained and the highest perfection reached. In much of
John's apocalyptic vision, I believe that he is trying to help us see that
heaven makes earthly reality intelligible. A continuity of order exists
between the earthly beatitude accessible here below and the heavenly
beatitude to which we are called.

All our desires, when properly governed and interpreted by heaven
on earth, have legitimate significance. Here below we desire health
and material well-being; and these, indeed, are favorable conditions
through which human happiness is attained. In this life we desire riches,
health, power, sex, and other corporeal goods because they enable us
to live and to perform the works of contemplative and active virtue.
They may not be essential for heaven, but they are at least instruments
of it. Here, in this life, we desire a society of friends, and rightly so
because anyone who is happy in this world must have friends. This is
the effect of heaven. Heaven shows us that one does not have friends
as useful objects—a friend must always be an end, not an object. One
who is heavenly minded now sees only injustice in treating others as
objects. Heaven shows us that others are not a source of pleasure—
only God is. Heaven shows us that we have friends because we need
a community in which to practice becoming more the persons we are
created to be. Friends are there to receive our good deeds, and they
provide us with opportunities to acquire virtue or to perfect it. This is
why Jesus speaks as he does:

> When the Son of Man comes in his glory, and all the angels with
> him, then he will sit on the throne of his glory. All the nations
> will be gathered before him, and he will separate people one from
> another as a shepherd separates the sheep from the goats, and he
> will put the sheep at his right hand and the goats at the left. Then
> the king will say to those at his right hand, "Come, you that are
> blessed by my Father, inherit the kingdom prepared for you from
> the foundation of the world; for I was hungry and you gave me food,
> I was thirsty and you gave me something to drink, I was a stranger
> and you welcomed me, I was naked and you gave me clothing, I was
> sick and you took care of me, I was in prison and you visited me."

Then the righteous will answer him, "Lord, when was it that we saw you . . . ?" And the king will answer them, "Truly, I tell you, just as you did it to one of the least of these who are members of my family, you did it to me." (Matt. 25:31–40)

If heaven is in mind, ethics takes on a whole new meaning. No longer can one look at creation solely from the utilitarian perspective. If heaven impinges upon this world, Jesus' words are real, for heaven is already in our midst. When we mistreat the littlest one of us, we abuse heaven. If heaven is real, if living with God is possible and actual, God must be preparing us on earth to live in its environment. We must wake up to this possibility and actuality.

Even when one sees God face to face in heaven, and even when the soul has come to resemble God completely, our soul will not be separated from its body. This is what is beautiful about Christianity— the natural perfection of the soul cannot exclude the perfection of the body. Before we reach heaven, the body is the soul's minister; it is the instrument of those spiritual operations that facilitate heaven's arrival. But in heaven, the soul rewards the body by conferring incorruptibility upon it and lets it share in its own immortal perfection.

Dante, a student of Aquinas, provides poetic imagery of the soul and body in heaven.[6] In paradise, souls await the resurrection of their bodies so they may enter the empyrean, the highest state of heaven, completely with God. When body and soul are united, then the joys of the soul shall redound upon the body, and the consummation shall be complete. Therefore the souls in Dante's paradise are still on a journey. Even though we see God as human bodies see, we will be emancipated not only from time, but also from space itself in such illumination of God. What manner of vision is this? C. S. Lewis describes it in *Surprised by Joy* as

> something which, by refusing to identify itself with any object of the senses or anything whereof we have biological or social need, or anything imagined, or any state of our own minds, proclaims itself sheerly objective. Far more objective than bodies, for it is not, like them, clothed in our senses: the naked Other, imageless (though our imagination salutes it with a hundred images), unknown, undefined, desired.[7]

In other words, we cannot see divine substance by means of our creaturely capacities, which creates an inherent problem since they are created. In other words, human beings need God to help us see and understand God. We cannot do this by ourselves. Therefore, if God's essence is to be seen at all, it must be that we see God through God's divine essence itself; so that in that vision the divine essence is both the object and the medium of vision.

It would be impious to understand our face-to face-vision of God in a material way and imagine a material face in the Godhead. So turning the book of Revelation into a literal encounter with God is itself offending to God because we rely on our own intellect and imagination to determine John's Apocalypse. Nor is it possible to see God with a bodily face, since the eyes of the body can see only bodily things. Seeing face to face means we shall see God *immediately*. John's Apocalypse invites us to imagine what we cannot imagine. It is through this vision that we become most like God on earth and participators in God's divine life. Therefore it is said: When God shall appear we shall be like to God; because we shall see God as God is (1 John 3:2).

> Be thou my vision, O Lord of my heart; naught be all else to me, save that thou art; thou my best thought, by day or by night, waking or sleeping, thy presence my light.
> —"Be Thou My Vision," Irish poem

In conclusion, no intellectual substance can see God through the divine essence, unless God brings this about. The vision of God surpasses the ability of every creature, and it is impossible to attain it except by God's gift. God attaches God's self to the intellect as an intelligible form that allows our sight of God. But God does not become the intelligible form of a created intellect unless the created intellect participates in God. This participation is necessary in order that the divine substance be seen. Since the divine essence is a higher form than any created intellect, the created intellect needs to be raised to that capacity by some higher disposition.[8]

God continues nature into supernature. God is not satisfied in smiting and throwing fire and brimstone. Through the revelation of Jesus, we are clued into the deeper motivations of God. Jesus shows us a different destiny. It is a destiny not merely of the human soul but of the total person in community. God is this destiny, and even on earth we are being made to abide with God in heaven. So beware:

> It is a serious thing to live in a society of possible gods and goddesses, to remember that the dullest and most uninteresting person you can talk to may one day be a creature which, if you saw it now, you would be strongly tempted to worship, or else a horror and a

corruption such as you now meet, if at all, only in a nightmare. All day long we are, in some degree, helping each other to one or other of these destinations. . . . There are no *ordinary* people. You have never talked to a mere mortal. Nations, cultures, arts, civilizations— these are mortal, and their life is to ours as the life of a gnat. But it is immortals whom we joke with, work with, marry, snub, and exploit—immortal horrors or everlasting splendors.[9]

14

All Roads (and Rivers) to Heaven?

On the banks, on both sides of the river, there will grow all kinds of trees for food. Their leaves will not wither nor their fruit fail, but they will bear fresh fruit every month, because the water for them flows from the sanctuary. Their fruit will be for food, and their leaves for healing.
—Ezekiel 47:12

Then the angel showed me the river of the water of life, bright as crystal, flowing from the throne of God and of the Lamb through the middle of the street of the city.
—Revelation 22:1

Do all roads go to heaven? We need each other to know the answer to this question. Heaven as a state of being here on earth rather than a "place" only out there means that we need each other to know God's transcendence; otherwise, our lack of heavenly vision perpetuates oppressive structures on earth. In other words, where there is no vision the people perish. How do we have vision, however, especially when the picture of heaven seems so confusing? I illustrate this confusion with the following questions. Is heaven a place, or a perspective for why we exist, or a utopia that provides a model for a truly communal, peaceful, nonracist society, or the end product of God's creative acts, or uninhibited presence with God, or the contemplation of the divine Trinitarian essence by the human intellect, or the return of the soul to God, or a metaphor (an analogue) for earthly existence, or the potential—that is, the "form" (à la Plato)—of this present reality that sustains this reality in existence and of which this reality is but an image? One could ask equally whether heaven intersects the earth, transcends the earth, or is on earth, connatural with the earth, contingent with the earth, and so forth; and whether heaven is a future to which all of creation tends or a memory of the eternal present. After reading an earlier draft of this book, a book reviewer raised these questions in order to encourage me to face up to the Pandora's box that my theological project is likely to open.

In John's fifth vision in heaven (Rev. 14:1–5), we discover those who survived the tribulation and are trying to pick up the pieces of their lives. Let us remember the state we are in and the many broken pieces resulting from the fourth vision on earth that described the tribulation and how the one hundred forty-four thousand refused to worship the beast. Now in this fifth vision only those who had gone through tribulation seem to understand a new song. They can all understand and appreciate this new song because of their suffering. It is important to understand that it is not so much because of their resilience that they are able to begin picking up the pieces but because of the different experience of singing a new song.

We also discover in this section the fifth vision on earth (Rev. 14:6–20). Angels have been scarce since the seventh angel sounded the seventh trumpet (11:15), but now six angels appear. It is the third angel who makes us worry about picking up the pieces. This angel screams, "Those who worship the beast and its image, and receive a mark on their foreheads or on their hands, they will also drink the wine of God's wrath, poured unmixed into the cup of his anger, and they will be tormented with fire and sulfur in the presence of the holy angels and in the presence of the Lamb. And the smoke of their torment goes up forever and ever" (14:9–11). Here we have the problem of theodicy again. Cornel West states, "Christianity also is first and foremost a theodicy, a triumphant account of good over evil."[1]

> As you looked on, a stone was cut out, not by human hands, and it struck the statue on its feet of iron and clay and broke them in pieces.
>
> —Daniel 2:34

It is difficult if not impossible for us to put together the pieces of why a good God would allow torment forever. In addition it is surprising to know that other Christians seem to have little struggle with such passages of Scripture and receive them as solemn warnings that must not be toned down in the slightest degree. After all, some Christians believe, God is helping the chosen to resist the temptations of the beast and the false prophet. But the revelation of God in Jesus Christ is such that God knows our weaknesses—and knows that no one on their own can survive such impossible odds. After all, that is why Jesus came the first time. So how do we put these pieces together—the goodness of God known through Jesus with the perils of beasts and evil?

The Christian concept of heaven, as I've argued, should be experienced here on earth and should be a collective venture, not an individualistic one. In fact, some may accuse me of heresy in doing this. What I along with well-respected church theologians argue for, however, is that heaven is unintelligible apart from earth; and earth is unintelligible apart from heaven. In other words, we need both of them to know each of them. We have been given the image of God, and, even if we see this image piecemeal, we have responsibilities in the practice of God's presence (heaven) here and now. For too long we have used the concept of heaven to justify postponing correct behavior and responsibilities that Jesus gives us. The church has even condoned horrendous behavior in the name of Christian realism this side of heaven—whether that is keeping black people in slavery, offering them a better life in heaven, or going to war, offering soldiers the ultimate prize of heaven. It is time now to see why Jesus tells us not to wait for heaven because it is already among us. Such context of how heaven can already be among us deeply matters for correcting bad behaviors and dysfunctional beliefs in the apocalypse.

Why do we use apocalyptic discourse as an excuse to behave badly on earth? Malcolm Gladwell is helpful here. In his book *The Tipping Point*, he tells the story of a group of psychologists at Princeton University who decided to conduct a study on Good Samaritans. The story of the Good Samaritan, in which a beaten traveler lies by the side of a road, comes from Luke 10:30–37. In the story two upstanding persons, even a priest, come upon a person in distress and do not stop to help. The only one to help is a Samaritan, a cultural identity ostracized at that time. The psychologists decided to replicate this scenario for a study of students at Princeton Theological Seminary—a place dear to my heart, since I also graduated from there.

> A theological education can be a bit like assembling a child's toy on Christmas Eve. Lots of pieces, no idea how they fit together.
>
> —Frederick W. Schmidt,
> *Conversations with Scripture: Revelation*

The psychologists met with this group of seminarians and asked each of them to prepare a short sermon and then walk over to a nearby building to present it. An experiment was set up so that along the way to that nearby building, each seminarian would encounter someone slumped over in an alley in apparent pain. The question of the study was this: Which of the seminarians would stop and help the person in pain?

The psychologists introduced three variables into the experiment. First, the seminarians had to fill out a questionnaire about why they chose to study theology. For example, they were asked how religion was a means for personal and spiritual fulfillment. Or were they studying theology to find tools to figure out meaning in everyday life? Second, the seminarians were given different topics for their sermons. Some were asked to preach on vocation, others on the parable of the Good Samaritan. And third, the instructions varied. Sometimes the experimenter would look at her watch and say, "Oh, you're late. They were expecting you a few minutes ago. We'd better get moving." Other seminarians were told, "It will be a few minutes before they're ready for you, but you might as well head over now."

One would think that a seminarian, someone training to be a minister, would more naturally stop to help anyone in distress. And yet, these psychologists provide the sad evidence that being a seminarian does not predict the behavior of a Good Samaritan. The psychologists conclude, "Indeed, on several occasions, a seminary student going to give his talk on the parable of the Good Samaritan literally stepped over the victim as he hurried on his way." Seminarians in this study were no better than the average bystander at giving a helping hand. An important discovery, however, was made. Of the seminarians who felt rushed, only 10 percent stopped to help. Of those who knew they had a few minutes extra, 63 percent stopped.[2] The key to helping, it seems, was whether the seminarian was in a rush or not.

How does this Good Samaritan study help us discuss heaven on earth? I think it teaches us that in the end our beliefs are less important than our habits. Our beliefs about heaven are essentially dependent upon habits.[3] Without the character that comes from good habits, our belief systems will be immature—and even worse, destructive. For example, many things have been condoned in the name of Christianity—even slavery as the will of God. As an African American Christian spiritual leader, my beliefs in heaven are informed by ancestors who developed habits of survival in a violent world. The beautiful thing about their heaven was that God was big enough to save them and their oppressors. For many of my ancestors, reaching heaven was not a personal goal; it was a communal journey. This is why attention to how heaven can be on earth matters. No longer could there be the justification to keep systems of oppression in place because this is the way life is on this side of heaven.

My particular perspective of heaven challenges much of the rhetoric of Western Christianity that places a heavy emphasis either on personal salvation or on the European Enlightenment approach of only thinking about heaven. This book is important because *I want us to practice the habits required to see heaven on earth.* Even if you are not a Christian, I invite you into habits through which heaven on earth is imagined and realized. There can be no justification for violence on earth in light of the rewards of heaven. This leads me to Frederick Buechner's definition of vocation. Those who hear God's call to impact the world know "the place where your deep gladness and the world's deep hunger meet."[4] Buechner is right to call this a place. I envision such a place as heaven on earth—where deep gladness and the world's deep hunger meet. After all, a banquet is a chief metaphor for heaven. Habits are required to find heaven because we need practice to find where our deep gladness meets the world's deep hunger. Therefore, I invite readers from a variety of contexts into a strange worldview in which we practice the impossible heaven on earth.

> I saw no temple in the city, for its temple is the Lord God the Almighty and the Lamb. And the city has no need of sun or moon to shine on it, for the glory of God is its light.
>
> —Revelation 21:22–23

IMAGING HEAVEN

What will heaven be like? I have always been fascinated by this question. Social psychologists say that this question becomes more acute as one gets older and seeks meaning in one's life here and now. For example, in 2001 in what he said could be his last interview because of the cancer that had struck him, Archbishop Desmond Tutu talked about his view of heaven. "I wonder," said Tutu, "whether they have rum and Coke in Heaven? Maybe it's too mundane a pleasure, but I hope so—as a sundowner. Except, of course, the sun never goes down there. Oh, man, this Heaven is going to take some getting used to."[5] Tutu provides us the wisdom to know how to find heaven. The wisdom is this: despite our longing for that place that meets and surpasses our needs, we may seem to behave on earth as if heaven is not really our desire. Later, in Revelation, John seems to convey Tutu's insight that heaven as a concept requires a paradigm shift. The writer of Revelation is clueing us in that his desire for a temple was changed in heaven. Also, images of sunsets and sunrises would no longer help to describe heaven. What will heaven be like? The simple answer here is God. This is a difficult answer because it implies that God will have to be enough to satisfy our needs and desires.

ETERNAL GOSPEL

John's voice in the first section of chapter 14 seems to convey this theme of paradigm shift—of picking up the pieces to put together a whole new picture, or as he says, to "sing a new song" (Rev. 14:3). Well, it seems as though Scripture leads us to believe that heaven will be our completion, but not in the way we may have expected. John's vision, as throughout Revelation, is in pieces. His stream-of-consciousness dream moves from a new song and the one hundred and forty-four thousand to an angel flying in something called "midheaven" proclaiming something that I very much want to hear, "an eternal gospel . . . to every nation and tribe and language and people" (14:6). This "eternal gospel" comes in the midst of beasts and angels wielding sharp sickles and fire and sulfur. Shouldn't this "eternal gospel" make us rejoice? Shouldn't we take great delight in the knowledge that we will live in such a way that the gospel will be eternal? We should, but I am afraid we do not rejoice. I guess it is hard to imagine in John's vision that one can rejoice while still running from reaping angels and ravenous beasts. But I think Tutu puts his finger on a deeper issue of why it is hard to rejoice about John's "eternal gospel." As Tutu's humor exemplifies—will there be rum and Coke in heaven?—we have our own image of what delights us. And unfortunately, some of us would be delighted if those reaping angels and ravenous beasts exterminated the people we wanted to get rid of.

If I asked you in secret—all of you who read this book—what it is that you truly desire the most, that would complete you and satiate your desires, I imagine I would have as many answers as there are readers. Despite our diversity, however, I argue that there should be at least one common desire. I imagine this common desire as heaven. It is not a desire that should fall under a wish deferred or for some far-off utopia. The desire I imagine along with John in the book of Revelation is for heaven here and now. In the Western world, influenced so much by individualism, it is difficult to find a majority who would agree with my approach to heaven—that is, a heaven for everyone. This is counterintuitive: one would think most Western people socialized in an individualistic worldview would think heaven to be a good idea. It would allow everyone to pursue personal happiness. I argue, however, that personal happiness is an oxymoron. "Personal happiness" is akin to "limited freedom"; the adjective cancels out the subject. So my counterintuitive problem of a heaven the vast majority of Western

Christians believe in leaves me with a confused audience. It is an audience that thinks heaven is a good idea for personal fulfillment but that cannot really imagine communal or universal fulfillment.

When I use the pronoun "we" for Christian identity (at least in the Western world), it is unclear who that entails. I have this problem largely because of an individualistic Christianity. It is almost as if Christian identity can no longer be claimed in common. Perhaps we all have been trained to be suspicious of those who claim to be Christians, and rightfully so. After all, just look at the atrocities that have been done in the name of Christianity (war, genocide, Crusades, slavery, holocaust). By looking for heaven with common ground, I imagine a Christianity in which Protestants, Orthodox, Catholics, evangelicals, fundamentalists, and liberals help the world rather than make matters worse.

In all of the ways that I fail to provide this common vision, I hold out a baton to those with greater minds and hearts than my own to move all of us beyond contentious presumptions and worldviews. By addressing the question of how a communal understanding of heaven got lost, I hope to bring the reader up to speed on an ancient conversation and help them understand what is at stake in John's apocalyptic vision. Without additional and informed background to frame John's apocalypse, I am afraid the concept of heaven will continue to be conceived solely for individualistic and personal ends. After all, even though John speaks of an "eternal gospel" we are still not clear who gets to be in receipt of such a beautiful concept. In other words, even though the "eternal gospel" is for "every nation and tribe and language and people," John has yet another piecemeal vision in which this time a third angel says, "And the smoke of their torment goes up forever and ever. There is no rest day or night for those who worship the beast and its image and for anyone who receives the mark of its name" (14:11).

When asked, "what will heaven be like?" we cannot answer in our typical ways of who is in and who is out; too much is at stake within our ecosystem of being human and a planet to continue practicing exclusion. Jesus gives us a better answer to what heaven will be like, "I am going away, and I am coming to you" (John 14: 28). *The ultimate answer to what heaven is like is this strange movement of God—going away and coming to.* The confluence of heaven and earth is embodied in Jesus. If you want to know what heaven is like, you and I will have to know what God is like through this strange movement of incarnation.

Western individualists may not like this answer because it may mean finding a communal solution rather than a personal one. Or it may mean the painful process of waiting on consensus. After all, Christians believe heaven is simply God's communal presence—a communion so sweet that heaven laughs, applauds, and rejoices when those who are lost are found. Jesus tells us as much—"I tell you, there will be more joy in heaven over one sinner who repents than over ninety-nine righteous persons who need no repentance" (Luke 15:7).

15

Martin Luther King's Heaven

But let justice roll down like waters, and righteousness like an ever-flowing stream.

—Amos 5:24

United States citizens are far more socially isolated today than at any other time in history. More and more people say they have no one in whom to confide, according to a comprehensive evaluation of the decline of social ties in the United States. A growing number of persons say they have no one with whom to work out personal troubles. This comprehensive study displays the stark reality of an increasingly fragmented America in which intimacy and community are becoming unattainable. Far too many people are now suffering alone in the United States. Lynn Smith-Lovin, a Duke University sociologist who helped conduct the study, states, "That image of people on roofs after Katrina resonates with me, because those people did not know someone with a car. There really is less of a safety net of close friends and confidants."[1]

What I am afraid of is that not many people really know how to want a communal heaven—one in which we all will be healed. In fact, few of us realize how spiritually sick all of us are. There are a few, however, who dream of heaven. Martin Luther King Jr. dreamed of heaven in the United States:

> I have a dream that one day [people] will rise up and come to see that they are made to live together. . . . I still have a dream this morning that one day every Negro in this country, every colored person in the world, will be judged on the basis of the content of his character rather than the color of his skin, and [everyone] will respect the dignity and worth of human personality.[2]

King's dream is unusual for most of us in the Western world. For example, most of us are socialized to accept the United States' hierarchical existence as a superpower. We do this by seeing television images of black children in Africa sitting in arid places with flies around their mouths. We do this by watching warring people running from mortar fire. Evangelical television stations take advantage of these images and prey upon those who may feel that our place at the top is being threatened. As I look at Christian television programming on the TBN Cable Network, it is dominated by these images in such a way that the assumption becomes that many people around the world see the United States as the promised land and feel lucky to reach its soil. Many US evangelicals and evangelicals around the world are socialized to believe that the United States has become Noah's Ark while the rest of the world goes to hell. King's dream in the midst of this is unusual. He is not only aware of how US citizens see their place in the world but also how people elsewhere see the United States. Perhaps King's unusual dream gave him keener vision to resist the socialization processes that say heaven is for certain individuals. King realized that much of what happens in the Western world is not the goal of the healing of the nations.

As many spiritual leaders will tell you, we cannot assume that the West is the promised land, especially given the decline of Christianity and the demographic shifts to the global south. This is so because Western answers to what heaven is like are usually understood in personal terms and personal rewards. In this worldview, there is no contradiction between a personal heaven and the rest of the world going to hell. Such a European Enlightenment heaven, however, leaves out what should be our common answer, uninhibited presence with God.

How can we be in heaven, knowing that others are in hell? How can heaven be the place where we find our complete state of being if I still realize someone is in hell? How could I still be happy knowing someone else was suffering, weeping and gnashing their teeth forever? This conundrum is really not unlike our current dilemma on earth. How can we find contentment in our suburbs and Western affluence knowing that much of the world continues to suffer—in many instances needlessly?[3] I learn from such questions that if we do not understand heaven as God's presence in which healing occurs for all, then we face the dangerous kinds of heaven so well imagined by John's Revelation.

Instead of a common vision for what ultimately satisfies us, we often have fragmented and individualistic visions in which material goods are our bases for understanding our deepest needs. As for delusion, often we think about heaven when we're really thinking about a small fortress built to keep others out. Heaven gets even more complicated as we consider those in history who oppressed the poor while theologically justifying their own reward in heaven. And boredom is usually what happens when we cannot imagine rum in heaven. Strangely enough, this last conundrum may be the most dangerous, as I explained in chapter 7, "Yawning in Heaven." Spiritual people need the capacity to be bored but not boring.

Many people use Scripture to justify their imagination of their own utopia. For example, they would argue that one need not wait until reading the last book in the Bible to know that some people belong in hell; after all, Jesus warned us. So instead of seeing a biblical worldview of communal salvation in Matthew 13:11–13, they see only certain folks in heaven. In the conclusion of the parable of the Sower, Jesus seems to divide those going to heaven from those going to hell. According to verse 13, Jesus said, quoting Isaiah 6:9–10, "The reason I speak to them [the crowds] in parables is that 'seeing they do not perceive, and hearing they do not listen, nor do they understand.'" In the same way that I think John is trying to pick up the pieces in Revelation 14:1–20, I think Jesus is challenging us to move out of our narrow views of heaven. Jesus is not trying to further divide us with talk of heaven because Jesus is already heaven in the people's midst. They just cannot see this heaven yet.

It appears as though Jesus sanctions a separation of those going to heaven or hell. These appear to be those separated by God's angels to be routed to the furnace and the place where there will be weeping and gnashing of teeth (Matt. 13:41–42). On the contrary, those who think Jesus wants some to go to hell do not understand how Jesus teaches through parable; such exclusive exegesis or biblical interpretation misses Jesus' point about the kingdom of heaven. Jesus' point is this: "Seeing they do not perceive" (Matt. 13:13). Jesus is heaven—a most extraordinary revelation that most of us still fail to see. Jesus invites us to actively imagine and practice a more rich and flourishing existence than is readily perceived, not only for particular individuals but for all of creation.

And yet the critic tells me, one only needs to read Matthew 13:11–13 itself to realize that the text is setting up a separation between "them" (not Jesus' disciples) and "you" (Jesus' disciples). This is amply confirmed by a similar passage in Mark 4:10–12:

When he was alone, those who were around him along with the twelve asked him about the parables. And he said to them, "To you has been given the secret of the kingdom of God, but for those outside, everything comes in parables; in order that 'they may indeed look, but not perceive, and may indeed listen, but not understand; so that they may not turn again and be forgiven.'"

This passage seems to challenge my premise—that heaven is the realization of God's communal presence on earth—to its core. The critic would say that I might not like it, but in fact absolute religions engage in the business of boundary setting to determine and separate those who are inside from those who are outside, those who are saved from those who are damned and are perishing, the vessels of mercy from the vessels of wrath, the children of light from the children of darkness. The critic would say that Christian theologians who have argued that God is available to others outside of their (particular) Christian fold do so on grounds other than biblical exegesis. The problem with this criticism can be found in one's point of view.

Those who claim to interpret religion and the Bible as the absolute word see but do not perceive. The absolute word is Jesus—at least, this is what Christians believe. And the current problem with Jesus is not so much that Western people see Jesus as controversial, or even that Jesus orders angels to send people to hell; rather, the problem is that many people are bored with Jesus. The cliché "show me the money" comes to mind. This is similar to the thief on the cross who said to Jesus, who was also hanging on the cross—if you really are God, why are you dying like a criminal with me? (Luke 23:39). There is an apathy in the thief's reasoning—there's no way that Jesus could be God squirming like a tortured worm. The challenge of this book throughout is to move beyond this apathy that Jesus could matter in a universal way. In order to change this apathy in the twenty-first century, we need some good guides.

Contemporary figures like Desmond Tutu and Martin Luther King Jr. guide us to heaven. Both understand how Jesus truly matters and are not afraid of how such relevance builds bridges to those who may not even believe in Jesus as heaven's presence. Also, both do not get the attention they deserve as theologians who help us see how to navigate God's kind of apocalypse. Those who tend to write about the book of Revelation often overlook the marginalized prophets (the seers of heaven) who were insistent that heaven was already in our midst. Daniel Berrigan is helpful here when he says, "Our poor show us who we are. Our prophets show us who we can be. So, we hide our poor and kill our prophets."[4] Instead of killing or dishonoring our prophets, let us now learn from them.

The concept of the angel's proclamation of an "eternal gospel . . . to every nation and tribe and language and people" (Rev. 14:6) corresponds in a powerful way to Martin Luther King Jr.'s beloved community. Such a community spawned the black church. Noel Leo Erskine is correct in his conclusion that "Martin King was a son of the Black church, and his theology cannot be understood without referring to those origins. Because his social activism was based on theological convictions about God and humanity, he gave particular attention to an explication of Christian faith in a situation of oppression."[5] So the particularity of the black church helped King to think through the concept of community that included everyone. King's vision of community is best characterized in his metaphor of the "great world house" or the "world-wide neighborhood," which suggests a totally integrated human family, unconcerned with human differences and devoted to the ethical norms of love, justice, and community. King states:

> We have inherited a large house, a great "world house" in which we have to live together—black and white, easterner and Westerner, gentile and Jew, Catholic and Protestant, Moslem and Hindu—a family unduly separated in ideas, culture and interest, who, because we can never again live apart, must learn somehow to live with each other in peace.[6]

King's beloved community became the organizing principle of his thought and activity. This beloved community organized his ultimate goal of nonviolence. King writes: "In other words, our ultimate goal is integration, which is genuine intergroup and interpersonal living. Only through nonviolence can this goal be attained, for the aftermath of nonviolence is reconciliation and the creation of the beloved community."[7]

One could say that King's beloved community found partial fulfillment in South Africa, after Nelson Mandela and political prisoners were freed and the first democratic elections took place in April 1994. The beloved community manifested itself in the Truth and Reconciliation Commission that gave the country a new future, despite the critics who wanted more retributive justice. King's beloved community saw fulfillment through Mandela becoming South Africa's first black president. And closer to home, King's beloved community saw fulfillment in the first black president of the United States. In his second inaugural address, Barack Obama said:

> We, the people, declare today that the most evident of truths—that all of us are created equal—is the star that guides us still; just as it guided our forebears through Seneca Falls, and Selma, and Stonewall; just as it guided all those men and women, sung and unsung, who left footprints along this great Mall, to hear a preacher say that we cannot walk alone; to hear a King proclaim that our individual freedom is inextricably bound to the freedom of every soul on Earth.[8]

Yes, indeed, this is the ideal corporate expression of the Christian faith, that God's will be done on earth as it is in heaven. The beloved communal vision was consistent with King's understanding of the Christian doctrine of the kingdom of heaven on earth through Jesus' method of nonviolence, which in fact was Jesus' ethic of heaven. King writes, "There is the more excellent way of love and nonviolent protest. I am grateful to God that, through the influence of the Negro church, the way of nonviolence became an integral part of our struggle."[9]

The African American church, the extended family network, and the southern black experience in which King was nurtured constituted the most important formative influences in the shaping of his ideas about community. King argued that making ethical decisions was impossible without rediscovering the transcendent values of community. King charged that many people, including those who attended church every Sunday, had lost their faith in such concepts of community. We must remember that it is possible to affirm the existence of God with your lips and deny God's existence with your life. The materialism of American consumer culture had caused some to lose sight of God, and King cautioned that automobiles and subways, televisions and radios, dollars and cents, can never be substitutes for God. It is through this vision of God that King understands this commentary of Revelation—namely, that John's Apocalypse should not be read through the interpretive lens as to who is in or out, but how to finally see the conclusive healing vision of John's new heaven and new earth. King similarly concludes: "Here is the true

> We cannot take a single step toward heaven. It is not in our power to travel in a vertical direction. If, however, we look heavenward for a long time, God comes and takes us up. He raises us easily.
> —Simone Weil,
> *The Simone Weil Reader*

meaning and value of compassion and nonviolence, when they help us to see the enemy's point of view."[10]

King helped those in the twentieth century pick up the pieces of community broken by a violent world, one in which white segregationists saw the white race as genetically and spiritually superior to all others. For King and the civil rights movement, such a concept of a white segregated heaven included only dragons.[11] It was not only a white segregationist world that offered the antithesis to heaven on earth, it was also modernity's obsession with mass destruction. King warns us how modernity "continues to flirt unhesitatingly with war and eventually transforms . . . earthly habitat into an inferno such as even the mind of Dante could not imagine."[12]

A Western world that institutionalized systems of segregation and the modern decline of spirituality into individualism and materialism broke the world into pieces. The richer we have become materially, the poorer we have become morally and spiritually. Convinced that community is the ultimate goal of human existence, King insisted upon a Christian ethic of nonviolence that could help us all pick up the broken pieces of what God created. John's apocalyptic vision, in which he tries to connect the dots between the Lamb with power and beasts gone mad, is one symptomatic of a world problem; namely, the lack of imagination for looking for heaven on earth. Instead, there seemed to be only heaven's antithesis. The need for whites to dominate and control peoples of color, and the failure of persons to grasp the extent to which they are interrelated and interdependent, are indeed the antithesis of heaven.

16

King's Practice of Heaven

Those who say, "I love God," and hate their brothers or sisters, are liars; for those who do not love a brother or sister whom they have seen, cannot love God whom they have not seen.

—1 John 4:20

For Martin Luther King Jr., the vision of heaven included work on earth. To him, heaven and earth were not mutually exclusive. King's prophetic vision—of a future society in which those now in conflict will one day live in peace—led directly to civil rights action. In order to bring others along with his vision of the mutuality of heaven and earth, King articulated how Jesus related to political action. King used his encounter with the Rev. E. Stanley Frazier, minister of St. James Methodist Church, to describe those Christians who have impractical vision. Frazier, King said, preached about an impractical heaven on earth in which segregation was part of the beatific vision:

> [Frazier] made it clear . . . that the job of the minister . . . is to lead the soul of men to God, not to bring about confusion by getting tangled up in transitory social problems. He moved on to the brief discussion of the Christmas story. In evocative terms he talked of "God's unspeakable gift." He ended by saying that as we moved into the Christmas season our hearts and minds should be turned toward the Babe of Bethlehem; and he urged the negro ministers to leave the meeting determined to bring this boycott to a close and lead their people instead "to a glorious experience of the Christian faith."[1]

King went on to correct Frazier's false dichotomy between religion and politics by explaining how devotion to Jesus is indeed political. King writes: "We too know the Jesus that the minister just referred to. . . . We have had an experience with him, and we believe firmly in the revelation of God in Jesus Christ. I can see no conflict between our devotion to Jesus Christ and our present action. In fact I see a necessary relationship. If one is truly devoted to the religion of Jesus he will seek to rid the world of social evils. The gospel is social as well as personal."[2] King's prophetic vision which included politics was for a nonviolent world rooted in his heritage of longing for heaven as a Baptist preacher. In fact, King saw the world on a pilgrimage to this nonviolent heaven.[3]

Like John the writer of the apocalypse, King also had prophetic vision deeply rooted in Christian faith. King writes: "I am many things to many people; Civil Rights leader, agitator, troublemaker and orator, but in the quiet recesses of my heart, I am fundamentally a clergyman, a Baptist preacher. This is my being and my heritage for I am also the son of a Baptist preacher, the grandson of a Baptist preacher, and the great-grandson of a Baptist preacher. The church is my life and I have given my life to the Church."[4] It is from this identity in the black church that I think King relates well to the book of Revelation.

Like the book of Revelation, with its pervasive influence from many biblical sources, King's vision is shaped by Scripture in a way that shapes his thought and action, but not in a literalistic capacity. At the heart of these biblical sources is Jesus, who King believes will lead the people and nations to that healing tree at the end of the book of Revelation.[5] Shaped by the black church's pilgrimage in the United States, King naturally gravitated to such redemption of the people and how such stories parallel the black experience of the church. Erskine is helpful here as he writes, "Freedom is never won without struggle and the struggle is never primarily against persons but against the vicious systems and structures that would deny God's children their freedom."[6] It is through this struggle envisioned as God's eventual redemption of humanity that King articulates his theological vision. King states:

> Looking back, we see the forces of segregation gradually dying on the seashore. The problem is far from solved and gigantic mountains of opposition lie ahead, but at least we have left Egypt, and with patient yet firm determination we shall reach the promised land. Evil in the form of injustice and exploitation shall not survive forever. A Red Sea passage in history ultimately brings the forces of goodness to victory, and the closing of the same waters mark the doom and the destruction of the forces of evil. All this reminds us that evil carries the seed of its own destruction. In the long run right defeated is stronger than evil triumphant.[7]

Jesus becomes King's embodiment and incarnation for what God's presence means now. King states, quoting Galatians 3:28:

Racial segregation is a blatant denial of the unity which we have in Christ; for in Christ there is neither Jew nor Gentile, bond nor free, Negro nor white. Segregation scars the soul of both the segregator and the segregated. The segregator looks upon the segregated as a thing to be used, not a person to be respected. Segregation substitutes an "I-It" relationship for the "I-thou" relationship. Thus it is utterly opposed to the noble teachings of our Judeo-Christian tradition.[8]

King's vision is rooted in the biblical story that functions as the critical norm for his prepositional positions. The best succinct statement of King's conception of the dream in concrete terms is as follows:

The dream is one of equality of opportunity, of privilege and property widely distributed; a dream of a land where men will not take necessities from the many to give luxuries to the few; a dream of a land where men do not argue that the color of a man's skin determines the content of his character; a dream of a place where all our gifts and resources are held not for ourselves alone but as instruments of service for the rest of humanity; the dream of a country where every man will respect the dignity and worth of all human personality, and men will dare to live together as brothers. . . . Whenever it is fulfilled, we will emerge from the bleak and desolate midnight of man's inhumanity to man into the bright and glowing daybreak of freedom and justice for all of God's children.[9]

As this dream indicates, King envisaged a new social order wherein all kinds of people would live in harmony in creation. He writes, "My friends, the Christmas hope for peace and goodwill toward all men can no longer be dismissed as a kind of pious dream of some utopian. If we don't have goodwill toward men in this world, we will destroy ourselves by the misuse of our own instruments and our own power."[10] This belief was consistent with King's conception of the biblical God who had inspired the prophetic teachings of Amos, Micah, and Isaiah about justice, mercy, and peace. By looking at biblical prophets, some connections to King's vision of heaven and nonviolence can be made.

King often quoted the prophets, especially Amos 5:24, "Let justice roll down like waters, and righteousness like an ever-flowing stream,"[11] and Isaiah 40:4, "Every valley shall be exalted and every hill and mountain shall be made low. The rough places shall be made plain and the crooked places will be made straight, and the glory of the Lord shall be revealed, and all flesh shall see it to enter."[12] King writes:

> I still have a dream today that one day justice will roll down like water, and righteousness like a mighty stream. I still have a dream today that in all of our statehouses and city halls men will be elected to go there who will do justly and love mercy and walk humbly with their God. I still have a dream today that one day war will come to an end, that men will beat their swords into plowshares and their spears into pruning hooks, that nations will no longer rise up against nations, neither will they study war any more. I still have a dream today that one day the lamb and the lion will lie down together and every man will sit under his own vine and fig tree and none shall be afraid. I still have a dream today that one day every valley shall be exalted and every mountain and hill will be made low, the rough places will be made smooth and the crooked places straight, and the glory of the Lord shall be revealed, and all flesh shall see it together.[13]

Although King is a dreamer, like John with the apocalypse, King's visions are practical—sanitation workers need a decent wage, the aged need adequate health care. That is, those who are most vulnerable in society, along with children and the aged, will be given the support they need. King's practical vision, informed by his dreams, is for children to grow to maturity and the elderly to live out their lives in dignity. King's vision of heaven is in the concrete realities of earth. He makes us consider the content of heaven in all its concreteness and contemporary significance as they help us consider also how heaven relates so directly to our present struggles for a more just society. King writes:

> It's all right to talk about "long white robes over yonder," in all of its symbolism. But ultimately people want some suits and dresses and shoes to wear down here. It's all right to talk about "streets flowing with milk and honey," but God has commanded us to be concerned about the slums down here, and his children who can't eat three square meals a day. It's all right to talk about the new Jerusalem, but one day, God's preacher must talk about the new New York, the new Atlanta, the new Philadelphia, the new Los Angeles, the new Memphis, Tennessee. This is what we have to do.[14]

As early as 1956, King made the connections between Jesus and politics: "The gospel at its best deals with the whole man, not only with his soul but also his body, not only his spiritual well-being but also his material well-being. A religion that professes a concern for the souls of men and is not equally concerned about the slums that damn them, the economic conditions that strangle them, and social conditions that cripple them, is a spiritually moribund religion."[15] This connection between body and soul was deeply rooted in the prophetic tradition in which heaven and earth could not be separated.

Similar to John's apocalyptic vision of the exile in Babylon, much of the biblical prophetic tradition dealt with the high expectations of the returning Babylonian exiles when they began to rebuild Jerusalem. Obviously, as they faced the destruction of the temple, their expectations were not fulfilled in the way that they had hoped. In addition to gathering courage in the face of rebuilding a city, they also knew that only a remnant returned from exile. But even more, the situation in Judah was extremely difficult for them. Yet it is precisely in this context of disappointment that the Old Testament prophet speaks as he envisions "new heavens and a new earth." The prophet called Isaiah has a vision of God saying, "For I am about to create new heavens and a new earth; the former things shall not be remembered or come to mind" (Isa. 65:17). And this prophet, whom we refer to as Trito-Isaiah, was, of course, repeating what earlier prophets had declared, although their vision had also not been fulfilled.

The Jews returning out of exile and prophets who see better realities than actually exist lead us to how the prophetic tradition and nonviolence form one another. Are the prophets out of touch with reality when they see "new heavens and a new earth"? Are their visions illusions? Are they false prophets? What are the prophets trying to do? If King can be considered part of the prophetic tradition, then such questions are criteria by which to see the connections between the prophetic tradition and nonviolence. Amid all our frustration and despondency about the ways things are, we should never forget that hopes have been realized. People now live longer lives. More people are being educated. Some diseases have been eradicated or placed under control. Apartheid has been brought to an end. Of course not all our expectations have been met, for the reign of God is still coming and is, in a sense, always in the future, always beyond our grasp. Yet what we have experienced is connected to that future hope, it does bear a resemblance, it is a symbol of the "more" that we can still anticipate and work for.

Heaven is a hope that concerns the restoration of fertility, the yielding of the produce of the earth, so that there is enough for all. This is an extravagant promise that heralds the overcoming of everything that has gone wrong in creation, touching every aspect and phase of life and remaking them whole, and overcoming hostility at every level—not just in Israel or the human community, but throughout creation. Biblical scholar Walter Brueggemann writes: "It is clear that King claimed special experience and insight and therefore special authority that somehow was related to the powerful presence of God in his life. In some secret way never made public to us, Dr. King, like every authentic prophet, has been face to face with God's holy call."[16]

Isaiah's and King's visions continue to correlate the concreteness of heaven as they envision a particular economy in heaven. Heaven's economics includes a system of labor in which there is mutual exchange. There will be no scapegoats in heaven who never experience the benefit of their labor.

> They shall build houses and inhabit them;
>   they shall plant vineyards and eat their fruit.
> They shall not build and another inhabit;
>   they shall not plant and another eat;
> for like the days of a tree shall the days of my people be,
>   and my chosen shall long enjoy the work of their hands.
> They shall not labor in vain,
>   or bear children for calamity.
>
>   (Isa. 65:21–23)

Isaiah's vision is echoed by King, as both hold out the promise that everyone will have adequate housing and shelter, that laborers will receive just rewards, that all people, even black people, will have long and qualitative lives, and that there will be no institutions like slavery for which to bear children for calamity. In King's context, African Americans will be able to live in the homes they have built without fear of losing them. In Desmond Tutu's context, there will be no uprooting of people and dumping them onto unfertile regions of a country. For Tutu there will be no bulldozing of properties so that others can take them over; no apartheid legislation decreeing forced removals to distant alien lands.

King's heaven is specific. There will be no rampant capitalist exploitation that widens the gap between the haves and the have-nots. Labor, according to this vision, is not drudgery but a joy! It is not only for African Americans to possess their own homes; they will also have the freedom and right to grow their own crops and to eat what they have produced. Like Isaiah, in King's heaven there is no slave labor that provides food for the rich while keeping the poor in their place. This is why memory is so important. It calls to mind what God has done in the past. How easy it is to forget and, like the Israelites in the wilderness, to start complaining. "If only we had died by the hand of the LORD in the land of Egypt, when we sat by the fleshpots and ate our fill of bread" (Exod. 16:3). As we struggle with present realities it is easy, perhaps, to have a romantic view of the past, those good old days when things were better! But that they were days of slavery in Egypt or captivity in Babylon we forget. How many white people in South Africa, for example, look back to apartheid and say how much better it was then! They forget that everyone was on the verge of a civil war that would have devastated the country. They forget the "miracle" of transition. Only God has the right to forget. As our text puts it: "The former troubles are forgotten and are hidden from my sight" (Isa. 65:16). God blots out our sins from his memory. But we have the responsibility of remembering from what we have been rescued and redeemed.

The nightmare that John has in his apocalypse concerning Babylonian captivity should be seen in this light of the rescued and redeemed. It should not be used in misogynistic ways in creating narratives against women or justifying the violence displayed in John's vision. The whole of Israel's faith and hope is predicated on the conviction that God led them from the captivity of Babylon back to Jerusalem. In the same way, Christian eucharistic faith recalls the life, death, and resurrection of Jesus. Do this in memory of me. Such memories are not simply of the past; they bring the past into the present. The death and resurrection become present to our contemporary experience. But there is more at stake in our eucharistic faith, for we remember the death and resurrection of Jesus Christ in anticipation of the new heaven and new earth. We do this until he comes to practice heaven on earth. In other words, it is not only the past that becomes present, so too does the future.

This prophetic hope is no spiritualized fantasy world, a world of make-believe, but the promise of a transformed material world in which justice will prevail, there will be bread for all, and the human race will dwell securely. King is intensely aware of how pacifism may be perceived: "After reading [Reinhold] Niebuhr, I tried to arrive at a

realistic pacifism. In other words, I came to see the pacifist position
not as sinless but as the lesser evil in the circumstances. I felt then, and
I feel now, that the pacifist would have a greater appeal if he did not
claim to be free from the moral dilemmas that the Christian nonpacifist
confronts."[17] For King, nothing could be more embracing, more radi-
cally new, and yet so related to the world as we know and experience it
than nonviolence. It is literally the promise of starting again, a new creation brought about by the activity of God, and yet in continuity with
everything that we hold dear and for which we strive. But we must ask,
especially in light of King's violent end, can such a nonviolent promise
be fulfilled? King preaches:

> Well, I don't know what will happen now. We've got some difficult
> days ahead. But it doesn't matter with me now. Because I've been to
> the mountaintop. And I don't mind. Like anybody, I would like to
> live a long life. Longevity has its place. But I'm not concerned about
> that now. I just want to do God's will. And He's allowed me to go
> up to the mountain. And I've looked over. And I've seen the prom-
> ised land. I may not get there with you. But I want you to know
> tonight, that we, as a people, will get to the promised land. And I'm
> happy, tonight. I'm not worried about anything. I'm not fearing any
> man. Mine eyes have seen the glory of the coming of the Lord.[18]

Is heaven a totally unrealistic and romantic view of things, a utopian
illusion that must inevitably be thwarted by social and political forces
beyond our control? After all, this promise of heaven was uttered centuries ago and was repeated in the Christian Scriptures, and yet the vision
of a new heaven and new earth still seems beyond reach. King describes
such overwhelming feelings in one of his darkest nights of the soul:

> At that moment I experienced the presence of the Divine as I had
> never before experienced him. It seemed as though I could hear the
> quiet assurance of an inner voice, saying, "Stand up for righteous-
> ness, stand up for truth. God will be at your side forever." Almost at
> once my fears began to pass from me. My uncertainty disappeared. I
> was ready to face anything. The outer situation remained the same,
> but God had given me inner calm. Three nights later, our home was
> bombed. Strangely enough, I accepted the word of the bombing
> calmly. My experience with God had given me a new strength and
> trust. I knew now that God is able to give us the interior resources
> to face the storms and problems of life.[19]

There are many skeptics who say that Christian faith is ground-less and irrelevant. They say that it is a religion that slips like sand through our fingers. We learn, however, through exemplars like King that Christian faith can be practical. King expands our commentary on Revelation by demanding concrete responses to the end of the story—the healing of the nations. He helps us to deal not with the delayed Parousia, not just with the fulfillment of eschatological hope, but with this shattering of our more immediate hope for heaven.

The future of a new heaven and a new earth breaks into our present struggles, awakening hope and strengthening faith and love in the expectation that there is always more that God wants to give us. God is always ahead of us, always creating the new, always opening up new possibilities. So the true prophets are not awakening false expectations but rather proclaiming that there is always more that God wants to give us, more that God wants to do between heaven and earth. Moreover, the prophets know that unless that hope of the more is kept alive we will simply give up and begin to accept things as they are instead of reaching out to receive the more that God has in store for us. King states:

> We can remember the days when unfavorable court decisions came upon us like tidal waves, leaving us treading the waters of despair. But amid all of this we have kept going with the faith that as we struggle, God struggles with us, and that the arc of the moral universe, although long, is bending toward justice. We have lived under the agony and darkness of Good Friday with the conviction that one day the heightened glow of Easter would emerge on the horizon. We have seen truth crucified and goodness buried, but we have kept going with the conviction that truth crushed to the ground will rise again.[20]

Christian hope is rooted in such light, but it is also a hope against hope, a hope that often flies in the face of reality because it is based on the faithfulness of the God who surprises us in ways that enable us, in the end, to say Amen. King's life and thought help us understand the book of Revelation in healthier ways than those that only identify victims and retributive justice. King helps us identify what are John's nightmares and what are his dreams. King helps us understand that although we are called to participate with God in the struggle for justice and peace, in the end it is God who will surprise us. For it is God who finally creates the new heaven and new earth. We participate, as King envisions, "not through violence; not through hate; no, not even through boycotts; but through love. . . . But we must remember as we boycott that a boycott is not an end within itself; . . . the end is reconciliation; the end is redemption; the end is the creation of the beloved community."[21]

17

Desmond Tutu's Heaven Is Ubuntu

On that day you will know that I am in my Father, and you in me, and I in you.

—John 14:20

As Martin Luther King argued for perception of heaven on earth through the beloved community, Desmond Tutu argued for the synthesis of earth in heaven through his concept of Ubuntu.[1] In Tutu's theology of Ubuntu, God creates personhood in such a way as to allow the intelligibility of self as self loves others—even if the other is an enemy. Ubuntu is a proverb: A person is a person through other persons. In other words, without the correct relationship of persons, there would be no understanding of the self. It is this theological step that is missing in our current culture wars. The person's infusion of God's image of community is the needed light to see how to grow and what to grow toward in a suffering world. The miracle is this: God created us to be infinite because God instilled God's image in us.

Outside of the relationship of persons, self-identity is false. This idea influences Tutu's Ubuntu understanding of prayer. It is only in relationship that prayer occurs. Jesus tells his disciples, "Again, truly I tell you, if two of you agree on earth about anything you ask, it will be done for you by my Father in heaven. For where two or three are gathered in my name, I am there among them" (Matt. 18:19–20). It is only when two or three gather that self is led to the initial mystery of heaven.[2] Tutu states:

God is a fellowship, a community, God is a society from all eternity in which God the Son, who is coequal, coeternal with the Father pours forth in return His entire love and being on the Father. The love that binds them together is so immense that this love flowing between Father and Son is God the Holy Spirit. And so God created us wonderfully, not out of necessity. He did not need us; but gloriously, He wanted us.[3]

Tutu believes that human persons are especially born as potentiality; if human beings would grow up individually among wolves they would not know how to communicate as human beings. There would not be human posture or human ways of eating, sitting, and walking. Human beings become persons only by living in an environment conducive to the interaction of diverse personalities and cultures. If there is no such environment, personhood does not survive. Tutu illustrates this with an allegory:

> There was once a light bulb which shone and shone like no light bulb had shone before. It captured all the limelight and began to strut about arrogantly quite unmindful of how it was that it could shine so brilliantly, thinking that it was all due to its own merit and skill. Then one day someone disconnected the famous light bulb from the light socket and placed it on a table and try as hard as it could, the light bulb could bring forth no light and brilliance. It lay there looking so disconsolate and dark and cold—and useless. Yes, it had never known that its light came from the power station and that it had been connected to the dynamo by little wires and flexes that lay hidden and unseen and totally unsung.[4]

This means for Tutu that the African concept of Ubuntu is the environment of vulnerability, that is, a set of relationships in which persons are able to recognize that their humanity is bound up in the other's humanity.

Central to Tutu's theology is the fact that Tutu's life and thought appeal for competitive societies to move beyond contradistinction as determinative of human identity. Through Tutu's emphasis on the church's life of worship, in which human identity is elevated as persons find communion with others and God, Ubuntu makes sense of how the church should then proceed to operate on the basis of more than racial and sexual identity. In other words, people need not kill each other because they are black or white, gay or straight, but should instead rejoice in how God has created persons differently so that new meanings and identities are always possible.

Unlike many Western ideologies that seek to "fix" who a person or community is, Tutu's Ubuntu theology excludes tendencies of competitiveness.[5] The beauty of Ubuntu is that instead of forming warring factions, persons are "more willing to make excuses for others"[6] and even discover new meaning in other persons. Therefore Ubuntu is an attribute that distinguishes human community from the frenzied animal kingdom, as Tutu concludes, "If you throw a bone to a group of dogs you won't hear them say: 'After you!'"[7]

Most explicit for Tutu's context, the beatitude of Ubuntu is that it provides an alternative to vengeance. Tutu states, "I saw it in Zimbabwe yet again last week. It is what has allowed Mr. [Ian] Smith to survive in a post-independence Zimbabwe."[8] By this he means that South Africans—black and white—can be human together and will define tyranny only by first living together.[9] Again, perspective determines actions, and Ubuntu provides an invaluable perspective in which white and black people may see themselves as more than racial rivals. "When you look at someone with eyes of love," Tutu says, "you see a reality differently from that of someone who looks at the same person without love, with hatred or even just indifference."[10] Apartheid in all of its forms in the world in which human beings are victimized naturally creates hell rather than heaven.

Instead of perpetuating the system of apartheid, Tutu believes that Ubuntu's insight into what it means to be interrelated helps the church witness to the world that God is the one who loves human identities into being even before individuals could conceive of rights or perspectives of tyranny. In other words, God's relationship of persons is prevenient—it is there before everything else and calls all justifications for control into account. As a Christian, no one can claim complete control of determining self. To gain the vision to negotiate how to be in the world is to access the communal life of grace in God. I call this communal life the church. Any claim of control or power in the church is delusory and foolish, as Tutu explains about the apostle Peter: "Jesus gave a new, a very important responsibility to Peter. He said, 'Feed my sheep.' It's almost like asking a thief to become your treasurer."[11]

Through a theological concept of Ubuntu, the Christian recognizes the need to be transformed to a new identity, a new perspective that fully encompasses the truth which Tutu describes: "God does not love us because we are lovable, but we are lovable precisely because God loves us. God's love is what gives us our worth. . . . So we are liberated from the desire to achieve, to impress. We are the children of the divine love and nothing can change that fundamental fact about us."[12] And yet, as Tutu's Ubuntu theology unfolds access to a new identity for gays and lesbians in the church, it also appeals to ancient African concepts of the harmony between individual and community; in John Mbiti's words, "I am because we are, and since we are, therefore I am."[13]

Once persons learn to live in community beyond convenient arrangements of power and tolerance, they can act in clarity and operate prophetically in the world. As a result persons learn to abandon false identities and are set free from the desire to dominate others as a means of gaining self-identity. While identity definition through control is illusory, the death attached to giving it up is very real, and the result is weeping. In this experience of tears the presence of God becomes most real in the contradictions of the world. These tears are not tears of self-pity for loss but something of greater value than what we have lost, and the pain is as real as the desire. In this seeming polarity of love our tears become holy tears, and their salt lights God's fire upon the earth. The choice to return God's gaze brings us to tears because our relationship to God in a world such as this acknowledges the unconverted in us, and it is only when we weep—with or without physical tears—that we have any sure indication of changes occurring on a level beyond the merely conscious level. Tears are a sign that we are struggling with power of one sort or another: the loss of ours, the entering of God's.[14]

In the end, Ubuntu help us to move beyond the skepticism that heaven never intersects earth. Ubuntu trains persons beyond the contradictions of survival and grace. Perhaps this is what prayer simply is—the capacity to be in relationship with God through others. This kind of prayer depends not so much on the goal of penetrating God as an object of prayer as it does being penetrated by God. Tutu states:

> God gives us space to be persons who are moral agents, with the capacity to respond freely, to love or not to love, to obey or not to obey, free to be good or to be vicious. God has such a profound reverence for our autonomy and freedom that He had much rather see us go freely to hell than compel us to go to heaven. As they say, the doctrine of hell is God's greatest complement to us as humans.[15]

Tutu's Ubuntu seeks a paradigm in which the affliction of any person can be transfigured into divine relationship through communal living. Instead of retaliation and a further competition of Christian narratives for God's privilege, the church is to turn toward God and see God also as afflicted. Even if we seem hopelessly trapped in oppressive systems incapable of receiving the reality of heaven, the image of

God is planted in human beings in such a way that its slow, vegetative movements, responding to light, will one day manifest the kingdom of heaven. For those who doubt, there is a concrete miracle that has just occurred in South Africa.

> Apartheid in South Africa, and those who think like the perpetrators of apartheid in other parts of the world . . . say the thing that gives a human being his or her value is a biological attribute which by its very nature cannot be shared by all people everywhere. . . . It is the fact that each individual person is created in the image of God, that each person is God's viceroy, each person stands in the place of God and St Paul goes on to say, "you know you are the temple of the Holy Spirit." You are a sanctuary and to treat you as if you were less than this is not just wrong, which it is, is not just painful, as it often is, it is positively blasphemous. It is a sacrilege to treat the temple of God, someone indwelt by the Spirit of God and the Holy Trinity in such a way.[16]

Instead of typical Western dualisms of rationality and faith, freedom and will, Tutu's miracle of South African community follows an Eastern theological tradition that places revelatory emphasis on our relationship to what God has already revealed in the world. Most importantly, Christ reveals the salvation of the world, but such a revelation does not require control or domination on our part, nor does it claim a banal observation of a "new heaven and new earth" already complete on earth. Instead, Tutu's theological construct refuses the Augustinian and Pelagian split of grace and free will. God created us to be responsible for others, indeed, to know one's identity through others because God so desired that our movement toward God's life be a movement of participation in the divine life, a life that implies freedom. As Gregory of Nyssa writes:

> As the grace of God cannot descend upon souls which flee from their salvation, so the power of human virtue is not of itself sufficient to raise to perfection souls which have no share in grace . . . the righteousness of works and the grace of the Spirit, coming together to the same place . . . , fill the soul in which they are united with the life of the blessed.[17]

Instead of contradictions in creation, Ubuntu theology illumines the relationship between God and human beings who both toil together in the salvation of creation. In this light of salvation, individual persons need the full participation of other persons in order to move beyond the narrow definitions of self. An interviewer asked Tutu, "What do you think Heaven will be like?"

> The Archbishop closes his eyes to ponder and spreads his palms out on the table. "It will be spatially, temporally different, of course. It is difficult for us to conceive of an existence that is timeless, where you look at absolute beauty and goodness and you have no words. It is enough just to be there. You know how it is when you are sitting with someone you love and hours can go by in what seem like moments? Well, in Heaven, eternity itself will pass in a flash. In heaven we will never tire. We will never be bored because there will always be such new sides of God that will be revealed to us."[18]

Instead of Western individualistic interpretations of heaven as a personal reward system for individuals, innate to Tutu and King's communal ethic of heaven is the apprehension of mutuality with God and creation. From King and Tutu we learn the full meaning of God's edict: "It is not good that 'adam should be alone; I will make 'adam a helper as 'adam's partner" (Gen. 2:18). I have not tried to display historical thought on the Christian concept of heaven, nor tried to trace all the factors that led to the modern demise of writings on the concept of heaven. Rather, I direct the reader's attention to those whose images of heaven, earth, and communal salvation exist coterminously. In particular, my method is to display a constructive use of heaven through what I learned especially from the privilege of living with Tutu, who taught me that heaven is Ubuntu. And from growing up in North Carolina I implicitly know that King's beloved community approach to heaven is a natural fit with Tutu's concept of Ubuntu.[19]

Both views of heaven, from Tutu and King, offer the paradigm in which humans seek a heaven that is more about communal transformation than self-fulfillment. The problem for King, spawned from his Baptist theology in the black church, was how Christians could turn a blind eye to the horrors of racial injustice, especially before his eyes growing up in the southern United States. The otherworldliness of theology in which there was a lack of concern for earthly justice became a deep problem that King sought to rectify. There was more concern for a heaven beyond this earth than one on it.

18

Tutu's Practice of Heaven

And the king will answer them, "Truly I tell you, just as you did it to one
of the least of these who are members of my family, you did it to me."
—Matthew 25:40

Tutu's practice of heaven on earth, similar to Martin Luther King's, includes a sharper understanding of community. Tutu's understanding, however, is not so much through the language of a beloved community but through his concept of Ubuntu, which implies that persons discover identity through community. Tutu believes that God creates personhood in such a way that we resemble the very persons of God. The unbroken bond of God's persons known as Father, Son, and Holy Spirit are so interrelated that they are one God. Their communal being allows the intelligibility of heaven. If you stop to think about it, complete joy implies community. Without the other, laughter is incomplete. Without relationships, we would have no reference point in which to know we are happy. In other words, without the correct relationship of persons, there would be no understanding of what perfects the self. This is what Ubuntu is like.

The person's infusion of God's communal image is the needed light to see our truest identity and to see the perfection of such identity—namely, heaven. Ubuntu informs an image of heaven in that it displays a communal milieu in which God's persons reside in each other to make unity of the whole. Christians believe that God is not an individual—such belief is deemed modalism or false images of God. Neither is God "the Man upstairs," another way of imagining humanity writ large. The description of God's communal self is not a lapse into split personalities or three gods because God's persons are so interrelated

141

that they create one identity beyond human comprehension—we call this one identity God. In God's identity, human persons are created in God's image as infinite and are continually infused with God's triune, communal image. So how does Tutu make all of this practical?

Tutu relates such heavenly information about God to earthly realities in the following way:

> The tremendous thing about each one of us is that we have a value, which is an infinite value. It resides in the very fact of being created and so we say to the perpetrators of racism and apartheid, your policies are immoral, are unchristian, are unbiblical. You are taking on God for you are saying, God has made a mistake, that God, when he created some black, has made a ghastly mistake so that they have to go around apologizing for their existence. We don't have to apologize for our existence. God created us in his own image.[1]

Outside of the desire for communal relationship, there can be no beatific vision of God. This is why racism is sinful: it displays a power dynamic in which one demonstrates to the other, "I have no need of you as a mutual person."

Instead of the Western obsession with personal salvation, Ubuntu teaches us that deeper salvation comes through God's communal presence. Therefore something like forgiveness is not so much what we choose to do as what we practice when we live in God's presence. We really participate in the forgiveness that naturally flows from the community of God. In the deepest way, forgiveness is an act of theism—truly believing in God. It is not something we can really do; rather, forgiveness is a worldview in which God truly exists. This is why it is more difficult for us to know that we are forgiven than it is to forgive. At best, our efforts at forgiveness are coping techniques in the face of tragedies. We forgive according to our limits and tolerance of pain, but God is the only one who forgives completely. To understand this more fully, one can simply eavesdrop on Peter and Jesus' conversation about forgiveness. How many times should I forgive—seven times? Peter was trying to be a good rabbinical student and put the answer in the question. After all, the number seven meant perfection. Peter's definition of perfect, however, always rested on his limited patience. That is why Jesus constantly pushed Peter beyond his own definitions toward God's generosity.[2] Like Peter, we need to learn that forgiveness is really God's presence. Without such presence, Tutu teaches us, there is no future.[3] Without forgiveness there is never intelligibility of heaven on earth. In forgiveness the wound that makes creation groan in travail is slowly transfigured toward a new heaven and earth.

For Tutu, heaven on earth is the environment of vulnerability, that is, a set of relationships in which persons are able to recognize that their personhood is bound up in the other's humanity. Tutu's kind of heaven is practical in the sense that we practice healthy relationships on earth by which to appeal for how we all will live better in the future. For example, instead of seeing racial difference as a threat to one's own racial and economic identity, Ubuntu helps us see why racial difference is necessary in how God creates life—diverse and abundantly. As Tutu writes:

> We have in this land a pyramid of power and privilege based on color—the lighter you are of pigmentation, the higher you stand on the pyramid of privilege and power. In this pyramid blacks are the broad base of the exploited and oppressed. Next is the so called coloreds and then next Indians and right at the top Makulubaas, white. It is a pigmentocracy.[4]

Through John's heavenly imagination in which he dreams and does not have nightmares, human identity no longer competes as persons against other persons but discovers communion with others and God. Ubuntu behaves the same way as it makes sense of how South Africans should operate on the basis of more than racial identity, the *ethnoi* in Revelation 22:2. In the new heaven and earth, people need not kill each other because they are black or white but should instead rejoice in how God has created persons differently so that new meanings and identities are always possible. Unlike many Western forces that seek to compete in order to "establish" who a person or community is, Tutu's Ubuntu excludes Western tendencies of grasping competitive claims of authority which limit and define infinite personhood into racist categories.[5] The beauty of Ubuntu, however, is that instead of warring factions, we now have an imagination of community. When one lives in Ubuntu, instead of being manipulative and self-seeking, a person is "more willing to make excuses for others"[6] and even discover new meaning in other persons. Ubuntu is an attribute that distinguishes humans from mere animals. We are made in the image of God.

Most explicit for Tutu's context, the practicality of Ubuntu is that it provides another way to negotiate violent earthly realities which seem fixed and determined. Since perspective determines actions, Tutu's Ubuntu perspective provides invaluable insight into reality in which white and black people may see themselves as more than racial rivals.

"When you look at someone with eyes of love," Tutu believes, "you see
a reality differently from that of someone who looks at the same person without love, with hatred or even just indifference."[7] This is how
competitive worldviews like racism form persons and how the legitimiza-
tion of oppressive structures form, by which language of victimization
becomes utilitarian language of the common good. Instead of perpetuating violent earthly systems, Tutu believes that Ubuntu facilitates a deeper
understanding of earthly reality in which personhood forms ultimately
through the image of God who loves human identities into being.

Tutu's Ubuntu provides a corrective vision of John's nightmarish
heaven and earth that requires streets flowing with blood. This corrective is also deeply practical; after all, there is no better political project
practiced by a nation-state than South Africa's Truth and Reconciliation Commission (TRC). Concepts like Ubuntu and the leadership of
Tutu as an archbishop of Cape Town were catalysts that led to the first
major way of solving systemic political corruption through public confession and amnesty. Unlike any other truth commission, South Africa
gave the world a public means to solve political violence with public,
spiritual means.[8] So, for Tutu, proper attention to heaven produces the
desire for justice. Said another way, true attention to God disallows the
treatment of others as means for ends. Tutu writes:

> At the heart of things is an ultimate reality that is good and loving,
> concerned to see that justice and goodness and love will prevail. This
> ultimate reality I believe to be personal, a being with whom I can
> enter into intimate personal relationship. Despite all appearances to
> the contrary this ultimate reality, God, is in charge, but in charge in
> a way that does not cancel out our autonomy as persons. God gives
> us space to be persons who are moral agents, with the capacity to
> respond freely, to love or not to love, to obey or not to obey, free to
> be good or to be vicious. God has such a profound reverence for our
> autonomy and freedom that He had much rather see us go freely to
> hell than compel us to go to heaven. As they say, the doctrine of hell
> is God's greatest complement to us as humans.[9]

The problem of justice is in its definition of retribution or restoration. Tutu's vision of heaven causes him to depend on the definition of justice as restorative. Tutu's Ubuntu seeks a paradigm in which
the affliction of African people can be transfigured through forgiveness instead of vindictive vengeance.[10] Instead of retaliation and a further perpetual competition of Christian narratives for God's privilege,

Christians in South Africa made an unusual move toward practicing heaven on earth through the TRC.

Even if black and white people seem hopelessly trapped in the closed system of racial classifications, the image of heaven is planted in all human beings in such a way that its slow, vegetative movements, responding to light, will one day manifest the kingdom of heaven. Such an image of heaven is often taught through Jesus' agricultural parables in which the kingdom of Heaven manifests surreptitiously.[11]

In the end, Tutu's vision of Ubuntu collapses the hierarchy that engenders the idea that the oppressed are in such a condition because of a lack of intelligence—that darker-skinned peoples are naturally oppressed because of an evolutionary process that makes white people superior. Thus the opposite of hierarchy is not, as the revolutionists believe, equality, but rather anarchy; for when hierarchy is disrupted, there is a violent oscillation between one form of inequality and another, issuing in a confusion that may be mistaken for adjustment or progress. Uprooting people and dumping them as rubbish onto unwanted (and usually toxic) ground puts an end to the vestige of heaven on earth; the condition of being rootless was the impetus of the oppressor in implementing apartheid. The communal God that Christians worship is always recovering the broken pieces of heaven on earth. Tutu states:

> What we know is that God's intention, God's dream, is to establish a fellowship that includes us all, in which the physical, moral, and spiritual environment share, where there will be wholeness (shalom), where there will be physical and spiritual well-being, where all will care for each other, where laughter and joy, compassion and caring, peace and sharing, life without end, goodness and righteousness, justice and reconciliation, togetherness and fellowship will have prevailed over their baneful counterparts. This is sometimes called the Kingdom of God. God calls on us to be fellow-workers with Him, to be agents of transfiguration to help Him bring this to pass when the kingdoms of this world become the Kingdom of our God and His Christ and He shall reign forever and ever. Amen.[12]

To say with analytical philosophers that such a metaphysical world is impossible, or that Tutu's eschatology represents emotionalism, presents false dichotomies between rationality and Christian faith. Tutu helps us see how heaven can indeed be present on earth.[13]

Most important for Tutu's vision of heaven is that God does not remain inaccessible, like some Aristotelian unmoved mover. God emptied God's self and became involved with suffering people, even when they were cast into the fiery furnace. The oppressors then saw a fourth and mysterious figure walking about with the three that were originally thrown there (Dan. 3:24–27). The Old Testament, having struggled with the problem of righteous suffering, reaches a zenith in the teaching about the so-called Songs of the Suffering Servant of Yahweh, especially Isaiah (52:13–53:12), and how this text describes vicarious suffering, that is, suffering not for one's sake but on behalf of others, even on behalf of others for their salvation. Herein Tutu takes solace that there is a redeeming value for how black people have suffered, that perhaps here, with the Suffering Servant, there is a clue about the inevitability of suffering in the economy of salvation. Therefore, Ubuntu addresses the theodicy of African suffering in that their severe suffering is not in vain and that suffering has salvific significance given the perspective of heaven on earth.[14]

Similar to the mystery of how heaven can be on earth, how God can suffer defeats most of our imaginations. There is identity and solidarity with the Suffering Servant, an identification that happened when Jesus agreed to be baptized, causing for some a theological problem, as can be seen in the conversation Matthew records between John the Baptist and Jesus (Matt. 3:6, 13–16). If John's baptism was an acknowledgment of sin, how could the sinless one need to be baptized? We are again in the realm of mystery, the mystery of what it cost God to redeem us through suffering.

Jesus makes it abundantly clear that heaven without suffering is impossible (Matt. 10:17–39). In short, for Tutu, a person who is a person through others cannot follow Jesus into heaven without suffering (John 16:1–5; Matt. 10:38; 16:24–26).[15] And so a church that does not suffer cannot be the church of Jesus Christ. Christ calls forth a beatitude on behalf of those who suffer for the sake of the kingdom's righteousness (Matt. 5:10–12). Such beatitude is not delusional or utopian. The contradictions of utopian expectation are easily apparent. Instead of the assumption of much modern religious thought that attention to heaven is the onrush of delusion, Tutu believes that the social practices of the church derived from belief in heaven enable a true confrontation of evil. Tutu illustrates what a true confrontation of evil may look like in his response to seeing a "new level of poverty and squalor" in Calcutta:

I was truly devastated by what I had experienced. I wondered about God, about the reality of His love and caring. Why should so much unmitigated and seemingly pointless suffering be happening, especially when one looked on potbellied urchins who looked so dissipated and exhausted so prematurely? Was there any point in human existence? Now these and similar questions I could have asked in almost identical settings at home in South Africa. . . . So much avoidable suffering could happen just because human beings appeared to be incorrigibly selfish, for in my home country one had the distressing spectacle of the squalor and poverty of a Crossroads, a black slum near Cape Town, existing almost obscenely cheek by jowl with the affluence of white suburbia. Where *was* God in all of this? Was it all just sound and fury signifying nothing? Did human beings really count? Why did justice, righteousness and all the worthwhile things seem to bite the dust so comprehensively and often so ignominiously when their opposites strutted about arrogantly?[16]

In a suffering world seemingly void of heaven, Tutu believes that human persons are especially born as potentiality. Herein is Tutu's concept of Ubuntu in which a person is a person through the other. As stated above, if human beings grow up individually among wolves they would not know how to be human. The beauty of Ubuntu is also its curse. On one hand, Ubuntu helps us understand how dynamic human life is. No human being should ever be seen as anyone less than dynamic. And yet on the other hand, Ubuntu exposes us to the vulnerability of being human. There would not be human posture or human ways of eating, sitting, and walking. This dynamic vulnerability makes Tutu conclude that human beings become persons only by living in an environment conducive to the interaction of diverse personalities and cultures. If there is no such vulnerable environment, personhood does not survive. King indeed understands Ubuntu as he states, "No individual can live alone; no nation can live alone, and as long as we try, the more we are going to have war in this world."[17] Tutu agrees and proclaims along with Christ's teachings for a new heaven and new earth that we all must be born again. And through Jesus' own life he shows that even the reality of death may not hold us to meaninglessness. As Tutu states, "Who says that death is the worst thing that could happen to a Christian?"[18] The Western mind, on the other hand, asks the question of Nicodemus, "How can these things be?" Tutu adheres to Christ's response, "If I have told you about earthly things and you do not believe, how can you believe if I tell you about heavenly things?"[19]

Therefore, Tutu envisions the paradox of how heaven can still exist in a broken and contrite world such as this:

> Perhaps the greatest paradox then was the one of life coming as a result of death. If one denied oneself and did not seek to preserve one's life then paradoxically one found it enhanced the opposite to occur. A grain of wheat, He said remained alone if it did not die, but if it fell to the ground and died then life would come. . . . Has it not been wonderfully paradoxical that the way in which those whom the rulers of the world put to death because they were Christians had a way of haunting their killers for they seemed to live on after death, perhaps more potent in death than if those put to death had been alive. Just look at the impact the death of Steve Biko has had. Just think of the death of other Christians, e.g., Dietrich Bonhoeffer, Archbishop Luwum in Amin's Uganda, Archbishop Oscar Romero in El Salvador and now Pakamile Mabiya. They are witnesses to Christ and to the power of the resurrection over death.[20]

Through Tutu's Ubuntu, God gives us space to be human persons. In so doing, God respects human autonomy and freedom in such a way that God expects us to grow up and be born again.

19

Practicing Heaven Ourselves

If any of you put a stumbling block before one of these little ones who believe in me, it would be better for you if a great millstone were fastened around your neck and you were drowned in the depth of the sea.
—Matthew 18:6

A mighty angel picks up a great millstone and throws it into the sea, saying, "With such violence Babylon the great city will be thrown down" (Rev. 18:21). In this vision, heaven has come to earth with judgment. Jesus used such imagery of giant stones tethered to our judgments, especially as the consequences of leading little ones astray. Our language of heaven and earth may seem inconsequential, but as I have tried to argue here, there is much at stake when we speak of heaven and earth. Although heaven appears to be idealistic, it carries very practical consequences. No longer does an individual have to accept the contradiction between heaven and earth, infinite and finite, and individual and community. Heaven rescues our fall into dualism by uniting us with heavenly existence in such a way as to make our personal goals congruent with communal goals—and most of all, God's goals. This objective was most manifest in the incarnation of Christ. So how are we to recognize the incarnation of heaven and earth? The most feasible answer seems to abide in the concept of virtue. Victor Preller asks the pertinent question, "Against what standard are we to examine ourselves?"[1] Attention to heaven gives proper sight of this standard that is built into our existence. We know which particular acts we should repent of because we cannot picture a heaven in which life is unconscious of its infinity. Therefore, human beings are not allowed to snub each other here as mere finite existence.

We must repent of making a fellow creature an object, because heaven has taught us otherwise. Heaven reorients our finite perspective to contain the potential to see and be with God. With this insight, how shall we maintain our attention to heaven on earth? Are there rules or laws that we can consult in order to find our way continually to heaven? Preller believes that if our moral concern is only to avoid obvious actions of sin, like leaving a baby in a trash can, then rules and laws might be sufficient standards against which to gauge heaven. "If, however," says Preller, "our moral concern is to seek perfection in all that we do—to make the right decisions in all of the complicated circumstances of everyday life—then no list of laws, rules, or commandments, however long, will suffice."[2] Sets of laws, rules, or commandments do not make this world whole. Those who think laws and rules are ends in themselves are legalists who become opposed to true morality. Such people had an extremely difficult time with God in Jesus. They are like the Pharisee who praised God that he was not like others who do bad things.

The ethics of heaven is not an ethics that is derived from law alone. Instead, knowing how to apply a law to a specific case requires the ability to discern within the specific case the means available to us to serve God. The ability to discern what the moral law requires in each particular case is what classical ethicists call "the virtue of prudence." This ability requires something other than the grammatical and deductive skills of a legalist. It requires a particular kind of moral character that has learned to recognize heaven in strange places—after all, there is no other kind of place for heaven to be but strange places.

In classical terms, knowing how to relate earth to heaven requires the acquisition of "the virtues." Virtues are habitual orientations of the heart and the mind to those goods that are heavenly and good. The cardinal virtues of temperance, fortitude, justice, and prudence are those from which all heavenly actions flow. A communal ethics of heaven contains the virtues necessary to prevent individualistic and greedy kinds of heaven. So Jesus teaches us to pray for God's will to be done on earth as it is in heaven. Instead of being delusional, religious folk can imagine and practice flourishing existence not only for particular, like-minded individuals but for all people. Perhaps more controversial among some Christian constituencies, I claim in this book that the concept of heaven is not the goal of personal salvation that is taught in many churches today. There are indeed human frailties among those of us who imagine heaven; so, by holding up individuals like King and

Tutu as paradigmatic for understanding a heaven on earth I do not see their visions as wholly complete, nor is my vision of heaven wholly complete. They teach us, however, that heaven is not full of individuals wrapped up in their own personal salvation. My salvation is inextricably bound up in your salvation. This is why there is thunderous applause and joy in heaven when anyone lost is found.

The apocalyptic writer of Revelation sees an interdependent earth and heaven as well. "Then I saw a new heaven and a new earth. . . . 'See, the home of God is among mortals. He will dwell with them as their God; they will be his peoples, and God himself will be with them; he will wipe every tear from their eyes. Death will be no more; mourning and crying and pain will be no more'" (Rev. 21:1–4). Christians are discipled to dream of and envision God's act of communal salvation. Instead of causing us to lose our uniqueness and individuation, community makes individuals shine bright. We know our uniqueness only in community. Uniqueness is unintelligible without the reference point of the other. I need you to know myself—that I have a sense of humor or that my smile is infectious. We know our own salvation through others who are being saved. This is why Jesus says we must lose life to find it. Do not seek your personal salvation—in doing that we end up like those religious hypocrites that irritated Jesus the most. In fact, Jesus doesn't get angry at those who seem to be most worthy of our anger—those who embezzle money (the tax collectors) and those who commit sexual sin (prostitutes and adulterers). These were Jesus' best friends; he required from them conversion and fidelity. He became angry at the religious folk who sought only their personal salvation.

God requires the interdependency of heaven and earth to be so expansive that the lion and lamb rest together, little children can accidentally reach tiny and vulnerable fingers into a snake pit and not be harmed, and, most of all, political systems on earth reflect a good life for all. This is not simply a dream. Jesus' incarnation is the ultimate sign that God does not intend for us to wait for heaven. It has already occurred—among mortals. Our work is to cultivate and practice heaven already on earth. This book is such an attempt as I seek to envision a heaven that actually changes the world for the good, rather than exacerbating culture wars with our own personal (self- or group-interested) pursuits of salvation that only deepen divisions and rivalries. Instead of competing concepts of heaven, this book longs for God's kingdom come here on earth as it is in heaven. I am encouraged in this journey by Cate Waynick, the Episcopal bishop of Indianapolis. She wrote to me after reading my thoughts, "Thank you for this—I couldn't agree more, and I do hope you're including Jesus, who said repeatedly that 'the kingdom is among you' (Luke 17:21)." I worry, however, that many Christians really do not believe this.

In the cafeteria at Yale Divinity School seventeen years ago, I was praying before a meal when, to my surprise, I was interrupted by a voice full of compassion. Someone at my right whispered, "Are you all right?" Instead of seeing signs of prayer—bowed head and closed eyes— the person thought I was sick. It was such an episode that planted the seed for this book. I will never forget that instance of how prayer was confused for sickness. I will never forget because it represents the difficult matter of discerning how religion is helpful or hurtful. Unfortunately, much of human history is filled with religious wars and violent practices that create more of a hell on earth than heaven. The irony, however, is that such war is usually fought in the name of heaven.

What I want us to do is to remember heaven. Yes, the operative word is *remembrance*. As the desert fathers and mothers taught us, heaven is more of a return than a going forward. Practicing heaven is more akin to excavation of the garden of Eden. Instead of seeing heaven as an unattainable utopia, we would do well to see how this planet earth is miraculous enough, full of diverse and abundant life. We need not long for a future miracle of heaven; it is already in our midst for which to dig deeper. The good news is that we already have many examples of God's reign with us: for example, the miracle of South Africa. One may see my reflections on how South Africa is a sign of God's reign in my books on Archbishop Desmond Tutu.[3] I am shaped by my firsthand witness to South Africa's miracle, and this makes me ever more reliant on exemplars like Tutu, whose thought is grounded upon an experience in which God creates what is good by creating what is different. Consequently, there is no legitimacy in competitive heavens which form people into believing that God has a future for only certain groups or individuals (e.g., white heterosexual people). Further, in trying to distinguish prayer from sickness, as I experienced in the Yale cafeteria, my particular African American identity can benefit me. I am often overwhelmed by what is done in the name of God's reign on earth. As was done to my African ancestors in the North Atlantic slave trade, concepts of God's paradise often prove capricious, based upon whoever happens to be the dominant group of people doing the theology. Marginalized people rarely get to contribute to the vision of heaven on earth, except through personal labor. Because of such incongruence, it is easy to forget the ubiquity of heaven or not realize its usefulness.

Relating my African identity to my Anglican identity also proves difficult because of how colonial powers used their versions of Christianity to justify slavery and segregation. Having lived for two years with Tutu in Cape Town (1993–1994), I experienced Tutu's response to bad religion firsthand. As he said, "Who you are affects and determines to a very large extent what you see and how you see it."[4] This is important wisdom, because the content that I present in this book requires the reader's willingness to want God's will done on earth as it is in heaven. This raises the complex question: What do I mean by "heaven on earth"?

Frederick Buechner helps me explain my meaning of heaven on earth through his definition of vocation as "the place where your deep gladness and the world's deep hunger meet."[5] Buechner's concept of vocation proposes a kind of confluence similar to heaven on earth in which behavior is congruent not only with words and ideas but also with commitments and practices. In other words, our vocations must contain both the ideal and the practical. Similarly, we must learn to see what is heavenly in our earthly life. Visionaries like King and Tutu readily admit the incongruence between words and actions. In other words, we need to learn to see the world differently by learning to see first what is not there between what we say as Christians and what we actually do. By learning to see what is not there, we learn to see what should be there. And so, when I bowed my head to pray before a meal at Yale, I was practicing the frame of reference of God being there. By returning thanks to God, I was also practically reminded of the labors of migrant workers, truck drivers, cooks, and oven repair workers who helped the food to get to my table.

A rearticulation of heaven occurs when we practice heaven. In light of Jesus' resurrection, our images of heaven can no longer be individualistic or the justifications of the powerful. Heaven constantly entreats us to find our salvation in others—the greatest other being God. In such a search, Christ's resurrection offers us new images to understand a heaven capable of transforming and redeeming a world full of conflicts, a heaven that does not harm or exclude but instead speaks for the weak and voiceless. We begin to stride toward the United Nations' Millennium Development Goals and, better yet, insist upon debt relief for nation-states, an end to hunger, and cures for HIV/AIDS, malaria, and tuberculosis.[6] Likewise, understanding heaven on earth helps us imagine a new earth, where we flourish, not just exist. If our existence on earth is seen in light of heaven, then we may see more clearly the bounds of goodness—and what is out of bounds, sin and evil. We learn by practicing heaven, however, that even when we are out of bounds, God will find us and put us back in play.

HEAVEN'S PRACTICALITY

We now come to the last of the seven visions seen in heaven. This last vision in heaven is divided into two parts: heavenly voices and heavenly beings. It is the heavenly being riding to earth on a white horse (Rev. 19:11) that I find most interesting. Is it Jesus? If so, we see him coming forth in all his power and glory. The beast and false prophet were cast alive into the lake of fire and the rest killed by the rider with a sword flashing out of his mouth. And all the birds gorged on the flesh of the enemies. The devil is bound for a thousand years so that he should not deceive the nations any longer, until the thousand years be completed. Afterward, for some reason in John's dream, the devil must be loosed a little while longer.

Some practicality must be injected into John's dream concerning the powers that be—namely, there can be no real contest between God and the devil. To turn Jesus into the white horse rider lessens the provocative nature of John's apocalyptic vision, which has already established the paradox of Jesus being both the Lamb and the Shepherd. In this paradox we are called to glimpse how God is both subject and object. Not only does God create all things (Col. 1:16), but through God all things coexist (Col. 1:17). From this it follows that no created being, heavenly or earthly, can compete with God (Heb. 1:3–10). And so, to see the violent drama of Jesus riding on a white horse to compete with beasts or the devil does a disservice to the deeper paradox of what God is doing in John's vision. Paradox and mystery occur when one has visions of heaven and earth; and strangely enough, such paradox and mystery have practicality (Eph. 3:9–11).

> Our longing for heaven will manifest itself benevolently in the world. For as Cain indicated his state of mind by murdering his brother, so will the heavenly minded indicate their state with a new and transcendent ethic, contradicting the natural ethic in order to bring us to a new level of life.
> —Irenaeus, *Against Heresies*

So what are the practical lessons inspired by John's apocalyptic vision? And what are the lessons that God is now teaching us and the heavenly beings? To both questions the answer is simply this: no created being can stand apart from God made known in Jesus. The nations fail when they try to stand apart from Jesus' rule: do unto others as you would have done to you. Revelation is practical in that it shows that, apart from Christ, nothing can exist. As we will shortly see in the end of John's vision, the great lesson of the ages that Jesus reveals is that we not only need God to be saved, we need each other. And strangely enough to some, Christians need other religions to flesh out what salvation truly means. The United States, the country of which I am a citizen, needs other countries and nationalities in order to know what it means to be a good and responsible republic in which all people are created equal.

20

The Key to the Bottomless Pit

Then I saw an angel coming down from heaven, holding in his hand the
key to the bottomless pit and a great chain.

—Revelation 20:1

The problem with applying John's apocalyptic vision to our everyday
lives and our politics is that we fall into what seems to be a bottomless
pit of despair. We may envision such application. We may have an
exciting senator from Chicago, Barack Obama, campaign on a vision of
interdependence and change to become president of the United States.
We may have a lot going for us but inevitably the scale of friction in
the world is so enormous that we may feel as though there is really no
practical hope for heaven on earth.

John faced such a challenge as well when he saw an angel coming
down from heaven, holding the key to the bottomless pit. The mighty
angel seized the devil and bound it for a thousand years and then threw
the devil into the pit so that it would deceive the nations no more.
John, too, shows despair in his vision as he goes on to say that the
devil must be let out for a little while. The devil will be released from
the prison pit and will come out to deceive the nations yet again. The
deception entices the nations back into war with heaven (Rev. 20:1–9).

The bottomless pit seems to be the recidivism of violence. There is a
practical side of heaven that draws us away from destructive tendencies
and toward solutions best suited for the entire planet of earth and realm
of heaven. In other words, heaven's immortality is extremely practical. It teaches us that unless we practice realities beyond our normal
conflicts, there can be no future. Unless South Africa practiced a reality beyond normal conflicts, there would have been no future for that

society.[1] South Africa practiced something extraordinary—something most nation-states have not—a Truth and Reconciliation Commission (TRC). The idealism of moving beyond conflict was practiced in very practical ways in the South African context. Through the lessons of exemplars like Mahatma Gandhi, Nelson Mandela, and Archbishop Desmond Tutu, South Africa has modeled a Jesus way of making heaven practical to earth. Therefore, given the vision of Jesus' spirituality, we aim to bring our deep desires into conformity with the demands of heaven—a place contingent with earth that allows only those goods that perfect human nature.

Heaven's practicality does not define human nature as finite and stuck in sin. Nor does it view human nature solely in individualistic terms of relativity. From heaven we learn that sacrifice and covenant do not come naturally to an individual on earth. In a postmodern and Western way of life, the fundamental pursuit of an individual is to fulfill one's personal needs and desires. But in such a habitat, temperance means at best that one should not pursue one's own self-fulfillment by unfairly interfering with someone else's pursuit of individual goods.[2]

From this view of heaven, practical human response presupposes a social model of human nature. We become perfected only in the context of human community. Heaven teaches us that those goods that are perfective of human nature are not only identified with the personal pleasure that individuals experience through the satisfaction of their psychobiological needs and desires. From the practicality of heaven, we learn that when our nutritive and sexual desires are satisfied responsibly that this satisfaction is not the same as perfected human nature. In other words, the goods on earth that we pursue and enjoy are true goods and not idols because we live in community. They remain true goods and not idols to the extent that we pursue such goods in community. The moment community breaks down is the same moment those goods become idols and spoils of war.

The practicality of heaven teaches us that aesthetic pleasures are true goods as long as they are not intended as ends in themselves. From the seraphim and cherubim who sing "Holy, holy, holy" we learn that the goal of tempering our natural appetites is to allow our personal satisfaction to be complete in God. Earth's recognition of heaven provides this counterintuitive practicality in which the heavenly minded can be of earthly good. As demonstrated by Gandhi, Mandela, and Tutu, those who see ideal existence also help us to see the practicality of such existence. In South Africa's case, there was nothing more practical than establishing practices like the TRC to avert the cycles of civil war. The world looks curiously at such a miracle—one even stemming from Christian witness—and is transformed by creative practices caused by the idealism. This is the beatific vision that guides our destiny.

As mentioned before, the dynamics between heaven and earth relate both ways. So not only are we being led to heaven, but heaven is coming to us despite our resistance. In the church, the general description of such a movement to earth is in the form of miracle. The modern mind has lost its patience with the role of miracle as a heavenly force breaking into earthly existence. We must tread carefully here. There is a general misconception today that miracles happen in the most remote regions of the world—the skepticism being that technologically less advanced people still need the language and worldview of miracles. But this is not an accurate perception of miracles.

In his work *The Fear of Freedom*, concerning early Christian communities, Rowan Greer explains that the miraculous represents a heavenly power brought down to earth and tied to the life of the community. In these early Christian communities, no one raised the modern question of how there could be miracles at all; instead, the issue for the ancients was legitimacy and authenticity. It seems as though the modern believer may still learn from the ancient church that miracles are authentic when harnessed to the life of the community.[3]

Miracles seek to untie the unnecessary contradiction between heaven and earth. There is no miracle in heaven, just as there is no beatific vision on earth. Miracles occur when heaven touches earth in such a way as to make earth acknowledge what it can become. Beatific vision occurs when earth touches heaven in such a way that heaven cannot help but share some of its transformation.

Miracles disclose that heaven is not about length of life, or four dimensions, but quality of existence. Heaven touching earth makes us reject the tendency to make earth antithetical to heaven. Harmony between earth and heaven provides the insight with which to engage again with the great but controversial minds like Karl Marx and Sigmund Freud. To attend to heaven does not, as they might say, mean an escape from this earth or a delusional activity. Heaven makes us see that life is not a question of quantity and material but quality and transformation. Heaven allows the perspective that social class and capitalist economies are not the only systems that impede life on earth, but ultimately, it is practices that lead to death that cramp us the most.

The concept of heaven does not make us avoid the harsh realities of a suffering world. On the contrary, heaven enables the view that our corporeal existence is not as mundane and arbitrary as many secularists think. Heaven helps us see that more is here than meets the eye. Mother Teresa and Gandhi saw this. All of this creates the problem of who gets to determine human realities and systems. Lovers of the world's system discount the need for heaven and therefore feel there is a lot at stake when visionaries like Tutu challenge the status quo. Heaven threatens to rain down on our existence something different from finite existence—the freedom of eternal existence. And so language of heaven couches our material existence in meaningful terms like *Homo sapiens*. And instead of *Homo sapiens* seeing the concept of heaven as a means to subordinate a lower class of people, John's Apocalypse offers a rather different view. The revelation of heaven is not a place of delusion; instead, heaven is perceived as a place that inspires fire in the face of injustice (Rev. 20:9–10).

Both Tutu and Martin Luther King Jr. could not withdraw from the world and be comforted in the Western practice of personal salvation. Influenced by Karl Barth, whom he met in 1963, King says that the way from God to humanity is in Christ crucified and resurrected, who offers a bridge between heaven and earth.[4] King states: "It is in him that the impossibilities are combined, the irreconcilables are reconciled: God and man, eternity and time, death and resurrection. Here in him, the conflict is somehow resolved and we are saved."[5] But what is equally clear from Tutu and King is the way in which God fulfils the promise of heaven through a new earth and new heaven that encompasses both spiritual and political strategies of community.

Tutu and King teach us that heaven for South Africa and the United States, indeed for the whole world, cannot be achieved simply through diplomacy. For them it is God who creates the new heaven and the new earth. This does not mean that God acts without the cooperation of human agency. The prophetic vision of a new heaven calls for human repentance and faith; in the same way, the prophetic vision of a new earth calls us to struggle for justice and peace. The genius of Tutu and King's vision teaches us to image each other's heaven in the same way that Jesus taught us to do to others as we want done to ourselves. Both Tutu and King are aware of the difficulty of keeping human attention fixed both on the divine realm and on social transformation of current realities. In fact, both spiritual figures believe that without attention to both heaven and social transformation, human beings will err to either delusion or anarchy.

Tutu's and King's views of heaven on earth commend themselves to public dialogue because they both reorient Western imagination to the memory that persons are intentionally made for a perfect end, more than just by chance. In more of a communal ethics, their concepts of heaven are expansive enough to include more people than most can imagine getting there. They both resist the double standards that we use to talk about heavenly and earthly realities. It is interesting that in both Tutu's and King's doctrines of God, there is a universalism that lends itself to interreligious dialogue. For example, King's understanding of God was validated in the experiences of everyday life:

> God has been profoundly real to me in recent years. In the midst of outer dangers I have felt an inner calm. In the midst of lonely days and dreary nights I have heard an inner voice saying, "Lo, I will be with you." When the chains of fear and the manacles of frustration have all but stymied my efforts, I have felt the power of God transforming the fatigue of despair into the buoyancy of hope. I am convinced that the universe is under the control of a loving purpose, and that in the struggle for righteousness man has cosmic companionship. Behind the harsh appearances of the world there is a benign power.[6]

Among many spiritual and mystical traditions, attention to heavenly reality among earthly reality guards against a capricious understanding of existence, or a materialistic understanding of reality, which has become the heresy of Western religion. For example, Miles Krassen thinks detachment from corporeality was part of what might be termed a "Tantric" tendency in Hasidic "spirituality." Krassen also refers to the tantric practice in Tibetan Buddhism, in which there is a possibility of using transcendent aspects of experience considered outside of the parameters of the material realm, in some respects, beyond even what may be envisioned as spiritual.[7] For Tutu and King, there can be no such detachment from corporeality—any such religion was always impoverished in their eyes. King admired Gandhi and Jainism because they provided a way to understand religion in concert with the earthly life. Tutu also believes this way as his spirituality seeks God's presence made available to all of creation through the use of the concept of the *imago Dei*.

More specifically, Tutu and King could not afford to believe in a heaven detached from earthly existence. They acutely knew that in

the Christian church the problem of materialism raises its ugly head
through the racial divisions in the history of the United States, especially the denominational splits due
to differing positions on slavery. In
other words, for much of the history of the United States, people
could believe they were Christians
with disregard to earthly realities
like racism. King goes on to say
that such a double standard in the
church became part of the fabric of
society in the United States. King's vision of the deep double standard
in the church is further developed as he reflects:

> The Book of Revelation reads as if John
> had wrapped up all our worst fears . . .
> violence, plague, wild animals . . . earth-
> quakes, erupting volcanoes, and the
> atrocities of torture and war—into one
> gigantic nightmare.
> —Elaine Pagels, *Revelations*

> First the church must remove the yoke of segregation from its own
> body. . . . It is appalling that the most segregated hour of Christian
> America is eleven o'clock on Sunday morning, the same hour when
> many are standing to sing, "In Christ there is no East no West."
> Equally appalling is the fact that the most segregated school of the
> week is the Sunday School. How often the church has had a high
> blood count of creeds and an anemia of deeds.[8]

Despite these double standards, I am not trying to shame white
Christians—such shaming rarely produces constructive changes—
rather, I believe that one may learn from Tutu and King the desire to
pass beyond solipsistic existence into eternal participation with God,
who knows how to contain infinity in creation. I think this is why John
has his nightmare that Babylon the great has fallen, that "her sins are
heaped high as heaven" because "she glorified herself and lived luxuri-
ously" (Rev. 18:5, 7). In other words, God's real kind of heaven entices
us away from the double standards of being in heaven yourself (e.g.,
wealth and individualism) while others are weeping and gnashing their
teeth forever. A communal ethics of heaven passes beyond the double
standards between heaven and earth and seeks an integrity of faith that
heaven can be present on earth.

CONFLUENT VISION

To be sure, King's heaven was not precisely the same as Tutu's. The
contexts of the United States and South Africa are too different. But

both advocate a communal view in which heaven can only be intelligible through reconciliation, for both considered reconciliation to be a theological commitment. Such reconciliation is ultimately achieved in heaven—the grace, however, is that heaven has come to earth. For King, heaven looks like a peaceful, beloved community, and for Tutu, heaven looks like the interpersonalities of Ubuntu.

The greatest similarity between Tutu and King seems to be in their avowal that they are not politicians, but Christian leaders. This fact is more overlooked in King than Tutu, nonetheless it remains true for both. King's faith in Jesus was apparent:

> Where do we find this God? In a test tube? Where else except in Jesus Christ, the Lord of our lives? By knowing him we know God. Christ is not only Godlike but God is Christ like. Christ is the word made flesh. He is the language of eternity translated into words of time. If we are to know what God is like and understand his purposes for humankind, we must turn to Christ. By committing ourselves absolutely to Christ and his way, we will participate in the marvelous act of faith that will bring us to the true knowledge of God.[9]

Where King may have learned from Tutu's Ubuntu is in the interrelatedness of personality. King's formal education in the philosophy of personalism at Boston University's graduate school, under Edgar Sheffield Brightman, helped to form King's view of the vital nature of persons.[10] The term "personalism" is commonly used to designate a fairly significant nineteenth-century philosophical movement. The movement developed as a reaction to materialism, evolutionism, and idealism. Personalism, which places great stress on personality as a supreme value and as a key notion that gives meaning to all of reality, is usually theistic in orientation.

The differences between Tutu and King are in the unique circumstances in the United States and South Africa. For example, unlike King, Tutu had no Constitution to which he could appeal for political justice. But King states:

> One day the South will know that when these disinherited children of God sat down at lunch counters, they were in reality standing up for what is best in the American dream and for the most sacred values in our Judeo-Christian heritage, thereby bringing our nation back to those great wells of democracy which were dug deep by the founding fathers in their formulation of the Constitution and the Declaration of Independence.[11]

Tutu's and King's lives warranted and even demanded a change in the way heaven was expressed. One could say that Tutu learned from King, who was convinced of the ultimate, apocalyptic bend of human history toward God's justice. God's justice demanded human justice, and human justice demanded the equal treatment of all God's people. And so King pushed for what Tutu desired, a heaven that witnesses to an alternative and transformative truth that would obstinately resist the truth of the present segregationist age. Heaven called for a resistance that existed as a contrary witness to a corrupt age.

Again like Tutu, King also knew that such active resistance could entail persecution, suffering, and even death. He knew that the segregationist age would protect its concept of heaven with fierce hostility. Only through King's keen imagination of heaven would all of America see how bestial the system of segregation really was and see the hideousness of the evil that lay behind it. Enraged at what they saw, Americans, King believed, would then move to change it, to transform it.

Envisioning heaven for everyone helped bring about the segregationists' demise and society's movement toward integration. To be sure, King did not focus on the suffering or the dying, just as Tutu had not. They were evils that accompanied the witness of heaven. This witness, in King's case manifesting itself through sermons and marches, effected the positive societal change King and his civil rights compatriots sought. The concept of heaven commends, and Tutu and King exemplify, bold witness and active resistance to entrenched forces of institutional evil. Their confluent visions of heaven on earth helped Tutu answer King's question, "Can a nonviolent, direct-action movement find application on the international level, to confront economic and political problems? I believe it can. It is clear to me that the next stage of the movement is to become international."[12]

Tutu acknowledges a great debt to King as Tutu's role as leader of the anti-apartheid movement increased.[13] While in London in the early and mid 1960s, he was constantly exposed to media coverage of civil rights activities, an experience that would not have been possible in South Africa and one that undoubtedly reinforced his sense of the unity of the African American and black South African struggles. Thus, it is not surprising that by the late 1970s, as he rose in the ranks of leadership among his people, Tutu had begun to speak of the ways in which King's philosophy and praxis were instructive for oppressed South Africans.[14]

The Christian understanding that King brought to his rejection of apartheid influenced Tutu tremendously. Despite the different styles and traditions that separated King, a Baptist clergyman, from Tutu, an Anglican archbishop, their opposition to apartheid emerged out of a basic understanding of heaven on earth. Tutu agreed completely with King's insistence that racial separation in all forms not only degrades human personality and denies the interrelatedness and interdependence of human beings, but it also violates the parenthood of God and the essential oneness of God's creation. Throughout the 1970s, Tutu echoed King's belief that the love of God is inseparable from the love of neighbor. For Tutu, as for King, this conviction found its strongest support in the life and ministry of Jesus Christ.[15] This became Tutu's most consistent argument as he confronted apartheid laws and customs through nonviolent action.

Tutu fully embraced King's insights into the meaning, character, and actualization of human community. In 1978, he reminded fellow South Africans of King's challenge that "together we must learn to live as brothers or together we will be forced to perish as fools."[16] As was evident with King, Tutu stressed the communitarian ideal as the organizing principle of all his thought and activities. All other important concepts that pervaded Tutu's writings and public speeches—for example, love, nonviolence, forgiveness, human dignity, morality, freedom, justice, reconciliation—were explicitly related to his understanding of community. Tutu's Ubuntu can be seen in King's vision of humanity. King writes:

> As long as there is poverty in the world I can never be rich, even if I have a billion dollars. As long as diseases are rampant and millions of people in this world cannot expect to live more than twenty-eight or thirty years, I can never be totally healthy even if I just got a good checkup at Mayo Clinic. I can never be what I ought to be until you are what you ought to be. This is the way our world is made. No individual or nation can stand out boasting of being independent. We are interdependent.[17]

Here the spirit and influence of King were unmistakable for Tutu.[18] King's communitarian ideal became quite significant for Tutu as he promoted, with awesome precision, his own view of "a new South Africa that is just, nonracial, and democratic, where black and white can exist amicably side by side in their home country as members of one family."[19]

Tutu and King open the perspective that heaven can be like yeast in the world. Whereas attention to some faraway heaven is passive acceptance of the fallenness of creation, Tutu and King's prophetic vision of a new earth and a new heaven helps us create with God new realities. Their vision and hope alone provide us with the vision and motivation needed to bring about a new and just global society. Their vision for heaven centers upon how the imagination of a perfect environment of community—namely, heaven—provides the proper vision of how to live on earth. I admit in this book that the demise of the concept of heaven and the beatific vision of God is the same as the demise of the concepts of justice and peace. This demise of the imagination of heaven, I suppose, is caused by Western thinkers like Karl Marx and Sigmund Freud who believe that attention to heaven is an irrelevant criteria for revolution or is simply individual psychosis. Imagining heaven through Tutu and King, however, is to recover how imagination of heaven is healthy and provides integrity for earthly existence.

By seeing heaven through Tutu's and King's eyes, my assumption is that human imagination of heaven creates a connatural reality between realized eschatology of earth and heaven's supernatural intervention. In other words, for Tutu and King, imagination of heaven continually shows persons the goal of their createdness. This vision guards against fundamentalistic tendencies of an apocalyptic heaven in which one must conceive of hell before one conceives of heaven. This fundamentalist view of heaven is in an apocalyptic hope that assumes the world is in such a crisis that only a cataclysmic ending of the present order and the creation of a new heaven and earth could bring redemption.

Instead of such a destructive God, Tutu and King envision that God is more creative. Solving all of the problems on earth may indeed prove impossible for human beings alone, but with God all things are possible. Cooperating with God instead of fearing God's apocalypse is a much wiser approach. I think God longs for us to pay closer attention to how we are all made in God's image. God invites us to realize our distinction of looking like God's image of persons in one nature. And yet, God is only God. We are God's children with whom God interacts in such a way as not to allow the pantheism of God deleting human personality. Therefore, imagination of heaven is a divine gift that enables human vision to see through the finality of personal existence. This "seeing through" enables sacramental realities beyond the simple conclusion that life is inherently violent and finite. Therefore,

the practice of nonviolence sacramentally demonstrates in my framework that attention to heaven is not delusional; instead, such heavenly
imagination self-fulfills an attention span for justice and peace and
allows better vision of how to live here, now, and on earth. Simone
Weil's spiritual writings provide special insight here—whether a person
can maintain a fixed attitude of "attention," she writes, depends not so
much on the goal of penetrating God as an object of prayer as being
penetrated by God. She states:

> The key to a Christian conception of studies is the realization that
> prayer consists of attention. It is the orientation of all the atten-
> tion of which the soul is capable toward God. The quality of the
> attention counts for much in the quality of the prayer. Warmth of
> heart cannot make up for it. The highest part of the attention only
> makes contact with God, when prayer is intense and pure enough
> for such a contact to be established; but the whole attention is
> turned toward God.[20]

Prayer as "the orientation of all the attention of which the soul
is capable toward God" should shape Christian communities to live
beyond the contradictions of survival and grace. In other words, main-
taining attention to God should enable the mutuality of how heaven
and earth intersect each other. True attention or apprehension of God
shows persons that creation is at the point where love is just possible —
a "love," for Weil, which was "not a state but a direction."[21] In many
ways, heaven is such a direction. It is a love in proportion to the dis-
tance created between God and persons. The obvious question, however, that I must attend to at this point is why Christian communities
who pray for God's kingdom of heaven to come on earth rarely display
such a kingdom themselves.

Weil is accused of being heterodox in Christian faith, becoming as
it were a secular saint, able to draw upon the spirituality of Christianity without being officially a part of it.[22] Weil's marginality is useful
in my framework with Tutu and King because she offers a critique of
how modern societies often view justice as banal and self-serving. In
other words, Weil teaches the activist who is without spiritual depth
that any effort stretched toward goodness does not reach. It is only
after long, fruitless efforts toward heaven that end in despair—when
persons can no longer expect anything—that, from outside us, the gift
of justice comes as a marvelous surprise. God's gift of justice is the perfection of community. Weil's insights help me locate Tutu and King's

understanding of heaven and justice in such a way that attention to both destroys the false sense of finality found in individualistic hermeneutics of justice. What Tutu and King offer Weil are the practices of an institutional church seeking to realize heaven on earth. Not only to black and African people, but to others marginalized by the mistakes of the church and the world, Tutu and King offer a confluent vision of how those who have failed to reach their potential may still strive toward such potential. Through their witness, Tutu and King display to the world that the call of Christ to Christian persons is to believe in heaven even when it seems so far away.

21

New Heaven and New Earth

But, in accordance with his promise, we wait for new heavens and a new earth, where righteousness is at home.

—2 Peter 3:13

Then I saw a new heaven and a new earth; for the first heaven and the first earth had passed away, and the sea was no more.

—Revelation 21:1

John's concluding section of Revelation in chapters 21 and 22 focuses on people who will both survive the concluding days of the old earth and heaven and be revived in the new heaven and new earth. When many people think about the book of Revelation they envision the end of the world, not knowing that John's vision had a different reference point. There will be an end, but not of the earth. There will be an end of a way of being (see Matt. 5:18; 24:34, 25; Mark 13:30, 31; Luke 16:17; 21:33). All will be made "new" (*kainos*) which does not refer only to time but also to kind and to quality. The heaven will be new as well as the earth. In this *kainos* there will be no more curse and therefore no more sin or suffering or sorrow.

> If the sun is *cosmic* or universal and we are microcosmic, little worlds, then if I translate these findings into the spiritual dimension it means that exposure to the Sun of Righteousness will enlighten, irradiate and illumine all the dark places of our souls and fill us with glory.
>
> —Brother Ramon, SSF,
> *Heaven on Earth*

Among these new things will be the new Jerusalem, coming down out of heaven from God. Here is the complement of Genesis 1 and 2 in which beginnings and endings meet. Paradise renews itself and Eden is restored (Rev. 22:1). And there will no longer be any night because God will finally be our light. And there will be a tree there, one this time that will heal us instead of divide us. The tree of life in Genesis was intended to preserve

Adam and Eve in life but was used to strike death. But now the tree only brings life as we this time eat of its fruit. John's Apocalypse comes to its climax as we—once driven out of paradise, cut off from eating from the tree of life—are now restored.

As I have tried to articulate, "paradise" in Scripture is always a definite place, hence my premise for heaven on earth. Paradise is described in Genesis 2 but lost in Genesis 3. Then restoration of the specific place of paradise is spoken of in Luke 23:43. Paradise is seen in a vision in 2 Corinthians 12:2, 4. It is promised in Revelation 2:7. And finally in Revelation 22:1–5, 14, 17, we see the promise fulfilled. No one earns this paradise (22:17). This paradise is a gift. This climax to Revelation is brief, almost as if John reaches the point of the ineffable but assures us again and again as to the truth of his vision. And then perhaps the most important words are said to John by an angel: "Do not seal up the words of the prophecy of this book, for the time is near" (22:10). Proclaim this happy ending! Make it known. All is not lost.

WHERE IS HEAVEN?

There have been two responses to the question, where is heaven? The first response is a cry of frustration, and the second response comes out of desperation. It is because of these two responses that I think Tutu's and King's nonviolent views of how to locate heaven on earth become a crucial vision that keep the people from perishing. For many, the first response of frustration has been to take political responsibility for the creation of a new world order into one's own hands. That is, to seek to establish utopia either through hegemonic systems or through violent revolution if necessary. Inevitably, this first and seemingly natural response to where heaven is implies the destruction of current reality in order to achieve specific interpretations of what heaven should look like. We see this first response in what I describe as heaven's antithesis. Heaven's antithesis, I argue, is violence.

The second response, of desperation, has been to regard the material world as so evil that it is beyond redemption. Much of this view we inherited from ancestors trying to survive in a hostile world. I certainly see this in my own ancestors—African slaves who found in the black church some sense of consolation for their desperation. Thank God my ancestors channeled their desperation in such a way instead of relying on desperation's natural end: to scorch the earth. These black folk knew heaven was not on earth; and yet, they found a way, even in their desperation, to work for heaven on earth by imagining what God's kingdom would look like. King's statements about the kingdom of God may be seen in such light:

> The kingdom of God as a universal is not yet. Because sin exists on every level of man's existence, the death of one tyranny is followed by the emergence of another tyranny. . . . Even though all progress is precarious, within limits real social progress may be made. . . . And though the kingdom of God may remain not yet as a universal reality in history, in the present it may exist in such isolated forms as in judgment, in personal devotion, and in some group life.[1]

In one of King's few attempts to define what he meant by the kingdom of God, he writes:

> Jesus took over the phrase "the Kingdom of God," but he changed its meaning. He refused entirely to be the kind of a Messiah that his contemporaries expected. Jesus made love the mark of sovereignty. Here we are left with no doubt as to Jesus' meaning. The Kingdom of God will be a society in which men and women live as children of God should live. It will be a kingdom controlled by the law of love. . . . Many have attempted to say that the ideal of a better world will be worked out in the next world. But Jesus taught men to say, "Thy will be done in earth, as it is in heaven." Although the world seems to be in a bad shape today, we must never lose faith in the power of God to achieve this purpose.[2]

In order to participate fully in King's and Tutu's dreams and visions of the redemption of creation to paradisiacal state, we must remember that in the end it is God who creates the new heaven and the new earth. In other words, we do not directly cause the kingdom of heaven to appear. This is vitally important to understand so as not to advocate violence as a means to bring so-called justice.

In Christian theology, the only one who causes the kingdom of heaven is God. The role of human beings is to participate in how God gives birth to the kingdom of heaven. We participate through the practices of heaven. As Jesus taught his disciples through the Lord's Prayer to pray for heaven on earth, so too King and Tutu practiced heaven on earth through *remembrance, reconciliation,* and *restitution.* These three practices are appropriated into the vision of heaven.

First, we must *remember* heaven, or else we keep repeating the violence of hell. We must remember so that the ideal of a new heaven and new earth can be born into reality now. To remember heaven becomes the proactive vision for the city of God that demands an infrastructure in which we must remember to guard against not only racial injustice but injustice of all kinds against humanity. As King demonstrated so well in the civil rights movement and Tutu through the Truth and Reconciliation Commission, without truthful remembrance, there can be no healing. And as Tutu states, without forgiveness there is no future.

Second, this vision of the city of God demands an infrastructure in which we must always practice *reconciliation*. We must be reconciled in order to go to heaven, or else our created differences will always be perceived as threats and will cause us to rip each other apart—thereby returning to Beast Mode. Instead of Beast Mode and even retributive justice, King and Tutu dream of and envision a community of reconciliation reflective of heaven on earth. They both have prayed for the peace and reconciliation of Jerusalem, that biblical nexus where heaven and earth meet. For King and Tutu, such a Jerusalem need not inevitably be at war. Reconciliation is possible. The beauty of their perspectives is that they help us see how religion need not exacerbate culture wars. King and Tutu shed light on how religious perspectives can actually make the world a better place rather than a place of confusion and violence. Through spiritual and religious practices of reconciliation, especially among the Abrahamic faiths of Judaism, Christianity, and Islam, the whole world will be closer to a new heaven and new earth. We no longer need segregated heavens only for Palestinians, Jews, whites, blacks, Protestants, Catholics or those who make $100,000 a year or more. We cannot flourish in silos.

And third, we must practice *restitution* on earth as it is in heaven, or else there will be the contradiction of constant war in heaven (Rev. 12:7). We must pursue justice for the sake of our souls, but we must remember whose justice it is—God's—or else there will be no end to violence. In addition, and perhaps more controversial among some Christian constituencies, King and Tutu's heaven is not the goal of personal salvation that was taught to me so staunchly in the South. God's eschatological work is toward universal salvation. Restitution in heaven is not about individuals wrapped up in their own salvation and rewards. No, Tutu and King dream of and envision God's act of communal restitution in which whole political systems are restored.

Although heaven has been critiqued as unhelpful for modern humanity by Karl Marx and Sigmund Freud, such a concept can illustrate how human societies may imagine together what kinds of restitution are necessary to bring people back together again. This is especially important in this incipient stage in which some use the means of a crusade or jihad to solve incommensurate differences while others use oppressive economic structures to solve incommensurate differences. In these ways we are caught in a vortex of being unable to envision political futures, only war or the necessary dialectic of rich and poor. In other words, it would be wise for Jews and Christians to become familiar, for example, with many Muslims' concept of heaven in order to proceed forward toward a common goal. We need to further communal habits of seeking consensus instead of just sending individual talking heads to declare peace where there is no peace. We need to encourage human movement out of oppressive determinisms and into communal habits that image heaven. We need to seek heaven as the communal space and means of social salvation.

Vision beyond cultural wars becomes crucial to correcting a great deal of misconception of heaven, as a place far away and especially as a future place neglecting the quality of living here and now on earth. Tutu and King make us stop and think that a transcendent concept of heaven is only an invitation to quietism and passivity. King states, "As a minister, I take prayer too seriously to use it as an excuse for avoiding work and responsibility."[3] When it comes to seeking an understanding of heaven, many watch and pray for God's kingdom to come on earth as in heaven but do not feel a call to struggle and act on earth. These people believe that even if the prophetic vision and hope for heaven is not an illusion, there still is little we can do about heaven on earth except trust that God will fulfill God's promise.

MAKING ALL THINGS NEW

For many people caught in their own legitimate histories in which they have become victims to oppressors, either the hope for a new heaven does not include the hope for a new earth or a new earth has been spiritualized to the point of being irrelevant to ultimate dreams and visions of existence, having nothing to do with this world. In other words, Western spirituality often envisions heaven only in the absence of earthly existence. This kind of spirituality is represented among those who countered Tutu's and King's utopian visions. Such counterforces were right-wing Christians in the United States and Dutch Reformed Afrikaners in South Africa.

In many ways, Tutu and King resisted such forces. For example, they used the Bible to renarrate how heaven naturally relates to earth. Through their proclamations and their lives, Tutu and King rejected dualistic understandings of spiritual being that is somehow separate from earthly existence. Often, those more conservative Christian voices against King and Tutu remained in an individualistic framework in which little display is given to how our personal journeys in God relate to the redemption of world. For example, many of Tutu's and King's detractors often referred to the spiritual as that inner reality that is somehow separate from the material and political world. Tutu and King, however, provide a new way of thinking about spirituality and politics when thinking about heaven.

> The population of the richest among the first world countries shows the least belief in God and in life after death and has the lowest church attendance.
> —Albert Borgmann, *Power Failure: Christianity in the Culture of Technology*

It is an interesting notion to think that spirituality and politics are inextricably linked. Owen Thomas illustrates the integrity between spirituality and politics rather than a dualism as he believes that the key to spirituality is the "Reign of God." So, when Thomas acts as a spiritual director, he asks his directees who their municipal, local, state, and federal representatives are.[4] In other words, when doing spiritual direction, Thomas illustrates where the directee needs to go in order to find God in the world. God does not only sit on church pews. Tutu and King often challenged any notion that their political effect did not at the same time operate from a deep-seated spirituality, as King specifically states:

> To say God is personal is not to make him an object among other objects or attribute to him finiteness and limitations of human personality; it is to take what is finest and noblest in our consciousness and affirm its perfect existence in him. . . . there is feeling and will, responsive to the deepest yearnings of the human heart: thus God both evokes and answers prayers.[5]

This is powerful, spiritual insight by King that God both prays and answers prayers. King's struggle with a personal God is important because throughout the history of the United States, God has been identified with the ideals of democracy, and democracy has been viewed as the social expression of Christianity. For example, King readily confesses that his vision of the beloved community was "deeply rooted in the American dream."[6] For King, "America is essentially a dream." He states, "It is a dream of a land where men of all races, of all nationalities, and of all creeds can live together as brothers. The substance of the dream is expressed in these sublime words, words lifted to cosmic proportions: 'We hold these truths to be self-evident—that all men are created equal; that they are endowed by their creator with certain inalienable rights; that among these are life, liberty, and the pursuit of happiness.' This is the dream."[7]

James Cone goes on to say that King's dreams are "grounded not in the hopes of white America but in God."[8] An example of this grounding for King is found in his statement:

> From the beginning a basic philosophy guided the movement. The guiding principle has since been referred to variously as non-violent resistance, noncooperation, and passive resistance. But in the first days of the protest none of these expressions was mentioned; the phrase most often heard was "Christian love." It was the Sermon on the Mount, rather than a doctrine of passive resistance, that initially inspired the Negroes of Montgomery to dignified social action. It was Jesus of Nazareth that stirred the Negroes to protest with the creative weapon of love.[9]

One can also see in Tutu's context, South Africa, how spirituality becomes politics through the South African dream of a future utopia or holy commonwealth. Tutu's theology is characterized by deep reflection on creation and the image of God. Such reflection is necessary for Tutu; he seeks to do theology in a South African context that for most of its history has operated under the assumption that God's image reflects warring racial identities. Instead of God's image as persons at war, Tutu appeals to his society to see that the triune God encompasses the greatest mystery of how diversity can be unity. Tutu states, "It is no use trying to avoid [God] because we are face to face here not with a puzzle but with mystery. A puzzle in principle can be solved if you have enough data. A mystery can never be solved. It just deepens."[10] Since God's ineffable nature prevents ready definitions of how we, as God's creation, in turn participate in God's image, we are completely dependent upon the image of God revealed in Jesus Christ.

For the African, Christianity became more of a life manner, often affirmed already in existing cultural practices. Borrowing from these practices, theological convictions of cultural affirmation came into being and Africans distinguished a European gospel from an African one. Both were means of access, but neither was meant to stand alone. Instead of perpetuating conflictual gospels between African and Afrikaner, Tutu's theological convictions of "nonracialism" emerge from practices of the Christian life (i.e., prayer, liturgy, and conversion). The hard work of Tutu's witness of Ubuntu and Christian faith helps us understand John's Revelation in which idolatrous kinds of heaven like an apartheid system cannot work in God's scheme of things.[11] Amazingly, African Christians maintained these convictions in light of being defined by the dominant group as black and inferior.

Tutu inherited these theological convictions from his church and from African tradition which facilitated his strong appeal for South Africa (i.e., all its diversity of peoples) to be faithful to the particular nature and work of Christ's redemption in the world.[12] Christian spirituality for both King and Tutu is that interpersonal reality that cannot be separated from political action. King said in his Nobel Peace Prize speech:

> I cannot forget that the Nobel Prize for Peace was also a commission—a commission to work harder for "the brotherhood of man." This is a calling which takes me beyond national allegiances, but even if it were not present, I would have to live with the meaning of my commitment to the ministry of Jesus Christ.

> We are called to speak for the weak, for the voiceless, for the victims of our nation, and for those it calls enemy, for no document from human hands can make these humans any less our brothers.[13]

Interpersonal spirituality is that theology for both King and Tutu in which they both envision and act toward heaven on earth or earth in heaven. It becomes a mistake to separate the ideal of God's presence with us (heaven) from our reality toward God (earth).

Afterword

The Healing of the Nations

Although there is theological language here, this book is not meant so much for people to read while seated in church pews or academic hallways but in subways and everyday life. It is appropriate then that I end this book with a surprising message I read on the subway in Boston. Actually, it was a photo advertising a particular church with a quote from C. S. Lewis: "I believe in Christianity as I believe that the sun has risen: not only because I see it, but because by it I see everything else."

As the message streamed through my subway window, I found myself strangely moved because the message and its image resembled the stream of consciousness of John's vision of Revelation. If you interpret the photo and message in a literal way, you may easily dismiss it as medieval and naive in its idea that the sun actually moves. But as I was propelled past this photo by the powerful force of a T train, I noticed others trying to catch the address in the advertisement for Hope Fellowship Church. I do not know if this church is conservative or liberal, its people predominantly white or diverse; all I know is that they made me scramble to see their image in the darkness of Boston's underground subway. In many ways this is what I hope for this book using John's Revelation as a backdrop.

John began his vision falling down and scrambling to get up (1:17). In much the same way I scrambled to see a quote on a T train. Physics and centrifugal force tried to prevent my vision. But with a last burst of energy I caught a clear glimpse of what I wanted to see. My self-fulfilling prophecy was confirmed—that is, what I wanted to see could also be what I needed to see. John ends his vision with this same clarity and confirmation. As he leaves us provoked and yet comforted, in spite of his nightmares along the way, a

> And there will be no more night; they need no light of lamp or sun, for the Lord God will be their light, and they will reign forever and ever.
> —Revelation 22:5

paradigm shift unfolds before our eyes. All the dualisms of heaven and earth, us and them, light and darkness, slowly disappear. The reference point of God will no longer be one of contention and division. When we see God's face the most controversial reality will occur—namely, we will reign together. Because of human nature and political science, we all know such a vision goes beyond current culture wars and human perspectives. I do believe, however, glimpses of hope remain that we may one day see beyond our current frame of reference. Jonathan Kirsch states, in a History Channel documentary about the book of Revelation and scientific observation, "Scientists agree that the world will end. And scientists agree that many features of the end of the world may resemble phenomenon and catastrophes described in the Book of Revelation. What they disagree about is whether this is the will of God as prophesied in Revelation or whether this is just an accident of the natural world."[1]

This documentary posits that what scientists tend to agree upon eerily resembles the apocalyptic predictions from the seven seals of Revelation. Like John of Patmos, scientists, both natural and scientific, worry about famine, death, war, plague, disease, earthquakes, volcanic fury, blood-red oceans, and a scorched earth. John's worry, however, does not leave him in dismay. We know this because of how his vision ends.

The ending of Revelation is a fitting place to think of what "afterword" means. John ends his apocalyptic vision in a way that is more akin to paradigm shift than conclusion. He understands C. S. Lewis's message that there is another kind of light in which to see, a light in which there will be no more monsters and streets flowing with blood. So none of the monsters and consternation exist in the afterword of Revelation. John even says the whole paradigm of how he sees is no longer the same. He does not need the light of the sun or the moon to see. Now the uninhibited presence of God enables sight. In other words, revelation is complete when we face God.

I think John suggests a future direction for humanity in which we stop worrying over dualisms and political deadlock. That we stop conservatism's worry over who is in or out of heaven. That we stop also the liberalism that easily dismisses the value of a nonviolent confessional faith in a world full of violence and conflict. And that we stop the smugness of thinking we have figured out what 666 means or who the dragon is. I hope this book is in concert with John's afterword in which a paradigm shift occurs. The paradigm shift is this—we all scramble in darkness until we see God's reign on earth as it is in heaven. Even though such an image may be a blur from a passing train, Revelation points to a new frame of reference from which to see. This means more effort to stop stereotyping the other. More paradigm shifts in Christianity in which we realize a person's salvation is not independent of the other. But if truth be known, these paradigm shifts have occurred all along in the book of Revelation. In John's stream of consciousness he has interrupted our logic numerous times by making us see wars in heaven and a Lamb who, instead of being slaughtered, has the power to heal.

* * *

I discovered several things while writing this book. The first is that many of the culture wars today surrounding how to interpret Revelation remain the same as they have always been since the Bible was written; namely, we read Revelation through our own eyes and interest groups. This means that those in economic and political power tend to read Revelation in a more relaxed, "objective" way in which there can be a wide girth of interpretations as long as the reader and writer remain in control. Those without such power and resources are less inclined to such objectivity and instead embrace apocalyptic and literal tone.

For example, those who see themselves as up against powers and principalities will naturally identify with the one hundred forty-four thousand redeemed out of the great ordeal (Rev. 14:1–5). White evangelical Christians take great solace in seeing movies like the *Left Behind* series in which the majority of the raptured resemble themselves— white suburban folks speaking English. It is only natural to identify with one's own frame of reference. In this commentary, I have learned a much larger frame of reference from John of Patmos, one in which God's work of redemption is not only for those with whom we naturally identify.

John helps me see what many of us may not expect or even want. For example, in a recent *New York Times* article, there was rich discussion about 1.5 million black men missing from daily life in the United States because of early death—sometimes due to violence—or imprisonment.[2] As I read this article I could not help but rethink what the raptured one hundred forty-four thousand may mean. One of the most famous cases of disappeared people occurred during what was known as the Dirty War in Argentina. In the late 1970s a mechanic who worked near Buenos Aires said, "I remember seeing these military planes throwing these strange packages over the area. I did not know what they were. But I then saw these packages floating on the river banks. When I opened them I was aghast. The packages were dead bodies." These events happened when Argentina's last military government was in power, from 1976 to 1983. Official accounts say almost twenty thousand people were "disappeared" by the military regime, but human rights groups say the figure is at least thirty thousand.[3] Courageous steps to find the disappeared are occurring through the work of Pope Francis, who lived in Argentina during the dictatorship as Jorge Bergoglio, head of the Jesuit order. For example, Pope Francis has ordered the Vatican to open its files on Argentina in order to help families discover the fate of their loved ones.

Unfortunately, this apocalyptic cycle of the disappeared continues today. In New York City, almost 120,000 black men between the ages of twenty-five and fifty-four have been carried away from everyday life. Where have they been taken? Mostly, they died young or are locked behind bars. So for every one hundred black women there are only eighty-three black men. This gender disparity does not exist in childhood; there are roughly as many black boys as girls. An imbalance begins to appear in adolescence and increases with age. For white women there is near parity with white men, but black men are more likely to be in prison or die young. The endangerment of the black male identity is all the more highlighted by police killings and jarring gender gaps that leave many communities without enough black men to be fathers and husbands. Their absence accelerates far-reaching implications, according to research by Kerwin Charles, an economist at the University of Chicago. For example, "black women left behind, at least those who are heterosexual and seeking a partner of the same race, face a scarcity, while straight men have an abundant supply of potential mates and don't need to compete as hard to find one."[4] This imbalance has also forced women to raise families on their own.

Nationwide, almost one in twelve black men ages twenty-five to fifty-four are in prison, compared with one in sixty nonblack men. Black men are missing also due to homicide, the leading cause of death for young black men, and they also die from heart disease, respiratory disease, and accidents more often than other demographic groups, including black women. The *New York Times* article sums it up this way, "Perhaps the starkest description of the situation is this: More than one out of every six black men who today should be between 25 and 54 years old have disappeared from daily life."[5]

Apocalyptic situations do not happen by accident. The US city that has the largest proportion of missing black men is Ferguson, Missouri, where the fatal police shooting of Michael Brown occurred in 2014. For every one hundred black women in Ferguson there are sixty black men.[6] The shooting of Michael Brown helped to uncover this disparity and sparked international protests and a federal Justice Department investigation that concluded there were widespread discriminatory acts against black people committed by the city police and government. After the 2015 death of Freddie Gray in police custody in Baltimore, swift action by the prosecutor seemed to illustrate how much tension police violence has caused. It would usually require months before any charges or indictment would occur.

* * *

As I stated in the beginning of this book, I jumped at the opportunity to write this theological commentary because I share John's vision of the end, that there will be a healing tree beckoning us home. This tree will be a magnificent one whose leaves "are for the healing of the nations [*ethnoi*]." These ethnicities are not just black folk, they are a myriad of human identities trying to read themselves into God's salvation history. We do the brilliant yet controversial book of Revelation a great disservice if we are not aware of this fact. In other words, the reader must confess the social location that influences how she or he reads Revelation. Doing so can ameliorate our culture and religious wars over who is in or out of heaven. Most of us want to get there.

A good theology of Revelation is one in which we do not need to wait for heaven. We can find it beginning on earth through John's imagery of the leaves healing the *ethnoi*. Tom Shadyac, a Hollywood director, helps us conclude

> "If you become a bird and fly away from me," said his mother, "I will be a tree that you come home to."
> —Margaret Wise Brown, *The Runaway Bunny*

this book with what needs to be ultimately healed. He tells his story in a deeply reflective documentary about how his "end of the world experience" changed his life.[7] When Shadyac opens his documentary he notes that his story is about mental illness, but not the kind most people admit to. Shadyac would have been content being a Hollywood millionaire directing comedies, but he had to rethink his life when he faced his death. An accident led to severe postconcussion syndrome.

Often depression and suicidal tendencies develop with this syndrome. Nothing seemed to heal him. He welcomed death; and in so doing, a sense of clarity came to him. If he was going to die, there were specific things he needed to say and do before then. What he had come to know when facing his death was that the world he was living in was a lie. The power game of Hollywood and wealth in which he dominated and won, a game he thought would actually help the world, he realized was really destroying the world.

Unexpectedly, his postconcussion syndrome went away. A whole new heaven and earth opened up to him. He quotes Albert Einstein, "Humanity is going to require a substantially new way of thinking if it is to survive." Granted a new beginning, Shadyac went on a journey to spark a conversation around key questions to significant spiritual leaders, such as: Is there a problem that causes all the other problems? His answer is mental illness, but not the clinical kind of insanity. It is the kind of mental illness in which a society condemns a woman who goes through a trash can across the street, or a man who lies helpless on the sidewalk while others pass him by, or people who live in cardboard shacks.

The ultimate revelation that Shadyac helps us to see, and with which to conclude this book, is that God does not require sacrifice or Armageddon. Such a notion is in solipsistic streams of consciousness and nightmares. It is also in calmly reasoned theologies seeking only the apocalyptic end of those different from themselves. God does, however, require that the lost will be found. This is why truth telling and confession are important. We must participate in God finding us. When G. K. Chesterton was asked by the *London Times* to answer the essay question "What's wrong with the world?" he wrote: "Dear Sirs, I am.—Sincerely G. K. Chesterton." I agree. Much of this commentary on Revelation seeks to persuade all of us to answer the same. We need no longer interpret the book of Revelation as a cowboy western of us against them. We must cease and desist theologies in which we privilege ourselves in the narrative of Revelation as the raptured or saved. We must ask the same *London Times* question that is asked in the book of Revelation: What is wrong with the world? And if we want to move from mental illness as defined by Shadyac, we must all answer, "I am." By so confessing, we become open to the ultimate revelation that no matter how we try to hide from God, in the end God will find us all.

Notes

Introduction: Are We There Yet?

1. Rowan Williams, *A Ray of Darkness: Sermons and Reflections* (Cambridge, MA: Cowley Publications, 1995), 99.

Chapter 1. God, Are You There?

1. Charles Williams, *The Figure of Beatrice* (New York: Octagon Books, 1972), 190.

2. Rowan Williams, *A Ray of Darkness: Sermons and Reflections* (Cambridge, MA: Cowley Publications, 1995), 58, 59.

3. Robert A. Orsi, *Between Heaven and Earth: The Religious Worlds People Make and the Scholars Who Study Them* (Princeton, NJ: Princeton UP, 2005); Huston Smith, *Why Religion Matters: The Fate of the Human Spirit in an Age of Disbelief* (New York, NY: HarperCollins, 2001); Robert Wuthnow, *After Heaven: Spirituality in America since the 1950s* (Berkeley: University of California, 1998).

4. Martin Luther King Jr., *The Trumpet of Conscience* (San Francisco: Harper & Row, 1967), 76.

5. Martin Luther King Jr., "Honoring Dr. Du Bois," *Freedomways* 8, no. 2 (Spring 1968): 110–11.

Chapter 2. Context Matters

1. See Walter Wink's Powers trilogy: *Naming the Powers: The Language of Power in the New Testament* (Philadelphia: Fortress Press, 1984); *Unmasking the Powers: The Invisible Forces That Determine Human Existence* (Philadelphia: Fortress Press, 1986); and *Engaging the Powers: Discernment and Resistance in a World of Domination* (Minneapolis: Fortress Press, 1992).

2. Brian K. Blount, *Revelation: A Commentary* (Louisville, KY: Westminster John Knox Press, 2009), 1.

3. Justin Martyr, *Dialogue with Trypho* 81.4.

4. Blount, *Revelation*, 11–12. Here Blount provides primary historical texts from Pliny the Younger to the emperor Trajan (98–117 CE) indicating the laissez-faire approach to Christians. Trajan even says, "Christians should not be sought out."

5. Catherine Keller, *Apocalypse Now and Then: A Feminist Guide to the End of the World* (Minneapolis: Fortress Press, 2005).

Chapter 3. On Earth as in Heaven

1. E.W. Bullinger, *Commentary on Revelation* (Grand Rapids: Christian Classics Ethereal Library, 1902), 95f.
2. "CBS News Poll: Americans' View on Death," April 27, 2014, http://www.cbsnews.com/news/cbs-news-poll-americans-views-on-death/.
3. 2014 Religious Landscape Study; see http://www.pewresearch.org/fact-tank/2015/11/10/most-americans-believe-in-heaven-and-hell/.
4. For example, modern theologians like Rudolf Bultmann split hairs by distinguishing heaven as the conception of the transcending God through spatial terms and eschatology as the idea of transcendence of God through temporal terms. See Bultmann, *Jesus Christ and Mythology* (New York: Scribner & Sons, 1958), 20.

Chapter 4. Keys to the Kingdom

1. Rowan Williams, *A Ray of Darkness: Sermons and Reflections* (Cambridge, MA: Cowley Publications, 1995), 57.
2. Ibid., 58, 59.

Chapter 5. The Church of Zombies

1. See Willie Jennings, *The Christian Imagination: Theology and the Origins of Race* (New Haven, CT: Yale University Press, 2010).
2. Quoted in Philip D. W. Krey and Peter D. S. Krey, eds., *Luther's Spirituality* (New York: Paulist Press, 2007), 142.
3. Those who argue against my "progressive theology" usually perceive God as "He."
4. Catherine Shoichet, "Who Is Chapel Hill Shooting Suspect Craig Hicks?," CNN, February 12, 2015, http://www.cnn.com/2015/02/12/us/chapel-hill-shooting-suspect-craig-hicks/.

Chapter 6. Heaven in Beast Mode

1. For a powerful understanding of what the worthiness of a sacrificial lamb means, see René Girard, *Things Hidden since the Foundation of the World* (Stanford, CA: Stanford University Press, 1987), and "Are the Gospels Mythical?," *First Things* 62 (April 1996). Girard gives philosophical and anthropological insight into why Jesus puts an end to sacrifice. For an interfaith defense of Girard, see Roger Scruton, *The Soul of the World* (Princeton, NJ: Princeton University Press, 2014).

2. James Alison, *Faith Beyond Resentment: Fragments Catholic and Gay* (New York: Crossroads, 2001), 158.

3. Matt. 9:13; 12:7; quoting Hos. 6:6.

4. See also Gen. 48:16; Exod. 6:6; 13:13, 15.

5. Rowan Williams, *A Ray of Darkness: Sermons and Reflections* (Cambridge, MA: Cowley Publications, 1995), 86.

6. Richard Hooker, *The Laws of Ecclesiastical Polity*, book 5 (1597).

7. Miroslav Volf, *Exclusion and Embrace: A Theological Exploration of Identity, Otherness, and Reconciliation* (Nashville: Abingdon Press, 1993).

8. Brian K. Blount, *Revelation: A Commentary* (Louisville, KY: Westminster John Knox Press, 2009), 4.

9. For a more sustained meditation on the paradox of the Lamb, see Ward Ewing, *The Power of the Lamb: Revelation's Theology of Liberation for You* (Eugene, OR: Wipf & Stock, 2006).

10. Michael Battle, *Reconciliation: The Ubuntu Theology of Desmond Tutu* (Cleveland: Pilgrim Press, 2009).

Chapter 7. Yawning in Heaven

1. M. Masud R. Khan, introduction to *Holding and Interpretation: Fragment of an Analysis*, by D. W. Winnicott (New York: Grove Press, 1986), 1.

2. Robert Dykstra, "To Be Boring or to Be Bored: That Is the Question," *inSpire* 5, no. 2 (Winter 2001): 18. *InSpire* is an alumni journal of Princeton Theological Seminary.

3. Ibid.

4. Adam Philips, *On Kissing, Tickling, and Being Bored* (Cambridge, MA: Harvard University Press, 1993), 69–70.

5. Dykstra, "To Be Boring," 18.

6. Ibid., 19.

7. Philip Pullman has one of the best imaginations of hell in his fantasy series. See Pullman, *The Amber Spyglass*, His Dark Materials, book 3 (New York: Random House, 2000), 226–88.

Chapter 8. God's Time

1. Milton Sernett, ed., *Afro-American Religious History: A Documentary Witness* (Durham, NC: Duke University Press, 1985), 24.

2. Henri Nouwen, *Behold the Beauty of the Lord* (Notre Dame, IN: Ave Maria Press, 1987), 19.

3. Frederick Buechner, *Wishful Thinking* (New York: Harper & Row, 1973), 22.

4. Ibid.

Chapter 9. Individualism: Hell on Earth as in Heaven

1. Rowan Williams, *A Ray of Darkness: Sermons and Reflections* (Cambridge, MA: Cowley Publications, 1995), 58.

2. James Alison, *Faith Beyond Resentment: Fragments Catholic and Gay* (New York: Crossroads, 2001), 161.

3. Kim Paffenroth and Robert P. Kennedy, eds., *A Reader's Companion to Augustine's Confessions* (Louisville, KY: Westminster John Knox Press, 2003), 115. For this problem of compartmentalization, I am also indebted to my student Erin Hensley's paper "All Sides Being Equal: A Reflection on King's versus Augustine's Ideas of a Life."

4. Nikolai Berdyaev, "Studies Concerning Jacob Boehme: Etude I. The Teaching about the *Ungrund* [eternal nothing] and Freedom," 1930, http://www.berdyaev.com/berdiaev/berd_lib/1930_349.html.

5. Nikolai Berdyaev, "The Truth of Orthodoxy," in *Vestnik of the Russian West European Patriarchal Exarchate*, Paris, 1952. Available at http://www.chebucto.ns.ca/Philosophy/Sui-Generis/Berdyaev/essays/orthodox.htm.

6. Nikolai Berdyaev, *The Destiny of Man* (New York: Harper & Row Publishers, 1960), 293–94.

7. Michael Battle, *Reconciliation: The Ubuntu Theology of Desmond Tutu* (Cleveland: Pilgrim Press, 2009).

8. W. E. B. Du Bois, *The Souls of Black Folks* (New York: Pocket Books, 2005), 7.

Chapter 10. Learning a New Language

1. Rowan Williams, *Resurrection* (New York: Pilgrim Press, 1984), 72.

2. Gabriel Fackre, *The Christian Story* (Grand Rapids: Eerdmans, 1984), 213.

3. Ibid., 213.

4. Quoted in Charles Williams, *The Figure of Beatrice* (New York: Octagon Books, 1972), 196.

5. Charles Williams, *The Figure of Beatrice* (New York: Octagon Books, 1972), 197.

Chapter 11. Redemption Song

1. According to Origen, you cannot separate goodness and justice (*De principiis* 2.5).

2. See Plato, *Timaeus and Critias*, (New York: Penguin Books, 1983), 81–82. Uniformity is described through a Platonic worldview of interpenetration.

3. Origen, *Princ.* 2.9.2.

4. Origen, *Princ.* 2.8.3.

5. Rowan Williams, *Christian Spirituality* (Atlanta: John Knox Press, 1979).

6. Rowan Greer, *Origen: Selected Writings* (New York: Paulist Press, 2002), 11, 12.

7. Origen uses an illustration of a student of geometry or medicine to show the reason for hierarchy of souls (*Princ.* 1.4.1). Death does not finally decide the fate of the soul, which may turn into a demon or an angel. This ascent and descent goes on uninterruptedly until the final *apokatastasis* when all creatures, even the devil, will be saved. See also Plato, *Timaeus*, main section 1.10, for a discussion of the soul rising and falling. (See p. 58 in Penguin Classics.)

8. The soul is neither spirit nor body but the "sliding middle," according to Hans Urs von Balthasar in *Origen: Spirit & Fire* (Washington, DC: Catholic University Press of America, 2001), 46.

9. Ibid., 51.

10. Dale Andrews, *Practical Theology for Black Churches: Bridging Black Theology and African American Folk Religion* (Louisville, KY: Westminster John Knox Press, 2002), 18.

Chapter 12. A Theology of Proximity

1. For examples, see Ozer Bergman's *Where Earth and Heaven Kiss* (Jerusalem and New York: Breslov Research Institute, 2006); Pia Gyger, *That We May Join Heaven and Earth: Lay Religious Community for the 21st Century* (Lanham, MD: Rowman & Littlefield, 2006); Jeffrey Jue, *Heaven upon Earth: Joseph Mede (1586–1638) and the Legacy of Millenarianism* (New York: Springer Press, 2006); Stephen Nichols, *Heaven on Earth: Capturing Jonathan Edwards's Vision of Living in Between* (Wheaton, IL: Crossway Books, 2006); Alessandro Scafi, *Mapping Paradise: A History of Heaven on Earth* (Chicago: University of Chicago Press, 2006). These works focus on the apocalypse and the confluence or contradiction between heaven and earth.

2. Examples are Philip Gulley and James Mulholland, *If Grace Is True: Why God Will Save Every Person* (New York: HarperSanFrancisco, 2003); and Kerry Walters, *Jacob's Hip: Finding God in an Anxious Age* (Maryknoll, NY: Orbis Books, 2003).

Chapter 13. A New Ethic

1. Peter Kreeft, *Heaven: The Heart's Deepest Longing* (San Francisco: St. Ignatius Press, 1989), 105.

2. Etienne Gilson, *Thomism: The Philosophy of Thomas Aquinas*, trans. Laurence K. Shook and Armand Maurer (Toronto: Pontifical Institute of Mediaeval Studies, 2002), 400.

3. Ibid.

4. C. Gent. 4.54; Aquinas, *Summa theologiae* 1–2.2.8.

5. C. Gent., 3.48.

6. Philip H. Wicksteed, *Dante & Aquinas* (New York: Haskell House, 1971), is helpful in comparing Dante's and Aquinas's views of heaven.

7. C. S. Lewis, *Surprised by Joy* (New York: Harcourt, Brace & World, 1955), 221.

8. C. Gent. 3.43.

9. C. S. Lewis, *The Weight of Glory* (New York: Macmillan, 1949), 14–15.

Chapter 14. All Roads (and Rivers) to Heaven?

1. Cornel West, *Prophesy Deliverance! An Afro-American Revolutionary Christianity* (Philadelphia: Westminster Press, 1982), 35.

2. Malcolm Gladwell, *The Tipping Point: How Little Things Can Make a Big Difference* (New York: Little, Brown & Co., 2000), 163–70.

3. One of the best theological voices on this is Stanley Hauerwas. See his *A Community of Character: Toward a Constructive Christian Social Ethic* (Notre Dame, IN: University of Notre Dame Press, 1981).

4. Frederick Buechner, *Wishful Thinking: A Seeker's ABC* (San Francisco: HarperSanFrancisco, 1993), 119.

5. Desmond Tutu, interview by Gyles Brandreth, "My Idea of Heaven," *Sunday Telegraph*, April 27, 2001, http://www.telegraph.co.uk/culture/4723136/My-idea-of-Heaven.html. Today, Archbishop Tutu has found an equilibrium of wellness and continues to work on the international scene.

Chapter 15. Martin Luther King's Heaven

1. Shankar Vedantam, "Social Isolation Growing in U.S., Study Says," *Washington Post*, June 23, 2006.

2. Martin Luther King Jr., *The Trumpet of Conscience* (San Francisco: Harper & Row, 1967), 77–78.

3. For example, Jeffery Sachs thinks that global problems are not overwhelming but can be manageably solved. See Sachs, *The End of Poverty: Economic Possibilities for Our Time* (New York: Penguin Press, 2005).

4. Quoted in John Dear, "The school of prophets," National Catholic Reporter, November 17, 2009, https://www.ncronline.org/blogs/road-peace/school-prophets.

5. Noel Leo Erskine, *King among the Theologians* (Cleveland: Pilgrim Press, 1994), 9.

6. Martin Luther King Jr., *Where Do We Go from Here: Chaos or Community?* (Boston: Beacon Press, 1967), 167–68.

7. Martin Luther King Jr., *Stride Toward Freedom* (San Francisco: Harper & Row, 1986), 196.

8. Barack Obama, second presidential inaugural address, January 21, 2013, Washington, DC. Available at https://www.whitehouse.gov/the-press-office/2013/01/21/inaugural-address-president-barack-obama.

9. Martin Luther King Jr., *King, Where Do We Go from Here?*, 37.

10. King, *Trumpet of Conscience*, 29.

11. For an interesting appropriation of King's nonviolent resistance in the book of Revelation, see Brian K. Blount, "Reading Revelation Today: Witness as Active Resistance," *Interpretation* 54, no. 4 (October 2000): 398–409.

12. Martin Luther King Jr., *Strength to Love* (Cleveland: Collins Publishers, 1963), 32.

Chapter 16. King's Practice of Heaven

1. Martin Luther King Jr., *Stride Toward Freedom* (San Francisco: Harper & Row, 1986), 116–17.

2. Ibid., 117.

3. Martin Luther King Jr., "Pilgrimage to Nonviolence," *Christian Century* 77 (April 13, 1960): 439–41.

4. Martin Luther King Jr., "The Unchristian Christian," *Ebony* 20 (August 1965): 77. See also, King, "Letter from a Birmingham Jail," in *Why We Can't Wait* (New York: Signet Books, 1964), 91.

5. Martin Luther King Jr., "The Death of Evil on the Seashore," in *Strength to Love* (Cleveland: Collins Publishers, 1963), 58–66. Interestingly enough considering my Anglican background, King delivered this sermon on May 17, 1956, at the Episcopal Cathedral of St. John the Divine in New York City. Also see other references to King's eschatology in his *Where Do We Go from Here: Chaos or Community?* (Boston: Beacon Press, 1967); "Facing the Challenge of a New Age," in *Testament of Hope: The Essential Writings of Martin Luther King, Jr.*, ed. James M. Washington (San Francisco: Harper & Row, 1986), 140.; "I Have a Dream" and "I've Been to the Mountain," in *Martin Luther King, Jr.: A Documentary, Montgomery to Memphis*, ed. Flip Schulke (New York: W. W. Norton, 1976), 218, 223–24.

6. Erskine, *King among the Theologians*, 145.

7. King, *Strength to Love*, 82.

8. King, *Stride Toward Freedom*, 182; *Strength to Love*, 97, 130–31. Unfortunately, King omits "male nor female" from his allusion to Galatians. For an interesting discussion of an internal critique of King's work and the black church in relation to womanist theology, see Erskine, *King among the Theologians*, 159–73; Garth Baker-Fletcher, *Somebodyness: Martin Luther King, Jr., and the Theory of Dignity* (Minneapolis: Fortress Press, 1993), 165–93.

9. Martin Luther King Jr., "The Rising Tide of Racial Consciousness," *YWCA Magazine*, December 1960, 3.

10. Martin Luther King Jr., *The Trumpet of Conscience* (San Francisco: Harper & Row, 1967), 67.

11. King, "I Have a Dream," 218; *Stride Toward Freedom*, 186–87; *Trumpet of Conscience*, 92; and Kenneth L. Smith and Ira G. Zepp, *Search for the Beloved*

Community: The Thinking of Martin Luther King Jr. (Valley Forge, PA: Judson Press, 1998), 39.

12. King, "I Have a Dream," 218; *Trumpet of Conscience*, 9.

13. King, "I Have a Dream," 218.

14. Martin Luther King Jr., *I've Been to the Mountaintop* (San Francisco: HarperSanFrancisco, 1994), 16.

15. King, *Strength to Love*, 150.

16. Walter Brueggemann, "How Do We Know a Prophet When We See One: Martin Luther King Jr.," *Youth Magazine* 26 (January 1975): 54.

17. King, *Stride Toward Freedom*, 81; *Strength to Love*, 140.

18. King, *Mountaintop*, 33–34.

19. King, *Strength to Love*, 104; cf. *Stride Toward Freedom*, 114–15.

20. King, *Stride Toward Freedom*, 171.

21. Martin Luther King Jr., "Facing the Challenge of a New Age," 140.

Chapter 17. Desmond Tutu's Heaven Is Ubuntu

1. When referring to Tutu's writings, I rely upon my first hand access to his work when I lived with him in South Africa in 1993–1994. I had access to his unpublished various sermons, addresses, and other writings; therefore, many of my quotes of Tutu are from his primary sources, often handwritten texts. Where I am able to provide specific citations to Tutu's unpublished materials, I refer to my book, *Reconciliation: the Ubuntu Theology of Desmond Tutu.*

2. See Catherine LaCugna, *God for Us: The Trinity and the Christian Life* (New York: Harper One, 1993), 1. Also see Harry Williams, *The True Wilderness* (Harrisburg, PA: Morehouse, 1994) referred to in Tutu, "The Nature and Value of Theology." Cited in Battle, *Reconciliation*, 216. Tutu states that the doctrine of the Trinity assures us that we are not destined to eternal isolation.

3. Tutu goes on to give an illustration about the necessity of giving: one who only receives finds death, just like the Dead Sea, in which nothing can survive because it only receives its current. See Tutu, handwritten sermon, St. George's Cathedral, August 21, 1986. The text of the sermon is 1 Cor. 4:7: "For who sees anything different in you? What do you have that you did not receive? And if you received it, why do you boast as if it were not a gift?"

4. Tutu, "Response at Graduation of Columbia University's Honorary Doctorate" (address, University of the Witwatersrand, August 2, 1982 cited in Battle, *Reconciliation*, 219). The president and trustees of Columbia University came to South Africa because the South African government prevented Tutu from flying to New York.

5. Desmond Tutu, "A Christian Vision of the Future of South Africa," in *Christianity amidst Apartheid: Selected Perspectives on the Church in South Africa,* ed. Martin Prozesky (New York: St. Martin's Press, 1990).

6. Tutu, "The Nature and Value of Theology" (undated address).

7. Tutu, "Human Rights in South Africa," in *Monitor*, South African Council of Churches Library Resource Center, undated, cited in Battle, *Reconciliation*, 248

8. Ibid. Ian Smith was prime minister of Rhodesia from 1964 to 1979, when the country became Zimbabwe and he became head of the opposition party.

9. Ibid.

10. Tutu quoted in *Prayers for Peace: An Anthology of Readings and Prayers*, ed. Archbishop Robert Runcie and Cardinal Basil Hume (London: SPCK, 1987), 41.

11. Tutu, handwritten sermon for Sunday School Teacher's Eucharist, St. George's Cathedral, February 2, 1987.

12. Tutu, handwritten sermons, St. Philip's, Washington, DC, Christmas III, 1984.

13. John Mbiti, *African Religions and Philosophies* (New York: Doubleday, 1970), 141.

14. For tears as a sign of the presence of God, see Maggie Ross, *The Fountain and the Furnace: The Way of Tears and Fire* (New York: Paulist Press, 1987).

15. Desmond Tutu, "My Credo," *Living Philosophies: The Reflections of Some Eminent Men and Women of Our Time*, ed. Clifton Fadiman (New York: Doubleday, 1990), 234.

16. Tutu, "Birmingham Cathedral Address," transcript of Tutu's Sermon in Birmingham Cathedral, April 21, 1988, published by the Committee for Black Affairs, Birmingham, Diocesan Office, cited in Battle, *Reconciliation*, 225.

17. Gregory of Nyssa, quoted in Vladimir Lossky, *The Mystical Theology of the Eastern Church* (Crestwood, NY: St. Vladimir's Seminary Press, 1997), 197.

18. Desmond Tutu, interview by Gyles Brandreth, "My Idea of Heaven," *Sunday Telegraph*, April 27, 2001, http://www.telegraph.co.uk/culture/4723136/My-idea-of-Heaven.html.

19. Good sources for understanding the influences on King's thought are Lerone Bennett, *What Manner of Man* (Chicago: Johnson Publishing, 1968); Harold DeWolf, "Martin Luther King, Jr., as Theologian," *Journal of the Interdenominational Theological Center* 4 (Spring 1977): 7–9; James Hanigan, "Martin Luther King, Jr. and the Ethics of Militant Nonviolence" (PhD dissertation, Duke University, 1973); John Harris, "The Theology of Martin Luther King, Jr." (PhD dissertation, Duke University, 1974); David Lewis, *King: A Critical Biography* (New York: Praeger, 1977); Ervin Smith, "The Role of Personalism in the Development of the Social Ethics of Martin Luther King, Jr." (PhD dissertation, Northwestern University, 1976); Lois D. Wasserman, "Martin Luther King, Jr.: The Molding of Nonviolence as a Philosophy and Strategy, 1955–63" (PhD dissertation, Boston University, 1972).

Chapter 18. Tutu's Practice of Heaven

1. Tutu, "Birmingham Cathedral Address," p. 3.

2. See my discussion of Jesus and Peter's definition of forgiveness based on Matt. 18:21–35 in Michael Battle, *Practicing Reconciliation in a Violent World* (Harrisburg, PA: Morehouse Publishing, 2005), 22–23.

3. See Desmond Tutu, *No Future without Forgiveness* (New York: Doubleday, 2000).

4. Tutu, Handwritten Undated Address #5, cited in Battle, *Reconciliation*, 217.

5. Tutu, "A Christian Vision of the Future of South Africa."

6. Tutu, Address, "The Nature and Value of Theology," undated.

7. Tutu quoted in *Prayers for Peace: An Anthology of Readings and Prayers*, ed. Archbishop Robert Runcie and Cardinal Basil Hume (London: SPCK, 1987), 41.

8. See Michael Battle, "Truth and Reconciliation: From Chile to South Africa," in *Reconciliation, Nations and Churches in Latin America*, ed. Iain Maclean (Burlington, VT: Ashgate, 2006).

9. Tutu, "My Credo," 234.

10. One may see how Tutu operates from restorative justice through his work as chair of the Truth and Reconciliation Commission in South Africa, 1994–1997.

11. Cf. Luke 13:18–21; Matt. 13:31–33; Mark 4:30–32 (parables of Mustard Seed and Yeast).

12. Tutu, "Genesis Chapter 3." Handwritten Sermons, St Mary's, Blechingly, Surrey, October 6, 1985, cited in Battle, *Reconciliation*, 224.

13. Simone Weil presents an especially interesting concept of affliction, *malheur* in French. She believes that the human creature has the opportunity to "un-create" a fallen existence. This *malheur* is the only thing besides beauty with the capacity to convert one's attention toward God. In effect, "Affliction, when it is consented to and accepted and loved, is truly a baptism." See *The Simone Weil Reader*, edited by George A. Panichas (Mt. Kisco, NY: Moyer Bell Ltd., 1977), 439–68. Augustine Shutte states that he provides "detailed application of Weil's ideas to the South African Situation," especially her ideas of uprootedness. See Augustine Shutte, *Philosophy for Africa* (Rondebosch, South Africa: UCT Press, 1993).

14. Tutu, "Suffering and Witness" undated address, cited in Battle, *Reconciliation*, 216

15. Ibid.

16. Tutu, "My Credo."

17. Martin Luther King Jr., *The Trumpet of Conscience* (San Francisco: Harper & Row, 1967), 68.

18. Tutu, handwritten notes, undated.

19. John 3:9, 12.

20. Tutu, handwritten address, July, 1987, memorial to Pakamile Mabija, who died in detention in Kimberley, South Africa.

Chapter 19. Practicing Heaven Ourselves

1. Victor Preller was a well-known Aquinas scholar at Princeton University and an early mentor for me when I did my field education as a seminarian at Princeton Theological Seminary. Victor Preller, "An Introduction to the Virtues," All Saints' Church Newsletter, February 14, 1989.

2. Preller, "Introduction to the Virtues."

3. Michael Battle, *Reconciliation: The Ubuntu Theology of Desmond Tutu* (Cleveland: Pilgrim Press, 2009); *The Wisdom of Desmond Tutu* (Louisville, KY: Westminster John Knox Press, 2000); and *Desmond Tutu: A Spiritual Biography* (Louisville, KY: Westminster John Knox Press, forthcoming).

4. Tutu's undated handwritten speeches, "Perspectives in Black and White" cited in Battle, *Reconciliation*, 217. Tutu illustrates further with this story: "A little boy excitedly pointed to a flight of geese and shouted, 'Mommy, Mommy, look at all those gooses.' The mother replied, 'My darling, we don't call them gooses. They are geese.' Then the little darling, nothing daunted, retorted, 'Well they still look like goose to me.'"

5. Frederick Buechner, *Wishful Thinking: A Seeker's ABC* (San Francisco: HarperSanFrancisco, 1993), 119.

6. The Millennium Development Goals were adopted by world leaders in 2000. See "Millennium Project," United Nations, http://www.unmillenniumproject.org/goals/index.htm.

Chapter 20. The Key to the Bottomless Pit

1. Hence the title of Desmond Tutu's book *No Future without Forgiveness* (New York: Doubleday, 2002).

2. Victor Preller, All Saints' Newsletter, February 21, 1990. Preller provides much of the insight concerning virtue in this research.

3. Rowan Greer, *The Fear of Freedom* (University Park: Pennsylvania State University Press, 1989), 148.

4. For a reference to King's meeting with Barth, see Karl Barth, *Evangelical Theology* (Grand Rapids: Eerdmans, 1963), ix. Unfortunately, King does not give any reference for his meeting with Barth.

5. Martin Luther King Jr., "Karl Barth's Conception of God," 9 (unpublished manuscript, January 2, 1951), Archives of the Martin Luther King Jr. Center for Nonviolent Social Change, Atlanta. Quoted in Noel Leo Erskine, *King among the Theologians* (Cleveland: Pilgrim Press, 1994), 80–81.

6. Martin Luther King Jr., *Strength to Love* (Cleveland: Collins Publishers, 1963), 141. See King's references to God as "Universe," "Creative Force,"

"Cosmic Companion," in King, *Stride Toward Freedom* (San Francisco: Harper & Row, 1986), 88.

7. Miles Krassen, *Uniter of Heaven and Earth: Rabbi Meshullam Feibush Heller of Zbarazh and the Rise of Hasidism in Eastern Galicia* (Albany: State University of New York Press, 1998), 6.

8. King, *Stride Toward Freedom*, 184.

9. Quoted in Lewis Baldwin, *To Make the Wounded Whole: The Cultural Legacy of Martin Luther King, Jr.* (Minneapolis: Fortress Press, 1992), 61. See also Baldwin's very informative section on the theological and ethical influences on King, 59–162.

10. See Edgar Sheffield Brightman, *Persons and Values* (Boston: Boston University Press, 1952).

11. Martin Luther King Jr., *Why We Can't Wait* (New York: Signet Books, 1964), 94.

12. Martin Luther King Jr., *The Trumpet of Conscience* (San Francisco: Harper & Row, 1967), 62.

13. Desmond Tutu, "The South African Struggle," speech, Partners in Ecumenism Conference of the National Council of Churches, Washington, DC, September 26, 1984, 1.

14. Naomi Tutu, *The Words of Desmond Tutu* (New York: Newmarket Press, 1989), 101; Desmond Tutu, *Crying in the Wilderness: The Struggle for Justice in South Africa*, ed. John Webster (Grand Rapids: Eerdmans, 1982), 113; and Tutu, "The South African Struggle," 1.

15. Tutu, *Words of Desmond Tutu*, 26–91.

16. Desmond Tutu, *Hope and Suffering: Sermons and Speeches*, ed. John Webster (Grand Rapids: Eerdmans, 1983), 69.

17. Martin Luther King Jr., *The Measure of a Man* (Philadelphia: Christian Education Press, 1959), 52.

18. Tutu, *Hope and Suffering*, 9; *Crying in the Wilderness*, 113; *Words of Desmond Tutu*, 33, 38–39, 72–73, 83–91.

19. Tutu, *Words of Desmond Tutu*, 29.

20. Simone Weil, "Reflections on the Right Use of School Studies with a View to the Love of God," in *The Simone Weil Reader*, ed. George A. Panichas (New York: McKay, 1977), 44.

21. Simone Weil, *Waiting on God* (New York: Putnam, 1951), 77.

22. Diogenes Allen and Eric O. Springsted, *Spirit, Nature, and Community: Issues in the Thought of Simone Weil* (Albany: State University of New York Press, 1994), 3.

Chapter 21. New Heaven and New Earth

1. Martin Luther King Jr., *Stride Toward Freedom* (San Francisco: Harper & Row, 1986), 82–83.

2. Martin Luther King Jr., "What a Christian Should Think about the Kingdom of God" (Boston Collection), King papers, special collections, Boston University, 2. Quoted in Kenneth L. Smith and Ira G. Zepp, *Search for the Beloved Community* (Valley Forge: Judson Press, 1974), 129.

3. Martin Luther King Jr., *The Trumpet of Conscience* (San Francisco: Harper & Row, 1967), 59.

4. Owen Thomas, "Political Spirituality: Oxymoron or Redundancy," Journal of Religion & Society, Vol. 3, 2001, 10, http://moses.creighton.edu/jrs/2001/2001-3.pdf. (This journal articale was originally presented at the Christian Spirituality Group of the American Academy of Religion, Spirituality and the Civil Rights Movement, Nashville, November 21, 2000).

5. Martin Luther King Jr., "The Power of Nonviolence," in *I Have a Dream: Writings and Speeches That Changed the World*, ed. James M. Washington (San Francisco: HarperSanFrancisco, 1986), 61.

6. King, "I Have a Dream," *Negro History Bulletin*. 31, no. 5 (May 1968): 17.

7. Ibid. King said that America is a dream in a commencement address at Lincoln University. See Kenneth L. Smith and Ira G. Zepp, *Search for the Beloved Community: The Thinking of Martin Luther King Jr.* (Valley Forge, PA: Judson Press, 1998), 127.

8. James Cone, *Black Theology and Black Power* (New York: Seabury Press, 1969), 108.

9. King, *Stride Toward Freedom*, 84.

10. Tutu, Handwritten Sermon, Ninth Sunday before Christmas, St. George's Cathedral, 1986.

11. See the Freedom Charter of the African National Congress (ANC) drafted by three thousand delegates in June 1955. Christian leaders such as Lutuli were instrumental in proclaiming this nonracial theme. Nonracialism is still the theme of the ANC. For example, on May 10, 1993, when I attended the inauguration ceremony of Nelson Mandela as the president of the Republic of South Africa, I heard him refer to the ANC's commitment to nonracialism.

12. In South Africa approximately 70 percent of the population are Christian and of these almost one-third are members of independent churches.

13. King, *Trumpet of Conscience*, 25.

Afterword: The Healing of the Nations

1. Jonathan Kirsch, author of *A History of the End of the World: How the Most Controversial Book in the Bible Changed the Course of Western Civilization* (2006), quoted in the History Channel documentary "7 Signs of the Apocalypse," Morningstar Entertainment for History, A&E Television Networks, 2008.

2. Justin Wolfers, Kevin Quealy, and David Leonhardt, "1.5 Million Black Men, Missing from Daily Life," *New York Times*, April 21, 2015.

3. Vladimir Hernandez, "Painful Search for Argentina's Disappeared," BBC News (BBC Mundo, Parana Delta), March 24, 2013.

4. Wolfers, Quealy, and Leonhardt, "1.5 Million Black Men."

5. Ibid.

6. Ibid.

7. Tom Shadyac, "I Am," documentary, Shady Acres Production, 2011. Shadyac directs Hollywood comedies like *Ace Ventura*, but he also produced the comedies about God in the *Bruce Almighty* series. He also put Jim Carrey on the big stage from his early days as a cast member in the television series *In Living Color*.

Selected Bibliography

Influential Books (Annotated)

Bauckham, Richard. *The Theology of the Book of Revelation*. Cambridge: Cambridge University Press, 1993.

Bauckham provides a theological perspective from his situation as a New Testament scholar. His argument is that Revelation is not meant to be an esoteric forecast of historical events, but once properly grounded in its original context, Revelation becomes a vision for good use of how to talk about incessant social ills faced by the church.

Boesak, Allan. *Comfort and Protest: The Apocalypse from a South African Perspective*. Philadelphia: Westminster Press, 1987.

During the antiapartheid movement in South Africa, Boesak, like John of Patmos, had deep visions. He provides prophetic witness and theological insight into how Revelation remains a vital text in resistance to political evil.

Blount, Brian K. *Revelation: A Commentary*. Louisville, KY: Westminster John Knox Press, 2009.

As a biblical scholar, Blount provides a wonderfully textured commentary from which one may gain both theological and biblical insight. I especially liked his insight that although Revelation is full of violence, John of Patmos led his church communities to envision nonviolent resistance.

Bullinger, E.W. *Commentary on Revelation*. Grand Rapids: Christian Classics Ethereal Library, 1902.

Ethelbert William Bullinger (1837–1913), an Anglican biblical scholar, provides a comprehensive verse-by-verse commentary on Revelation. In the typology of dispensationalism (periods in which God relates differently to Israel, the church, and the world), Bullinger claimed seven dispensations. This was so provocative that "Bullingerism" was coined as a term.

Ewing, Ward. "Babylon the Great and the New Jerusalem." In *Politics and Theopolitics in the Bible and Postbiblical Literature*, edited by Henning Graf Reventlow, Yair Hoffman, and Benjamin Uffenheimer, 189–202. Sheffield: JSOT Press, 1994.

———. *The Power of the Lamb: Revelation's Theology of Liberation for You*. Eugene, OR: Wipf & Stock, 2006.

Ewing provides a helpful focus on the paradox of the Lamb with power.

Farrer, Austin. *The Revelation of St. John the Divine.* Oxford: Clarendon Press, 1964.
  Farrer, an Anglican philosopher and theologian, provides deep insight into the nature of vision and apocalypse.

Gilbertson, Michael. *God and History in the Book of Revelation: New Testament Studies in Dialogue with Pannenberg and Moltmann.* Cambridge: Cambridge University Press, 2003.
  An interdisciplinary study between biblical interpretation and systematic theology, by an Anglican priest.

Girard, René. *Things Hidden since the Foundation of the World.* Stanford, CA: Stanford University Press, 1987.
  Girard gives philosophical and anthropological insight into why Jesus puts an end to sacrifice. See also his "Are the Gospels Mythical?," *First Things* 62 (April 1996): 27–31.

Metzger, Bruce. *Breaking the Code: Understanding the Book of Revelation.* Nashville: Abingdon, 1993.
———. *The Text of the New Testament: Its Transmission, Corruption, and Restoration.* 3rd ed. New York: Oxford University Press, 1992.
———. *A Textual Commentary on the Greek New Testament.* London: United Bible Societies, 1971.
  Metzger is a well-known New Testament scholar who has trained numerous biblical scholars.

O'Donovan, Oliver. "The Political Thought of the Book of Revelation." *Tyndale Bulletin* 37 (1986): 61–94.
  O'Donovan is a moral theologian who unashamedly embraces how confessional Christian practices matter in the world.

Ramon, Brother, SSF. *Heaven on Earth: A Personal Retreat Guide.* London: Marshall Pickering, 1991.
  Brother Ramon provides a spiritual theology of retreat and helps the reader to plan one practically and specifically, even what to eat and when to go to sleep. Spiritual retreats become a means of practicing heaven on earth.

Sachs, Jeffery. *The End of Poverty: Economic Possibilities for Our Time.* New York: Penguin Press, 2005.
  Sachs provides a practical and economic vision for how we can make the world better. He thinks that global problems are not overwhelming but can be manageably solved.

Scruton, Roger. *The Soul of the World.* Princeton, NJ: Princeton University Press, 2014.

Tatum, Beverly Daniel. *Why Are All the Black Kids Sitting Together in the Cafeteria? And Other Conversations about Race*. New York: Basic Books, 1997.

Tatum provides a vital conversation in which the book of Revelation also addresses the question, who should be included and who should be excluded? Because worldviews are learned in classrooms, this is an important book in helping to train others that this is the wrong question. As an expert on race relations in the classroom and development of racial identity, Tatum helps us envision a better way to see community.

Williams, Rowan. *A Ray of Darkness: Sermons and Reflections*. Cambridge, MA: Cowley Publications, 1995.

Williams's writings and ministry powerfully reflect the struggles between heaven and earth. His profound theology seeks engagement with such struggle rather than avoidance in order to move toward God who first moved toward humanity.

Books on Heaven and Earth

The following works focus on the apocalypse and the confluence or contradiction between heaven and earth.

Bergman, Ozer. *Where Earth and Heaven Kiss*. Jerusalem and New York: Breslov Research Institute, 2006.

Gyger, Pia. *That We May Join Heaven and Earth: Lay Religious Community for the 21st Century*. Lanham, MD: Rowman & Littlefield, 2006.

Jue, Jeffrey. *Heaven upon Earth: Joseph Mede (1586–1638) and the Legacy of Millenarianism*. New York: Springer Press, 2006.

Nichols, Stephen. *Heaven on Earth: Capturing Jonathan Edwards's Vision of Living in Between*. Wheaton, IL: Crossway Books, 2006.

Scafi, Alessandro. *Mapping Paradise: A History of Heaven on Earth*. Chicago: University of Chicago Press, 2006.

Books on Martin Luther King Jr.'s Beloved Community

For King, the conception of the beloved community represented a view in which we could not wait for heaven to live with God. King provides a unique blend of insights from black culture, the Bible, Christian theology and ethics, the American democratic heritage, and Western philosophical traditions.

Ansbro, John J. *Martin Luther King Jr.: The Making of a Mind*. Maryknoll, NY: Orbis Books, 1982.

Baldwin, Lewis. *There Is a Balm in Gilead: The Cultural Roots of Martin Luther King Jr*. Minneapolis: Fortress Press, 1991.

———. *To Make the Wounded Whole.* Minneapolis: Fortress Press, 1992.

Fluker, Walter. *They Looked for a City.* Lanham, MD: University Press of America, 1989.

Smith, Kenneth L., and Ira G. Zepp. *Search for the Beloved Community: The Thinking of Martin Luther King Jr.* Valley Forge, PA: Judson Press, 1998.

Books on Restorative Views of Heaven and Earth

Gulley, Philip, and James Mulholland. *If Grace Is True: Why God Will Save Every Person.* New York: HarperSanFrancisco, 2003.

Walters, Kerry. *Jacob's Hip: Finding God in an Anxious Age.* Maryknoll, NY: Orbis Books, 2003.

Books on Desmond Tutu's Ubuntu

Battle, Michael. *Reconciliation: The Ubuntu Theology of Desmond Tutu.* Cleveland: Pilgrim Press, 2009.

Battle, Michael. *Ubuntu: I in You and You in Me.* New York: Seabury Books, 2009.

Tutu, Desmond. *No Future without Forgiveness.* New York: Doubleday, 1999.

Media Resources Helpful to Understanding the Book of Revelation

Battle, Michael. www.michaelbattle.com and www.peacebattle.com.

These websites will be continually updated to provide resources and events for how individuals and communities may participate in practicing heaven on earth.

Cosmos: A Spacetime Odyssey. Originally aired on National Geographic Channel and Fox, March 9–June 8, 2014. Available on DVD. 20th Century Fox, 2014.

"7 Signs of the Apocalypse." History Channel Documentary. Morningstar Entertainment for History. A&E Television Networks, 2008.

Shadyac, Tom. "I Am." DVD. Shady Acres Production, 2011.

Shadyac is a Hollywood director (*Ace Ventura, Bruce Almighty* series). A near-death experience put him on the road to look for ultimate meaning and how we can change the world seemingly headed toward a cliff. He interviews spiritual leaders like Archbishop Tutu in this documentary journey.

West, Kanye, and Jay-Z. "No Church in the Wild."

By the best-known hip-hop artists in the world. The music video has stunning visual imagery of a world in apocalyptic collapse.

CPSIA information can be obtained
at www.ICGtesting.com
Printed in the USA
BVOW06s2016240217
477043BV00008B/56/P

9 780664 262549